Making the grade

A study programme for adult students

This book is dedicated to all our students on New Horizons and other access courses. They have given us a great deal in terms of enjoyable teaching and satisfaction when they have gone on to sustain their studies in other ways. We also dedicate the book to Pat Barnett, an inspiring teacher who tragically died before this book saw the light of day.

Making the grade

A study programme for adult students

Volume I *Reading and learning*

Bill Jones and **Roy Johnson**

Manchester University Press
Manchester and New York
Distributed exclusively in the USA and Canada by St. Martin's Press

Copyright © Bill Jones and Roy Johnson 1990

Published by Manchester University Press
Oxford Road, Manchester M13 9PL, UK
and Room 400, 175 Fifth Avenue,
New York, NY 10010, USA

Distributed exclusively in the USA and Canada
by St. Martin's Press, Inc.,
175 Fifth Avenue, New York, NY 10010, USA

British Library cataloguing in publication data
Jones, Bill, *1946–*
  Making the grade : a study programme for adult students.
  Vol. 1. Reading and learning
  1. Adult education. Study techniques & teaching
  I. Title II. Johnson, Roy
  374.13

Library of Congress cataloging in publication data
Jones, Bill, 1946–
  Making the grade : a study programme for adult students / Bill
Jones and Roy Johnson.
      p. cm.
  Contents: v. 1. Reading and learning — v. 2. Thinking and
writing.
      ISBN 0-7190-3177-X (v. 1). — ISBN 0-7190-3178-8 (pbk. : v. 1). —
ISBN 0-7190-3179-6 (v. 2). — ISBN 0-7190-3180-X (pbk. : v. 2)
      1. Study, Method of.   2. Reading (Adult education)   3. English
language—Rhetoric—Study and teaching.   4. Distance education.
I. Johnson, Roy, 1939–   . II. Title.
LC5225.M47J66   1990
374—dc20   89-77465

ISBN 0 7190 3177 X *hardback*
       0 7190 3178 8 *paperback*

Photoset in Linotron Palatino
by Northern Phototypesetting Co Ltd, Bolton

Printed in Great Britain
by Dotesios Limited, Trowbridge

Contents

Foreword

As a university teacher I have watched the progress of mature students with great interest and often some anxiety. The good news is that adults who return to higher education several years after leaving school often achieve high standards, even first-class honours degrees. To confine higher education to eighteen-year-old school-leavers is absurd. Adults who abandon school at sixteen or eighteen, often with comparatively poor academic qualifications, can return to education ten or more years later with new abilities and motivation. They are very welcome in higher education, and a joy to teach because they are independent and sufficiently mature to challenge received opinions. In the 1990s higher education in Britain will be gradually transformed, as more and more people return to education for further qualifications. The system is beginning to open its doors to new groups of students, and I find this very exciting.

The bad news is that many people find the return to education difficult, for a number of reasons, and give up their ambitions too easily. Over the years I have often taught adults who have been away from education for several years, and who have lost the ability to write clear, accurate prose. Adults need to realise that the ability to write good prose depends on regular practice. If you have not written an essay for many years, then you will have difficulties, and this applies to everyone, even the most talented. But once you start a regular course of writing, and discuss your drafts with friends and tutors, you will be amazed how quickly your skills develop. I have watched adult students whose style at first was crabbed and tortuous move rapidly to high standards of fluency. Two of my students who were worried about their inadequacies as writers managed only a few years later to become regular contributors to literary magazines.

And it is vital to cultivate the right mental approach. When my students suffer from mental blocks, and perhaps cannot advance beyond the first paragraph of an assignment, I advise them to write their material to me in the form of a letter, as slap-dash as they please. Usually by the second or third paragraph they are writing satisfactory prose. It is important not to become too anxious, and self-confidence is vital. Many new adult students have false ideas about the brilliance of their teachers. We teachers often write badly, often become confused and often make mistakes. Everyone who studies and writes needs constant advice from friends and specialists. The main thing is to have the courage to start.

This study programme for adult students is based on an access course successfully piloted since 1979 at Manchester University, and converted into a distance learning course in 1986. In the past, teachers learnt to help students by trial and error, often working on their own initiative without help from colleagues. It is a sign of the increased importance of continuing education that this access course is based on collaboration between tutors, and on careful development of successful practice. The whole project originated from collaboration between the Manchester University Extra-Mural Department and the WEA in the North-West. The two volumes represent a comprehensive package which can be studied individually, as a classroom text or as part of a distance learning course.

When I started teaching for the WEA in 1952 I felt very much a pioneer, sent out to classes in small villages in Norfolk after only a two-week training course. Today the teaching of adults has become much more professional. *Making the Grade* is wonderfully organised to help real students tackle real problems. Nothing makes me happier than to recall adult students I have known in the past who renewed their lives by returning to education. I am confident these programmes of study will add to their number.

Brian Cox

Preface

In 1978 one of the authors (Bill Jones) organised a short experimental extra-mural course at Manchester University aimed at adults interested in finding out about different subjects and disciplines. This was organised in the form of introductory sessions on each topic, followed up by regular weekly written work. Interestingly, the participants proved to be more concerned to develop their study and writing skills than to pursue the original aim of the course. The following year the course content was adapted accordingly to reflect an emphasis upon study skills. A connection was also established at this time with the second author, Roy Johnson, who was developing a similar approach for the North-West District of the Workers' Educational Association. Eventually, a joint course was established, meeting for 25 one-day sessions throughout the year. We called it New Horizons.

It soon became apparent that a real need existed for a course like this which helped adults to develop their study skills and which introduced them to different areas of study. Since those early days hundreds of students have passed through these courses, many of them studying seriously for the first time in their lives.

Inevitably some (though a small proportion) dropped out, but of the majority who completed the course about one-quarter went on to enter higher education whilst over one-half continued their studies in one form or another.

We found these courses challenging to teach and great fun as well: once adult students gain confidence in their own abilities they develop very quickly and for any teacher this transformation is an exhilarating and satisfying process. So we decided to gather together and write up the study-skills teaching materials we have been developing over the years and to offer them to a wider public as a distance learning course.

A grant from the Department of Education and Science greatly aided this process on its way and three other colleagues, Pat Barnett (Open University), John Hostler and John McIlroy (Department of Extra-Mural Studies, University of Manchester), contributed various units.

The course ran successfully for a number of years and the materials were used by a number of other universities and colleges. In 1989 Manchester University Press agreed to publish the materials in their present form: a two-volume workbook which can either be studied by the independent learner or as part of organised open and distance learning courses. Material written by the other three colleagues has been retained in edited form.

We hope that this book enables users to return to study successfully and hope it succeeds in opening some of the doors indicated in the final chapter.

BJ
RJ
November 1989

Acknowledgements

The hundreds of students who have passed through our *New Horizons* course are too numerous to mention, but it is they who deserve the chief credit for this two-volume work. It is their interest and enthusiasm which encouraged us to develop the particular teaching approach reflected herein, together with the wide range of teaching materials and assignments. Next in the order of merit comes the Department of Education and Science which, in 1986, provided financial support for the conversion of *New Horizons* into the distance learning format. Then we wish to thank a number of colleagues for their support, encouragement and advice: John Hostler, the late Pat Barnett, John McIlroy, Kate Fisher, Sam Herman, Bryan Luckham and John Smith. Thanks are also due to former students who kindly gave permission for us to draw upon their work: Jean Day, Harold Carr, Terry O'Toole, Audrey Kay, Ian Churton, Ruth Ward, Jean Brooks, Freda Clarke, Sid Davies, Val Hands and Heather Leach. We wish to thank Sir Ian Gilmour for permission to use one of his articles (originally published in the *Guardian*) in the chapter on note-taking, and the editor of *Teaching Politics* for permission to use extracts of an article by Lorraine Culley. Thanks are also due to Gerda and Sixten Karlsson for their hospitality during a cold winter in northern Sweden when a substantial chunk of these two volumes was originally drafted. Finally, we owe a very considerable debt to Judith Martin in the Department of Extra-Mural Studies, University of Manchester, for her patience, accuracy and industry in typing the original manuscript and for her enthusiasm and ingenuity in helping to invent and run the distance-learning course upon which these two volumes are based.

The authors

Bill Jones comes from mid-Wales where his parents were both teachers. After attending the grammar school in Shrewsbury he went to Aberystwyth University to study International Politics, submitting his doctorate on Labour Party attitudes towards the Soviet Union. After two years as an Assistant Principal in Whitehall he joined Manchester University's Extra-Mural Department in 1973 where he was successively Staff and Senior Staff Tutor in Government and Politics before becoming Director in 1987. He was Chairman of the Politics Association 1983–85 and has written several textbooks and articles on British politics, in addition to undertaking extensive consultancy work for radio and television. As well as return-to study-courses he has a longstanding interest in Swedish adult and higher education.

Roy Johnson comes from a working-class background in Stockport. After attending the local grammar school and failing his A levels he joined Renold Engineering as an apprentice and later the Atomic Energy Authority as a technical draughtsman. At the age of 29 he decided to take his reading and other cultural interests seriously and, after attending various extra-mural and WEA courses, entered Manchester University as a mature student. He gained a first-class degree in English and American Literature and went on to write his doctorate on the political literature of the thirties. In 1975 he became a tutor-organiser in literature for the North-West district of the WEA. As well as New Horizons courses he has taught adult courses across a wide literary range specialising in twentieth-century novelists. He has published critical works on a number of authors plus a number of his own short stories.

Introduction   **1**

Contents

This book is also a course of study. It provides a programme of learning for adults wishing to return to serious study and, should they choose, proceed into higher education. It can be used either by you, the independent student working alone, or as part of a face-to-face or distance learning course. Based upon a successful access course at Manchester University it aims to help mature students acquire and refresh study skills, discover their potential as students and develop confidence in their own abilities. Volume I deals with effective learning techniques whilst Volume II concentrates upon clear thinking and the production of high quality written work.

Who is the book intended for?   1

Making the grade is designed for any adults wishing to develop their study skills and discover their potential as students, but the book is likely to be especially attractive to people

● specifically interested in entering the higher education system

● wishing to improve their performance on a course of study about to be or already being pursued

● wishing to develop the skills necessary to enjoy and make the most of other kinds of study

● wishing to pursue the course for its intrinsic interest

This book is also likely to appeal to the kinds of people with circumstances similar to those people who attended the access course upon which it is based. This course, New Horizons, attracted people from a wide range of backgrounds including

- *people wishing to change their jobs* but needing to study to achieve the new kind of job they prefer

- *women with grown-up families* who wish to 're-start their brains' (as one of them put it) and prepare for a new life when the child-rearing part of their life is over

- *unemployed people* who wish to use their enforced leisure more productively and improve their employment prospects

- *single parents* who wish and need to improve job opportunities or otherwise change their way of life sometimes after a separation or divorce

- *retired people* who wish to equip themselves with the skills necessary to make enjoyment of study an important part of their retirement.

Making The Grade is likely to appeal to all of these groups and in addition

- people in work who are unable to attend conventional courses

- women and men with heavy family commitments

- retired people or those living considerable distances from educational facilities

- people who, for one reason or another, prefer to study independently

Occupations of previous students have covered a very wide range: secretaries, business managers and executives, nurses, housewives, teachers, cleaners, social workers, lorry drivers, shop assistants, firemen, solicitors, salesmen and many others. Similarly, educational background has varied enormously from people who left school at the age of 15 to those with CSE O levels, degrees and various kinds of professional qualifications from HNC up to postgraduate qualifications.

There is no special level of attainment needed before you embark on this course. But you do need to be able to write reasonably clear English from the outset. If you have passed O level in English or any other subject at some time in your life your standard of written English is probably sufficient. Don't be in the

2

slightest deterred, however, if you have no qualifications of this or indeed any other kind: in the past such students on New Horizons courses have proved to have adequate written skills and have found no difficulty in keeping up with the work and doing well. You will, we hope, understand why some ability with English is a necessary requirement; if your standard is too low you will find so much of your time will be spent developing basic literacy skills that you will find it depressingly difficult to make progress. If you are in any doubt on this point, try working through some of the early chapters, or better still, have a word with someone experienced in this kind of work.

How to use this book   2

Making the Grade is constructed as a *workbook*: you learn through an *active* rather than passive involvement in the text. Throughout we pose questions, ask you to think and possibly write something, before moving on.

The book is divided for convenience into two volumes – each of which represent 'modules' which can, if you wish, be studied independently.

Volume I concentrates on	*orientation* – getting you used to the idea of being an adult student, organising your time efficiently, and so forth
	verbal communication, whether in small groups or when making a presentation
	learning skills like reading and note-taking
	generating ideas for written work
Volume II addresses	*clear thinking* and planning written work effectively
	good written work: grammar and punctuation, sentences and paragraphs, good style
	examinations
	further opportunities for study

How long will the course take to study? This will depend upon the context, your available time and your ability. Some people have worked through the course on an intensive basis in a month but three to six months would seem a more appropriate time-scale.

The book can be studied in three major ways:

(a) **Independent learning.** You may have bought the book for personal use and intend working through it on your own.

(b) **Full or part-time course.** This book may be part of a normal 'face-to-face' course at an adult centre, college of further education, polytechnic, Workers' Educational Association branch or extra-mural department of a university.

(c) **Distance learning.** You may be studying the book as part of a distance learning course run by a local centre. In this case you might be studying *independently* with the help of a tutor; as *part of a group* which meets up regularly at weekends or other convenient times; or via some other *open learning* system, depending upon the centre involved.

The *assignments* given at the end of each chapter are an integral part of the book, as are the *guidance notes* at the end of each volume. In the early part of the book the assignments are designed to get you writing in an easy and relaxed way and they often ask you to draw upon your own memory and experiences. They also aim to provide practice in the specific study skills covered in the chapter concerned, as well as building up your word power and providing further practice in skills covered in earlier chapters.

The guidance notes will be particularly useful for the independent learner as they provide a means of self-assessment. Where straightforward answers are possible, they are given, but where you are asked to write something, say a précis or an essay, 'model answers' are often provided, written either by ourselves or more often by former students. It should be stressed, however, that not all assignments (there are several score) receive comment.

Occasionally you are asked to *practise* a particular skill and comment in the guidance notes will not be appropriate. Other assignments are included for possible use within the context of a *taught* course where a tutor will need to provide a range of options and provide individual feedback to course members.

3   *Aims of the course*

(a) **Confidence-building** is the most important early objective of the course. Many adults undervalue the skills they acquired in school and fail to appreciate those they have subsequently

developed. Our experience is that the majority of students'
lack of confidence is the major initial problem which they
face. (See Chapter 1). The course is designed to reassure
adults that their brain *is* in good working order and is
perfectly adequate for the task of serious systematic study.

(b) **Breaking down barriers to study** is another initial aim of the
course. Possibly as the result of unhappy school experience,
many adults have developed something akin to a fear of
education or the feeling that study, especially in higher
education, is for someone else, not them.

(c) **Self-discovery.** The course becomes something of a voyage
into your own personality. You will find out more clearly
what you do know and do not know, what you can do and
cannot. You will occasionally surprise and perhaps even
astonish yourself with the talents and resources you did not
know were yours. During this process you will be led to
appraise yourself in a very honest way and, if you are
studying as part of a course, to learn the value of judgement
by others.

(d) **Identification of study problems.** The course will soon
identify, if you are not already aware of them, those areas
where special attention and help is required.

(e) **Improvement of study skills** is the obvious corollary of the
above. The whole range of study skills is attended to,
culminating in the production of good quality written work.
We stress the achievement of written skills as we feel that
they draw together and apply most of the others like
reading, note-taking, clear thinking, and so forth. The
emphasis throughout is on *method* rather than *content*; on the
way you think and write rather than upon *what* you think and
write about.

(f) **Preparation for further study, especially higher education.**
It is assumed that a proportion of those studying the course
are using it as preparation for further study. For example:
  ● part-time degree courses at a polytechnic or university
  ● the Open University (which also teaches via distance
    learning methods)
  ● full-time undergraduate or postgraduate study at a
    polytechnic, university or college of higher education
  ● adult residential colleges (like Coleg Harlech, Northern
    College or Ruskin College, Oxford)
  ● professional examinations (like those offered within local
    government, the Health Service, banking, accountancy).

For more information on opportunities for further study see Volume II, Chapter 9.)

No overall standard is expected One point which needs to be stressed is that there is no 'standard' or 'level' which you are expected to achieve. Some start with considerably more educational experience and resources than others who will need to work hard to develop their basic skills. The purpose of the course, however, is to enable you to take major steps forward in your own ability whether you start from a position of someone who left school at 15 or someone who is already a graduate. The emphasis, therefore, is on *individual* development.

No specialised knowledge is required to work through this course. Subjects dealt with are of a general nature, often drawn from everyday life. We also dip into a number of academic areas – literature, sociology, politics, history – but in each case the purpose is to illustrate and stimulate through easy-to-understand examples.

MOST OF THESE EXAMPLES ARE DRAWN FROM THE ARTS AND SOCIAL SCIENCES BUT PEOPLE WISHING TO STUDY SCIENTIFIC SUBJECTS WILL ALSO FIND THE COURSE USEFUL. STUDENTS IN ALL DISCIPLINES NEED TO THINK CLEARLY AND EXPRESS THEMSELVES WELL BOTH VERBALLY AND IN WRITING.

4   *Why concentrate upon study skills?*   4

Try to remember if you were ever taught how to study when you were at secondary school. The chances are that the subject was barely touched upon. The tradition in British schools is that once primary school is finished study skills are developed incidentally via courses in specific subjects – history, English, geography or whatever. Grammar and aspects of written style are tackled in English language of course, but note-taking, essay planning, clear thinking and the other topics studied in this course usually are not. It is assumed that such skills will be absorbed gradually and naturally through regular subject studies. In many cases this successfully occurs but in others – we suspect the majority – it does not. Thousands of young people leave school crammed with information but unable to argue or write clearly, to take good notes or structure a piece of writing coherently. University teachers will generally testify to the fact that most new undergraduates embark on their studies woefully lacking in the necessary **skills** as opposed to knowledge.

This emphasis on **content** rather than **method** in our educational system creates a need for courses like this one. But can study skills be taught in isolation? Our experience is that they can providing the approach is imaginative and varied (see case studies at the end of the chapter).

Skills are dealt with separately but all study skills are inter-related. This is particularly true, for example, of clear thinking, which can certainly be assisted by the chapter devoted to it but which will improve generally as a result of practising the other skills all of which require clarity of thought to a considerable degree. For this reason you will encounter some overlap and repetition in the chapters. This is inevitable, for example the need to review and revise throughout your course of study is dealt with in Volume I, Chapter 3 and again in Volume II, Chapter 8.

Study skills, which are in essence intellectual skills, are not easy to develop. They require considerable patience, practice and commitment. You have to realise that when jettisoning old ways of thinking and writing and adapting to new ones you may find that initially your level of performance falls below what it was before. But as in sport – learning a new tennis shot or golf swing – continued practice using a superior technique eventually produces much better results.

Be prepared therefore to be a little confused and disorientated at periods in the course. Our concentration upon individual skills may also confuse you a little. To focus on reading, note-taking or essay planning or grammar may seem a little unnatural at first but as the course is pursued and assignments are completed you will find things slotting into place; coming together. Your improved individual skills will start to reinforce, complement each other, and your overall study performance will make significant strides.

Remember too that this course will not make you any cleverer than you are: it will merely help you to discover where the limits of your ability may lie. You may have to come to terms with the facts that you never become especially good at certain skills and you may also in some cases have to realise that your ability is not what you thought it was. However, from our experience on New Horizons courses this is a rare occurrence: the majority of people are heartened and excited to discover that they are far more able than they initially believed.

Some sections will be more difficult than others but others will seem easy to the point perhaps of being banal, even patronisingly so. When you think about it, however, you will realise that this is bound to happen. Certainly some chapters *are* quite difficult and others relatively easy but the degree of difficulty you encounter will depend upon your level of ability: what might be easy for you might be difficult for someone else: on the other hand, what elsewhere seems obvious to someone else might appear completely fresh to you.

Finally on study skills; the course is basically applied common sense. There is no magic formula offered: merely sensible ways of setting about things. But our experience proves that with application, effort and encouragement, remarkable things can be achieved. The case studies of ex-New Horizons students we hope help to illustrate this.

5   *Case studies*

We asked some former New Horizons students to write about their experiences on the course and say how it helped to change their attitudes towards education. Provided below are edited versions of four fairly typical responses. For people who are hoping that studying this book will help them enter the world of higher education, these case studies will provide some encouragement.

HAROLD (late fifties)

66 I had recently retired on pension from the Fire Service and was in a position to change the direction of my life if I wished to do so. After about forty years in uniform (Army, Police, Fire Service) I felt that I needed a complete change of interest. The possibility of entering higher education had been in my mind for several years, but I had some doubts about my personal ability. A friend of mine at Surrey University Department of Adult Education gave me a contact at Manchester University who put me in touch with the New Horizons Course. Prior to this I had no idea that such a course existed.

From 1936 to 1939 I was at Grammar School. On the outbreak of war my parents only made a token resistance to my wish to leave school and, of course, at the end of the war I found myself without any formal education qualifications. Later I was to feel 'robbed' by the abrupt termination of my school education and in my late forties attended further education evening classes. It was here that I obtained O levels in English Language and English Literature followed by an A level in History.

It may seem surprising to some people but in spite of my maturity, considerable experience as a senior officer in the Fire Service and as a lecturer, I felt distinctly nervous when I started the course. Was I up to it? How would I compare with the other people on the course? This general feeling of uncertainty however was soon dispelled and I can honestly say that I did not have any important study problems after the first couple of weeks. The course helped me immensely. The subtly graduated progression of tuition combined with the sympathetic and supportive, yet positive and firm approach of the tutors quickly built up my confidence. I must say that I had not previously imagined that study skills could be studied as a subject in their own right.

The course was for me the ideal link between employment and full time education. It enabled me to assess myself in relation to the other students and the counselling I received from the tutors gave me a realistic view of my potential for acceptance for the various higher education institutions.

I was accepted to study for a BA degree in History and Human Geography at Crewe and Alsager College of Higher Education. Once I began the course I had no qualms about the work and felt very well equipped to tackle academic essays and seminar papers. New Horizons was *extremely helpful* in this respect. My further studies have no vocational value for me as I have already retired.

They have, however, opened up to me subjects of real interest; I am now a much more selective and discriminating user of the media and the pleasure I get from reading has been increased considerably by my studies. Contact with the young students at the college has been illuminating refreshing and very rewarding. (Note: Harold was eventually awarded an upper second-class honours degree.) 〞

TERRY (early thirties)

❝ I joined New Horizons because I desperately needed a diversion from my problems. My life was in a terrible – I thought irreparable – mess. I had become very depressed due to a number of misfortunes; long-term unemployment, a painful bereavement and a breakdown of a permanent relationship. At that time I had not really been thinking about further education but once the course had helped to lift me out of the mental rut I had occupied for so long I found that I wanted more from the world of study.

At the end of my undistinguished school career I had no qualifications or thought or hope of attaining any. It is hardly surprising therefore that my early study problems on the course were mainly lack of confidence. I found it so difficult to concentrate and had no idea at all about written style or how to plan an essay. The course served to gather my concentration by reinvigorating my old interests – I had always been a wide reader – and thus restoring my confidence. My written work problems were gradually ironed out by tackling the written assignments on the course. It helped a lot to receive constructive and encouraging criticism from the course tutors.

I was really surprised that study skills could be taught separately in this way. Note-taking, essay planning, syntax and grammar were all new things to me and I was surprised to discover that they were less difficult than I had imagined. With confidence and concentration restored (with a positive vengeance!) I continued studying extra-mural courses for a year before applying to the Northern College, an Adult Residential College. I found that New Horizons had given me a flying start regarding my ability to tackle a whole range of study tasks and the confidence to speak up on the new subjects which I was being introduced to. I soon discovered that progress becomes more difficult in higher education at times; one certainly has bad patches at times but they are never hopeless. I have now been accepted to study for a degree at Bradford University.

My life has been profoundly changed as a result of my further studies. From a personal point of view I have a much more optimistic outlook and have learned many things about myself and other people as a result of living in a residential college.
(Note: Terry went on to study for a degree at Bradford University and achieved upper second-class honours.) **"**

AUDREY (late forties)

" I joined the New Horizons course at a time in my life when my family had grown up and left home. I had given up a boring part-time job in a medical library and was seeking something which would relieve the monotony of an existence bounded by kitchen, neighbours' chat, and the usual sort of life in the suburbs. Until I read about the course I had no idea that it was possible for a mature person to get into higher education without first studying for A levels at night school. I suppose I automatically assumed that education was for young people and that I had missed the boat.

I had left school at 16 after five years at grammar school.

Although I obtained a fairly good school cert, my background – working-class – was such that it was considered an advancement to get work in an office. I subsequently worked in various office jobs for the whole of my working life as bookkeeper, library clerk, and so on. I certainly had not considered seriously the possibility of studying further.

My most important problem therefore was lack of confidence. I even had problems physically getting myself off the bus and into the university building! Meeting new people was an ordeal. Having got over that first hurdle successfully I discovered that my concentration and memory were terrible. The course helped me with my slow reading speed and my muddled thinking. Particularly useful was the work we did on the planning of essays; without this training I would never have been able to construct the type of essay called for later on my degree course. I was surprised that study skills could be studied separately – it really did work.

I can't say that I had any family problems whilst on the course but I did have problems with friends of many years who thought that I was out of my mind to contemplate putting myself through the trauma of serious study. But it was certainly worthwhile. The advantages I gained from the course were:

(a) Confidence gained from the support and encouragement of the course tutors as well as the moral support of other students.
(b) The skill of writing essays which has been of inestimable value.
(c) The ability to analyse a problem clearly and to get through to the heart of what a rather verbose writer is trying to say.

I never really mastered the art of note-taking, though; I still tend to try to take too much down. Not that this unduly hampered my studies at Manchester Polytechnic; I went on to get an upper second and am now studying for an MA. I would not have missed the experience of serious study for anything. **"**

JEAN (mid-thirties)

" I joined New Horizons on an impulse after reading about it. I had not thought about going on to higher education and had no definite objective in view. My parents, however, had very much wanted me to go to university when I left school but, conditioned by the dark ages of the late fifties to be cast as a woman in a supporting role, I elected to start work whilst my boyfriend, later my husband, went on to university.

We married at twenty and quickly produced four children. When my youngest child entered school I began work on statistics for a medical magazine. But it wasn't a fulfilling career and by the time I joined the course I had begun to feel that a new challenge was needed.

Contrary to expectations I had no family problems when I began to study. My husband and my children gave me lots of encouragement and support. My teenage children in particular were encouraged to see that I had homework as well and a kind of mutual support system came into operation. The need to succeed as an example to my children has been a powerful motivator; at times of low morale I always knew I could not quit because you cannot show children that this is ever an option. During the New Horizons course I had few problems with finding time but I had none of the skills – concentration, clear thinking, planning – which help to develop a written style, and after such a long gap in my education I was certainly lacking confidence in my abilities to either think or to write. I was surprised that study techniques could be improved so effectively by the approach adopted on the course and recall being particularly impressed by the 'brainstorming' techniques to which we were introduced. Each new skill learned was like a key to another door and through each door one gained access to others. The course was an exhilarating time and it changed my subsequent life immeasurably.

On one level the first major advantage I gained was contact with other like-minded but very different people on the course. Receiving well-informed guidance on possible avenues for further study was also very important; certainly without the course I would never have gone on to study Combined Honours at Manchester University, as I did. As a mature student I was initially wary at inflicting what I considered to be my middle-aged presence on the young people surrounding me. I need not have feared. I now have so many young friends and the twenty-odd-year age difference seems to be no barrier at all. Some tutors seem to find mature students a little threatening but this is very much a minority and most tutors welcome us as highly motivated and usually articulate, students.

Being a mature student is not easy. There are constant problems involved in balancing one's time and resources between study and family life. I also found it difficult to write essays – I always have, and I cannot say that I found examinations easy either. But my studies worked out astonishingly well in the end. One of the first things we had to do on New Horizons was to write a short piece on 'the happiest day of my life'. I wrote about passing my driving test because the intense joy of that day has always stuck in my memory! If I had to re-write that essay it would be about the day I received my degree result and learned that I had been awarded first-class honours. What made that day more magical was that my success was something that rippled outwards. The joy wasn't just mine but belonged to my family, tutors and fellow students. Education was the source of all this pleasure and the glow is still there inside me; not a personal pride – something much more intangible. I feel so unbelievably lucky that I was given this chance to live such a richer and rewarding life when at thirty I thought all the paths in life were closed to me. **"**

1 *Being an adult student*

What one knows is, in youth, of little moment; they know enough who know how to learn   *Henry Adams*

Only the educated are free   *Epictetus*

Contents

Introduction

This chapter is addressed to the problems of being an adult student. The topics are dealt with via a question-and-answer approach. The information is not simply presented to you: questions are posed and you are asked to think up the answers. The reasons for this approach are twofold: firstly, some of the answers relate to your own personal experience and secondly, others relate to things you possibly already know or can work out with a little thought. Indeed, one of the assumptions of this course is that much of what we are seeking to teach you is already known to you: the course will often ask you to think in ways which will demonstrate this fact. By finding the answers yourself you will be more likely to remember them and the invitation to think involves you more closely in the text. After a question is posed you will see the instruction STOP HERE, which means we would like you to stop and think through the question for a number of minutes. Space is allowed in the text for you to jot down notes.
The next message is a very important one!

Do not read on otherwise you will stray into the DISCUSSIONS, which are our version of the answers to the questions we have posed. To read on, without thinking, is to miss out an important requirement of the course: that you should begin to think for yourself right from the start. This chapter will encourage you to think about:

● our educational system
● problems of adult study
● the advantages of being an adult student
● your own attitudes towards education
● your present strengths and weaknesses as a student

ONCE AGAIN:
Don't forget to STOP and THINK before going on to the DISCUSSION!
You may find it helpful to cover up the Discussion whilst you are thinking.

The adult student in our educational system   1

The aim of this section is to help you realise that you are operating in an educational system which gives only limited support to adult students. The British system has been founded upon two important assumptions: that education is needed for the most part by young people; and that once they leave their schools or colleges at 16, 18 or 21 they have received sufficient formal education to last them throughout their lives. Do you think these assumptions are justified or can you identify any shortcomings which they might have?

5–10 minutes   Do *not* go on to discussion until you have thought   **STOP**
about this question for at least five to ten minutes. And write
down your responses on a piece of paper – just in brief note form.
Don't try keeping everything in your head.

There is an obvious logic about educating people when they are   *Discussion*
young. We *have* to learn how to speak, to read and write as clearly
as possible in order to understand and communicate with each
other. We also need to acquire some mathematical and scientific
skills, knowledge about the economy, society and subjects which
will help prepare us for employment and other aspects of the
adult world. It makes considerable sense, therefore, to establish a
system of primary and secondary education for young people

aged 5 to 16 and to make a variety of arrangements for those aged 16 to 21. However, to assume that this provision takes care of *all* educational needs ignores the following points:

(a) The economy is changing rapidly in response to recent technological advances. Many traditional occupations are disappearing, for instance – manufacturing jobs as a result of factory automation and clerical jobs as a result of computerisation. To re-train and re-employ people who have lost their jobs, to secure the future of those still working in occupations under threat and to help others keep abreast of developments, continual re-education is necessary throughout their working lives.

(b) These same technological advances have created the prospect and, for some, the reality of more leisure time – some of it welcome in the form of a shorter working week and some of it unwelcome in the form of unemployment. Work is not now sufficiently certain or time-consuming to fill our lives the way it used to: we need to learn how to enjoy our leisure time and to use it in a productive way.

(c) Some people – for a variety of reasons – fail to take advantage of educational opportunities when younger but develop a powerful interest later on. For example:

   (i) Many young people are bored at school and leave it with a sense of failure but find their own way to an interest in study when older.

   (ii) Traditional attitudes have tended to encourage women to see their main function as homebuilders and child-rearers and to dissuade them from studying seriously when younger. Later in life, especially when their children are older, many women question these assumptions and actively seek those opportunities they earlier let slip by.

   To make no provision for 'later starters' is to squander their potential contribution to society and prevent them from developing their personalities and abilities to a fuller extent.

(d) Study is something which people can and arguably should enjoy all their lives, not just for the first part of it. Education, moreover, is mind-enhancing in that it increases the ability to understand and do things. To assume that it should be abandoned after a certain age is to deny adults an important dimension to their lives.

(e) The argument that people should pay for their own education when they are adult is unsatisfactory in that it discriminates against the lower-paid and people with family commitments, especially when the course of study contemplated requires times off or a substantial break from work.

(f) Children are powerfully influenced by the behaviour and

habits of their parents. A home in which study is an integral part will reduce youthful resistance to study and help establish interests to cultivate and standards to aim for.

How did your response to the question go? Most likely you identified some of the points I have mentioned – quite possibly you have listed all my points plus a few more of your own besides, in which case, well done. You may have found, however, that your mind went blank: maybe you felt a bit threatened and even found you could write nothing at all. If this happened to you, don't worry – it frequently happens to adults returning to study and is caused mostly by anxiety which is itself a consequence of lack of confidence (on which more below). Don't worry, either, if you did not elaborate your points as fully as I have – I am deliberately using the 'discussion' in places to convey quite a bit of information.

To give you a little bit more practice here is another question. Try to think what extra facilities and financial arrangements adults need to help them pursue their studies more effectively. For instance, one might be the building of more purpose-built adult or community centres as opposed to evening use of school facilities.

---

5 minutes   Don't forget to make a written note of your answers.   **STOP**

Some parts of the country have very good adult education facilities and your impression may even be, in consequence, that they are adequate – especially given the availability for everyone of the excellent Open University (OU). However, in other parts of the country local facilities have declined over the last few years as a result of financial cuts. Your list might include:
(a) **Better grants for adult students.** At present adults receive at maximum little more than younger students yet may have considerably more financial responsibilities – for instance, a house and family. Nor do they receive any maintenance grants for studying part-time degrees and usually have to pay a proportion of their tuition fees for such courses. To study with the OU is still beyond the means of many potential adult students.
(b) **Paid educational study leave from work.** Few people are able to receive this in Britain, unlike adult students in Germany and Sweden. Swedish law actually protects the security of your job so that your return to it after study is guaranteed. For many adults substantial periods of study are completely ruled out through the lack of such possibilities.
(c) **More flexible ways of studying within higher education.**

Universities and polytechnics still concentrate on offering full-time three-year degree courses instead of the wide range of part-time and distance studies which are now available in other countries. Under government pressure the British system is slowly changing.

(d) **More plentiful and cheaper day and evening classes.** In some parts of the country evening classes have almost disappeared and costs have risen so as to exclude large groups of people. Indeed, many argue that retired people, the unemployed and those living on social security should be allowed to study such classes free of charge.

(e) **Crèche facilities for mothers wishing to study during the day.**

(f) **Easier access for adults to higher education.** The present entry requirements for most universities makes it difficult for adults lacking traditional qualifications to enter higher education even though their abilities might be quite high (see Chapter 9, Volume II for more information on this).

(g) **More opportunities for adult residential study.**

(h) **Better teaching materials in adult education:** too many are at present designed either for schoolchildren or for under-graduates.

The list is potentially much longer, of course, and I hope on this occasion you identified some requirements which I have not mentioned. I would now like to try asking you a more difficult question, but an intriguing one. There are so many excellent reasons for developing and changing our educational system to take account of the adult students that it sometimes seems extraordinary that more development has not taken place and that adult education should command much less than 1% of the educational budget. Can you think of any explanations?

STOP   **5–10 minutes**

Your points might include:

(a) The shortage of and shift away from public expenditure in the late 1970s and 1980s; governments are no longer so willing to spend money on expanding public services.

(b) The constant struggle by *other* parts of our vast educational system – universities, nursery education, secondary schools, multi-racial education – to gain increased resources or at worst, to minimise cuts.

(c) The invariable reluctance of established institutions to change their way of thinking and operating.

(d) The rise of the idea that individuals should not rely upon the state but should pay their own way.

18

(e)   The acute problem of youth unemployment and related law
       and order problems which help push adult education lower
       down the scale of priorities.

If you have better explanations perhaps you can send them to me,
as I would be interested! Having looked briefly at the educational
system as it relates to adults, I now move on to the specific study
problems which they face.

Problems of adult study   2

From the exercises above it is obvious that whilst opportunities
for study certainly do exist, life is not made especially easy for
adult students, at least not in relation to their younger
counterparts. Adults face in addition a number of specific study
problems. As your next exercise try to identify, in order of
importance, the five most important problems which you face as
an adult undertaking a substantial course of study.

---

15 minutes   **STOP**

You may have given different names to the problems facing you   *Discussion*
but in the past our students when asked this question have
identified:
(a)   Lack of confidence.
(b)   Lack of time.
(c)   Poor concentration.
(d)   Poor self-discipline.
(e)   Negative family attitudes.
(f)   Confusion over direction of future study.
(g)   Lack of finance.
(h)   The time lapse since last experience of study.
(i)   Lack of perseverance.
I will elaborate a little upon each problem and say a few initial
words on how they can be counteracted.

(a)   Confidence
I have quite a bit to say about confidence, and we will touch on it
again throughout the course. Lack of it can cause great
apprehension regarding any aspect of study and in many cases
prevent adults from contemplating any kind of course
whatsoever. One adult student once confessed to me that it was
her grown-up children who insisted that she fill in the application
form for the return to study course she attended and who walked
her to the post-box to make sure it was sent off. The fact that she

went on to gain an upper second-class honours degree at Manchester Polytechnic reveals that in reality she had far more grounds for confidence than for apprehension. Why do adults so often suffer from such chronic lack of confidence? Perhaps you can spend a few minutes trying to puzzle this out, especially if this is a problem which affects you to a greater or lesser extent.

STOP   10 minutes

Discussion   The reasons are obviously complex but in my experience they frequently include:

(i)   A home environment which did not encourage study.

(ii) An unhappy experience of school, producing a sense of failure.

(iii) For women, several years of child-rearing which, whilst fulfilling and enjoyable, can break up concentration (young children often see study or even book-reading as rivals for the attention they desire) or be so all-absorbing that they claim the time previously given to other interests.

(iv) A feeling that the proper time for study was at school and that adult study is somehow inappropriate or even foolish in the eyes of family and friends.

(v) A sense that serious study, especially within higher education, is not for them but is reserved for some special breed of 'clever people'. Some students have even said that the knowledge dealt with at universities was of a different kind to that used by 'ordinary people' like them!

(vi) The fear of being assessed by someone else, of maybe having one's inadequacies painfully exposed. Some people prefer to go living with the hope that they *might* be capable of studying successfully than actually putting it to the test and risking the disappointment of failure.

It is important to realise that these barriers are mostly psychological: they diminish rapidly once study commences and in their acute form usually rapidly disappear. Points (i), (ii) and (iii) are obviously considerable disadvantages but can be overcome more easily than might be thought with a little sustained effort and dedication. Points (iv), (v) and (vi) invariably prove to be groundless when it is realised that: it is quite normal for adults to study seriously and that many of them do; knowledge is not changed by the people who study it; and that tutor's comments on students' work are almost always helpful and constructive.

(b) **Time**
As a general rule adults have less time available for study than younger students: parents have to look after children, householders to take care of their houses, and those in work to devote

the considerable amount of time needed to do their job properly. Most adults have to find time to study in the evening or on a distance learning basis. This course offers an advantage in that you can study it in a way which gives you plenty of time to study at any time of the day or evening, depending upon your circumstances and your mood. Chapter 2 will help you to organise your time more efficiently.

(c) Concentration

Adult students often complain that their concentration span is very short: five, ten minutes or even less! And they frequently complain that after a short time reading they realise their eyes have been following the text but nothing has been really going in. Even worse, others complain that after sitting down, full of determination to study they wake up an hour later with barely three or four pages turned. Problems of concentration are dealt with in Chapter 3, so no more will be said here except that it is a familiar problem which is easily overcome once genuine interest is aroused.

(d) Self-discipline

Adults who remember their study habits as being slack or carefree when in school often fear that they will prove equally lacking without the external encouragement and pressure of teachers, parents, school expectations, examinations and so forth. It is certainly true that effective study requires self-discipline and an efficient routine, but good study habits are not impossible to achieve: adults must give themselves the credit for having matured and changed since their schooldays (see Section 3 below).

(e) Family attitudes

Usually (but often with great difficulty) the practical problems associated with adult study, like daytime collection of children, can be solved. What is harder to get around are the negative attitudes towards study by other members of the family: a wife or husband who resents and feels threatened by this potentially far-reaching departure; families which refuse to adapt and help and who inspire guilt and depression instead of enthusiasm and support. If faced with concerted family opposition anyone might have second thoughts about serious study.

It is highly desirable to have family support and if it is not forthcoming potential students should undertake a subtle but determined family education campaign to convince them of the merits of study. My own view – widely shared by adult educators – is that women with children in particular have no reason to feel guilty at reducing their domestic commitments to fit in some serious study. After years of giving to their families women deserve to spend some time on their own self-development. Families should appreciate this and realise that mothers have to make some preparation for what they will do when their children leave home.

(f)   Direction of future study

Adults returning to study are often unsure about what they can go on to do and feel they ought to have their objectives clearly defined. But there is no reason why you should know about your own potential and goals in advance. One of the reasons for returning to study is to discover what they *might* be! This problem usually solves itself as the course progresses and people on it develop a fuller idea of their own abilities and interests. Chapter 9 in Volume II will be of assistance here.

(g)   Finance

The lack of public financial support for adult students has already been mentioned. Short courses are obviously less of a problem but, depending on your circumstances, it can become acute for the larger and more expensive courses. It is usually possible, however, to pay your fee in instalments if this makes things easier for you. If this is a problem discuss it with your tutor or the course administrators. This may seem like cold comfort, but many adult students entering further and higher education accept that they might have to take a drop in living standards for a while – and they regard the intellectual stimulation they receive as a sort of compensation.

(h)   Time lapse since last experience of formal study

Many adults, especially the older ones, claim that their educational experience is so dead and buried in the past that there is little or no chance of exhumation. However, as with most of the other fears, this too usually proves groundless. This is not to deny that the higher the level studied at school the easier and quicker it is for skills to return. Those who left school at 15 will usually – though not necessarily – need to work harder and longer to reach a given level that someone who left at 18 with a couple of A levels. And it usually follows that the more recent these school experiences the shorter the skill recovery time, but in our experience:

(i)   School skills return surprisingly quickly – a matter of a few weeks – even for older students.

(ii) Most people have kept contact with reading and writing through their hobbies or their work.

(iii) Many older students were never tested or encouraged to use their full potential when in school and soon find out they are outperforming anything they achieved years ago in school.

Finally, no evidence exists that intellectual as opposed to physical ability declines with age: the brain survives generally much better than the rest of the body and has usually benefited from a lifetime's experience and regular use.

(i) Perseverance

As an extension of the last two problems mentioned, many adult students fear they will not stay the course but will fall behind and eventually give up. The best guarantee of successful study, as already mentioned, is interest in the subject. You will know from your hobbies and other leisure activities – sport, reading, gardening – that things which capture the interest give enjoyment and what you enjoy you normally want more of. If you find the course has caught your interest and you feel that you are making progress there will be no serious problem in seeing it through to the end. But something needs to be said to qualify this.

Your motivation will not be constant. It will vary according to the part of the course you are taking, the response you have been receiving to your work assignments from your tutor, and your own moods and problems. Over the years, Roy Johnson and I have noticed a typical profile of student morale emerge. We have have half-jokingly called this the 'Jones/Johnson curve' as illustrated below.

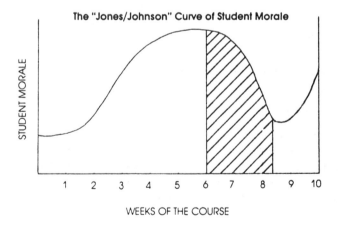

The "Jones/Johnson" Curve of Student Morale

STUDENT MORALE

WEEKS OF THE COURSE

We observed – and students confirmed our observations – that over the first ten weeks of our New Horizons course student morale began at a low point (reflecting the apprehension of the first day) and climbed rapidly during the first few weeks. This part of the graph reflected relief, growing confidence and (we like to think) enjoyment. Morale then often dips steeply when the novelty of the course begins to wear off and the work becomes more demanding. The shaded section on the graph between weeks 6 and 8 was the danger period when people were likely to drop out. If students survived the downward dip of the 'Jones/ Johnson' curve they were more likely to stay the full 25 weeks. We always took care to explain this phenomenon so that students could anticipate possible fluctuations in their morale and steel their determination to see them through. Naturally, the morale profile of a distance learning course (if you are studying in this mode) will be different but similar variations in your resolution will almost certainly occur, so you have been warned!

It ought to be said at this point that there are no easy routes with serious study. You have to accept that it requires considerable determination, discipline and application. But all this invest-ment of effort pays a rich dividend.

3 *Advantages of being an adult student*

So far this chapter had dwelt – perhaps excessively – upon all the problems that you face. That was the bad news. But there is, you will be relieved to hear, good news as well. There is a much more positive aspect to being an adult student and you enjoy several advantages compared with your younger counterparts. Try to entertain this welcome thought for a few minutes and then try to identify as many of those advantages as you can.

STOP   **5–10 minutes**

Discussion   (a) **Strong motivation**
This is probably the major advantage which adult students enjoy. Unlike younger students, who have been led along the path of study often without making any particular conscious choice, adults usually study through choice and interest. They are mature enough to feel a genuine curiosity and experience keen pleasure when it is satisfied or when a skill is developed and practised to a new level. A vocational motive can also serve to sharpen the interest, especially if studies relate closely to work requirements. Adults, therefore, frequently have clear objectives and are genuinely motivated instead of simply wishing to 'do well' like so many younger students.

(b) **Maturity**
For an adult student, new information and ideas are integrated

into a more extensive stockpile of knowledge and experience. Study, therefore, is more meaningful and exciting.

(c) Organising skills
Often without realising it, adults have learnt habits of discipline and organisation through work of childcare (a family requires considerable planning and management skills) or leisure activities (for example, working with voluntary bodies, organising football matches, etc.).

(d) Effective management of time
Paradoxically, their very lack of time helps adults to organise what they have more efficiently. Nor are they normally so diverted by the fun-seeking activities which claim – albeit pleasantly – so much of younger students' time.

(e) Communication skills
Though they are often surprised to discover it, adults are generally more articulate and confident than younger students. They operate more effectively in group work where they are able to bring to bear their experience of life: many university tutors rely heavily upon contributions from the mature members of their tutorial groups.

(f) Perseverance
Adults are often more resilient than youngsters and in spite of fears mentioned in the previous section, are aware that things which become difficult have to be struggled with until they are overcome.

A final note in this section needs to be added on the subject of 'guilt'. Psychology books often tell us that this is a harmful and unnecessary feeling but when adult students tell me they are worried about their feelings of guilt at not doing their background reading, not completing their work assignments, I always point out the beneficial aspects. Guilt is, paradoxically again, an advantage to be exploited. Those who feel no guilt at falling behind in their work are less likely to catch up than those who do. There are a few, very few, students of all ages who feel no guilt because they always complete their work on time, fulfil all their reading commitments and are generally beyond reproach. These saintly few are indeed fortunate (though sometimes irritatingly self-righteous). I always explain that one of the things you take on with study is the perpetual feeling that you are not doing enough, that work obligations will hang heavy on your conscience from time to time. This is a natural part of the student condition and should be recognised and valued as such. Be careful, though, not to overdo it; don't allow yourself to be eaten away by the feeling but keep it in perspective and in its place.

4   *Getting to know your own strengths and weaknesses*

As already mentioned in our Introduction this is to some extent a course of self-discovery: you will find out something about your own limits and potential. As a first step in this process of self-analysis I want you to consider the evolution of your own attitudes towards education. First, a little background is necessary, together with a related exercise.

Attitudes towards education
A. L. Rowse was a working-class boy who won the only scholarship in his county to Oxford University where he eventually became a distinguished professor. But Professor Rowse is very much a member of the minority. Children from professional homes are much more likely to go to university than those from working-class homes. Professor Edwards of Nottingham University has calculated that males born into the professional class have an 80% chance of entering full-time higher education whilst at the other end of the scale females born to the families of unskilled workers have about a 1% chance. Are middle-class children more intelligent than working-class children? Most research into the subject suggests that the differential rate of success has little or nothing to do with this; most groups of children display the same range of intellectual potential irrespective of class. It is the culture within which children from different social groups are brought up which is decisive. In what ways, though, do you think a middle-class social background gives greater encouragement to children to study compared with a working-class background?

STOP   **10 minutes. (Don't forget to stop at these points in the chapters: to read on without pause for thought is to squander an advantage of the 'workbook' approach.)**

Discussion   This is a much debated and complex question and you may very well disagree with some of my analysis which follows.

(a) **The greater financial resources** of middle-class families enable them to give their children a number of advantages: the possibility of high-quality private education; residence in a catchment area of a school with a high proportion of other advantaged children; good study facilities; educational leisure pursuits (for example, home computers); plentiful books and other study materials.

(b) **An atmosphere more conducive to study** is found in middle-class homes with books being available and parents who read regularly as part of their work or leisure.

(c) **Schools speak a 'middle-class language'.** Some sociologists argue that working-class children develop a distinctive language style which is not inferior but different to the more formal and elaborate middle-class way of speaking. As schools are run by teachers mostly using the middle-class 'code', working-class children are at a considerable disadvantage and are more likely to feel that school is not for them.

(d) **Middle-class children receive constant encouragement to study and 'do well'** as their parents did before them and to gain interesting, prestigious and well-paid jobs. They are made to feel that they ought to study and that it is the natural thing for them to do. Some working-class families place great emphasis on study but others regard it as part of an alien and antagonistic culture.

(e) **Children pick up the occupational expectations of their parents.** Those of you who have seen the excellent Granada programme '7 Up' will have seen well illustrated how a group of children drawn from across the social spectrum will tend to want to do the kind of jobs which their parents do. The 7-year-old working-class children interviewed on the programme expected and looked forward to manual-type occupations whilst the middle-class children expected to enter higher education and go on to professional jobs. Those of you who also saw the follow-up programmes will have seen how these expectations were fulfilled to a remarkable degree.

Do you see how the process works? Our attitudes to study and education are closely connected to the occupation and income of our parents. We tend to follow the paths already pursued by our parents and this pattern is a persistent one all over the world. In Sweden, for example – the country in Western Europe most concerned with social equality – a new admissions system to higher education was introduced in 1977. The idea was to make it easier for working-class people to enter higher education. After six years of operating the new system the results were as follows:

Population entering higher education in Sweden according to social class, 1983 (%)

Social class	Upper middle	Middle	Lower middle	Skilled workers	Unskilled workers
% of population (approximately)	6	13	24	19	38
% of class entering higher education	69	35	23	16	9

How did you get on with this topic? Quite possibly you disagreed with my analysis as many people have their own distinctive ideas on what is a politically controversial subject. However, if you did disagree try to see precisely where and how you did so and try to identify the evidence which supports your ideas rather than mine. Remember it is no use just *feeling* that you disagree or arguing purely from your own personal experience: on questions like this you must be able to cite evidence relating to substantial samples of the population.

5 *Overcoming writer's block*

If you have any difficulty in getting started on the self-assessment questions at the end of each chapter (or any problems with writing later on in the study programme) then consult this section on overcoming writer's block.

When confronted with the task of producing a piece of writing, many people develop a mental block. It can be like a state of panic, or emptiness, or paralysis – or just a sheer inability to get started. The sheet of blank paper stares you in the face, and you cannot think what to write on it. Your mind is just as blank as the paper or you simply cannot make the pen move across the page. Suddenly all sorts of other tasks seem very attractive – washing the car, tidying the cupboards, taking the dog for a walk. You *want* to write your essay or letter or report. You may even have a deadline to meet. But the last thing you can bring yourself to do is start writing. And to make matters worse, the longer you worry about it, the more intractable the problem seems to become.

If you sometimes suffer in this way, here's the first piece of good news: it is a very common problem. Even experienced writers sometimes suffer from it. So do not imagine that you are the only person in the world who has ever had such a difficulty, or that it is caused by some deficiency in your brain. What you need to know is how to get out of the blocked condition. And to do this it may help if you can identify the cause.

What I am going to offer in this note is a series of the most common statements people make when suffering writer's block. This should help you identify your own case. Then I offer in explanation one or two of the most probable *causes* for the condition – followed by tips on how to effect a *cure*.

Read through all the examples given. It will help you to

understand that the cure for writer's block often involves engagement with other parts of the writing process which *precede* putting pen to paper.

1 'I'm just terrified at the very thought of writing'

Cause Maybe you are just not used to writing or are out of practice. Maybe you are over-anxious and possibly setting your standards too high.

Cure Limber up and get yourself used to the activity by writing something else first. Scribble something on a scrap of paper which nobody else will see – a description, a letter to yourself, anything just to put words on to paper.

2 'I'm not sure what to say'

Cause Maybe you have not done enough preparation for the task in hand. Maybe you haven't yet accumulated enough ideas or comments.

Cure Sort out your ideas before you start writing. Make rough notes on the topics or comments you wish to make. These can then be expanded when you start writing. 'Brainstorm' your topic; read around it; put all your preliminary ideas on paper, then sift out the best ones.

3 'My mind goes blank'

Cause Maybe you have not done enough preparation. Maybe you do not have rough notes or a working plan. Maybe you are frightened of saying the wrong thing.

Cure Make notes for what you intend to do. Try starting yourself off on some rough paper – which nobody else will see. Write anything: you can always change it later.

4 'It's just a problem of the first sentence'

Cause These can be quite hard to write! Maybe you are setting yourself standards which are too high. Maybe you are fixated on order (or using this as an excuse?)

Cure The first sentence can be written later. Make a start somewhere else and come back to it. Alternatively write any sentence, knowing that you will change it later.

5 'I'm not *quite* ready to start yet'

Cause This *may* be procrastination, or maybe you have not finished digesting and sorting out your ideas on the topic in question.

Cure If it is procrastination, then use the warming-up device of writing something else just to get into the mood. If it is not, then maybe you need to revise your notes or drum up a few more ideas.

6 'I've got *too much* information'

Cause If you have several pages of notes, then maybe they need to be digested. Maybe you have not *selected* the details which are most important, or eliminated anything non-essential.

Cure Digest, then edit the information so as to pare it down to what is essential. Don't try to include everything. Draw up a plan which includes only that which is necessary. If your plan is too long, then condense it.

7 'I've not got the right information or book'

Cause If this is not just an excuse, then it may be that a crucial book or small piece of information is holding you up.

Cure Make a start anyway, without it. You can always leave gaps in your work and add things later. Alternatively, make a calculated guess – which you can change if necessary at a later stage when you have the correct information.

8 'I'm frightened of producing rubbish'

Cause Maybe you are being too hard on yourself and setting standards which are too high (or it's possibly a form of pride).

Cure Don't worry. Be prepared to accept a modest achievement at first. And anyway it is very unlikely that anybody else will be over-critical. If you are a student, it's the tutor's job to help you improve.

9 'I'm stuck at the planning stage'

Cause This may be a hidden fear of starting or it may be a sort of perfectionism. It may be that you are making *too* much of the plan itself.

Cure Make a start anyway. You can write a first draft which may help you to clarify your ideas and finalise your plan – which can then be used as the basis for your second draft.

10 'I'm not sure in what order to put things'

Cause Maybe there are a number of possibilities, and you are seeking the *best* order. Or maybe there is no 'best' or 'right' order. You are probably looking for some coherence or logic.

Cure Draw up a number of different plans. Lay them out together, then select the one which seems best. You might even do this literally, with pieces of paper on the floor. Be prepared to chop and change the order of your information until the best order *emerges*.

Some general guidelines

1 Don't imagine that you should be able to write impeccably at your first attempt. Many writers make several drafts of their work: they edit what they say, correct mistakes, and re-write extensively before they produce what they consider the final result. Writing well is a fairly skilled business – so nobody can expect you to have that skill if you are still at the learning stage.

2 Don't just sit staring at the blank piece of paper: it will only make you feel worse. Do something else, then come back to the task. Best of all, *write* something else – something you know you can write. This will help you feel better.

3 Do some different type of writing as a warm-up exercise. Write a note or a letter, re-write some of your earlier work, write something just for your own amusement.

4 Get used to the idea of using plenty of paper. Make a start: if it is no good or you make mistakes you can scrap it and start again. If you are writing more than one draft you might well be using scrap paper for your first attempts.

5 Don't try composing in your head if you get stuck. Put even your scrappiest ideas on paper, so that you can see what you are dealing with – and maybe identify the problem. Put it on paper. You can always cross it out or change it if it is wrong.

6 Get used to the idea of planning and making notes for what you are going to write. Don't try to work with all the information stored in your head. A plan and good notes will take the strain off you – and will prompt you with ideas, which in turn will prevent a 'block' developing.

7 Be prepared to make two or three attempts at anything you write. The first may not be very good – but it can be corrected, altered, changed, or thrown away. Nobody need see your first attempts, so you needn't worry how bad they are – provided you pass on to a second or third.

Self-assessment exercises

First let me just remind you what these exercises are for and advise you how to make the best use of them. We are including them to give you a chance to check that you have understood each chapter and to prompt you into further thought on the topics raised in them. If you are serious in your desire to acquire the study skills you will need for further education you should get used to exercises like these which ask to you recall information, make notes in response to questions, or write short, imaginative or explanatory pieces. You may be tempted to just skim over them or even pass them by, but we strongly urge you to resist this temptation – for your own sake.

And we also urge you to *write down* your responses and answers. Don't try to just hold the information in your head. Condensing your response into brief notes is a fairly useful skill you will be developing if you go the trouble of putting pen to paper. We, of course, have no way of knowing what you write, but we will be offering you a range of *possible* responses and occasional model answers against which you can check your own. If you are wide of the mark we suggest that you read through the chapter again to gain a firmer grasp of the issues, but if your response is more or less on target you will have the satisfaction of knowing that you have understood what is required and are making progress.

Exercise 1
Can you recall the main elements we have covered in this chapter? Try to list them without looking back in the book.

Exercise 2
Using a couple of sheets of paper, and informed by the topics discussed in this chapter, write out in brief note form (or as extended prose if you wish) a summary of your own experience of education from when you were a child up to the present. This should include both the influences on you and your responses to them, as well as any phase your personal life may have passed through which has brought you to your present interest in education.

Exercise 3
Can you list all the study skills you think you will need for progress into further or higher education?

Exercise 4
Write 2 to 3 sides upon a moment in your life which you will never forget.

Recommended further reading
We are offering these suggestions for further reading at this stage in order to help you sift through the thousands and thousands of books available – and to encourage you to get into the habit of reading as widely as possible. Not only will regular reading put you in touch with new ideas, it will also help you develop your own writing skills by bringing you into close contact with writers of proven quality.
The list is split into two parts – fiction and non-fiction. We have chosen books which are well known, and therefore easily available in libraries or as cheap paperbacks.

Fiction

Jane Austen	*Pride and Prejudice, Emma, Mansfield Park*
Saul Bellow	*Henderson the Rain King, Seize the Day*
Joseph Conrad	*The Secret Agent, Heart of Darkness*
Charles Dickens	*Hard Times, Great Expectations, Bleak House*
E. M. Forster	*A Room with a View, A Passage to India*
Nadine Gordimer	*Burger's Daughter, July's People*
Walter Greenwood	*Love on the Dole*
Thomas Hardy	*Tess of D'Urbervilles, The Mayor of Caster-bridge*
Henry James	*Washington Square, The Europeans*
D. H. Lawrence	*The Rainbow, Women in Love*
Katherine Mansfield	*The Collected Short Stories*
George Orwell	*Animal Farm, Nineteen Eighty-Four*
Evelyn Waugh	*Scoop, Decline and Fall, A Handful of Dust*
Virginia Woolf	*Orlando*

Non-fiction

John Berger	*Ways of Seeing*	(A)
E. H. Carr	*What is History?*	(H)
Simone de Beauvoir	*The Second Sex*	(P)
Sigmund Freud	*Introductory Lectures on Psychoanalysis*	(P)
Shere Hite	*Women and Love*	(S)
Eric Hobsbawm	*Industry and Empire*	(H)
Arthur Marwick	*British Society since 1945*	(H)
Margaret Mead	*Coming of Age in Samoa*	(S)
George Orwell	*The Decline of English Murder*	(E)
Henry Pilling	*The History of British Trade Unionism*	(H)
Robert Roberts	*The Classic Slum*	(S)
Sheila Rowbotham	*Women's Consciousness, Man's World*	(P)
A. J. P. Taylor	*English History 1914–45*	(H)

(A) Art   (S) Sociology
(H) History   (E) Essays
(P) Psychology

2 *Organising and planning your time*

Learning is its own exceeding great reward   *William Hazlitt*

The roots of education are bitter but the fruit is sweet   *Aristotle*

Contents

Introduction
1   Creating more free time
2   Making more efficient use of existing time
3   Combining study with other activities
4   Conclusions
    Self-assessment exercises

Introduction

When young people study at school, college and even university, they usually have three enormous advantages:
(a)   They are studying full-time.
(b)   They rarely have any other responsibilities or commitments.
(c)   Their study time in the classroom is planned for them.

Adults, on the other hand, returning to education as mature students, often have a number of disadvantages:
(a)   They can only afford to study *part*-time.
(b)   Many have full-time jobs and responsibilities to families.
(c)   They are not used to organising their own studies.
The net result of this can be a severe shortage of spare time in which to study.

It is for this reason that any adult student should confront this problem head-on before undertaking a serious course of study. It is no use thinking that academic advance can be made on a casual basis where work is just done occasionally when there happens to be free time. Systematic progress requires a regular and disciplined attitude to study in which a great deal of work gets done. All this will require a considerable amount of well-spent *time*. But where will this time come from? How can a mature student combine studying with a normal life which might include work and family commitments?

The answers to these (very common) problems fall into three categories:
(a) You should be prepared to *create* more free time by rearranging and maybe sacrificing some of your other activity.
(b) You should *make more efficient use* of your existing spare time by careful planning and a disciplined use of it.
(c) You should try to *integrate* study activity with other parts of your life where possible.

We will look at each of these categories in turn to see how the problem can be tackled at a particular level – but first a word of encouragement. Many mature students think that they work at a disadvantage compared with younger students, but in terms of organisation and discipline regarding their time they are often far more experienced. Anyone who has had to accept the disciplines of regular timekeeping at work or who has organised the routine of family life and childcare knows what it means to establish priorities, meet deadlines, and stick to plans.

What may come as a novelty to many mature students is *voluntarily* turning such discipline, restraint and planning on to the development of their own intellectual life. But it can be done!

Creating more free time

Here are two average days in the life of Ray Abbot and Gaynor Reynolds. How do you think they could create more time for themselves in which to study? (It is usually easier to solve this problem for others than for ourselves.) You should also try to take into account what possible effects making a change might have.

Your objective is to find or 'create' spaces in their days which could be used for studying. At this stage, look for larger blocks of time – say around an hour – but later we will show you how even smaller units or just the odd few minutes can be put to good use. You will probably have to look for spots of 'dead' time in which nothing special is being done.

Ray Abbot – single

8.00 a.m.	Gets up – breakfast.
8.30 a.m.	Travels to work on bus.
9.30 a.m.	Works in Town Hall.
12.30 p.m.	Lunches in staff canteen.
1.30 p.m.	Works.
5.30 p.m.	Travels home.
6.30 p.m.	Evening meal.
8.00 p.m.	Plays badminton.
10.00 p.m.	In pub with friends.
11.00 p.m.	Reads paper in bed.
11.30 p.m.	Falls asleep.

STOP   10 minutes

Discussion   Ray has the disadvantage (from the study point of view) of having to spend seven hours of his typical day at work – time which we assume he cannot use for study. But the rest of his day presents a number of possibilities.

(a) 'Travels to work on bus'

Two hours (total) is available every day travelling to and from work. This is time which could be used for reading or looking over notes instead of looking out of the bus window. Obviously nothing very strenuous or demanding can be done under such conditions, but the time is lost otherwise. Many people spend such time reading newspapers: why not a textbook instead?

(b) 'Lunches in staff canteen'

Many people could put this hour to use by having sandwiches for lunch and spending the time on a little reading or revision. Again, nothing very extensive need necessarily be undertaken, but keeping in touch with the subject will be beneficial – and perhaps even a refreshing break from work. Imagine how usefully such time would be spent if you were learning a foreign language. A one-hour slot is available every day of the week during which you could test your knowledge of vocabulary or acquire more.

Ray would be sacrificing the company of colleagues for the hour, but this is a case of deciding priorities. Which is more useful to him – a chat with workmates, or time spent in study on, say two or three of his five weekdays?

(c) 'Plays badminton'

Physical fitness can help promote mental fitness, but does he *have* to play in the middle of the evening? If he could play either earlier or later he might free a couple of extra hours for study. This is an example where studying comes into conflict

with social life, and it might require understanding on the part of his friends and the disruption of his normal routine.
(d) 'Reads the paper in bed'
Not everybody can study efficiently late at night, and this is obviously a suitable time and place for relaxation, but look how long Ray spends in bed – nine hours in all! He could surely make do with less time there, either getting up earlier in the morning or rearranging his evening and going to bed later. Both of these strategies could lead to an extra two to three hours free time.

Now we will try a more difficult case – a busy day in the life of Gaynor Reynolds.

Gaynor Reynolds – Husband and two children

7.30 a.m.	Gets up – makes breakfast.
8.00 a.m.	Dresses and feeds children — takes them to school.
9.30 a.m.	Cup of tea and rest – listens to Radio Two.
10.30 a.m.	Housework.
11.30 a.m.	Goes to shops.
12.30 p.m.	Lunch.
2.00 p.m.	Sewing – listens to Woman's Hour.
3.30 p.m.	Collects children from school. Calls at shops.
4.30 p.m.	Feeds children. Prepares evening meal.
6.00 p.m.	Evening meal with husband. Washes up.
7.30 p.m.	Prepares children for bed.
8.30 p.m.	Relaxes – watches TV.
10.30 p.m.	Makes supper.
11.30 p.m.	Bed.

---

10 minutes   STOP

Gaynor's day is typical of someone with a family to look after. She has children and a husband making demands upon her time. But she *does* have the advantage of potential free time during the day. To take advantage of this, however, she would have to be prepared to rearrange her activities.
(a) Housework
The amount of housework necessary in a home and the frequency with which it needs doing is very much a subjective matter: opinions on it (and standards maintained) vary enormously. Married women who become students often discover that they feel less oppressed by housework when they have the new project of self-education in their lives. Gaynor only spends an hour on this task, but if she did it as soon as she came in at 9.30 she could then have her cup

Discussion

37

of tea and start studying at 10.30 with two hours free up to lunch. But what about shopping?

(b) Shopping

You will perhaps have noticed that she goes to the shops *twice* in this one day. Are both trips really necessary? If she could eliminate her morning expedition and combine it with that later in the day, this would leave her most of the morning free.

(e) Lunch

If Gaynor had been studying between 10.30 and 12.30, a short break for lunch would be a good thing. But does she really need one and a half hours for it? A *short* break here – of say half an hour – could save another hour for study purposes.

(d) Sewing

Perhaps this is Gaynor's hobby, or she is doing essential repair work to the family's clothes – but couldn't she do this in the evening, perhaps whilst watching TV? Sometimes routine tasks can be performed at the same time as doing something else, just as we can sometimes combine some study tasks (rewriting notes) with some other activity, such as listening to the radio.

(e) The evening

The amount of time she spends in some shared activity (even watching TV) with her husband will be another very subjective matter. Some couples are quite happy to do things separately in the same house so long as they share the closing hour or two of the day. Others prefer to do things 'jointly'. This is an issue we will take up later in this unit. For the time being we have created quite enough free time for Gaynor during her day. Now it is the time to apply the same discipline to yourself!

Pick a typical day in your own life and list your activities in the way we have done for Ray and Gaynor. The important thing here is that you should be as honest and accurate as possible. Don't cheat by picking your busiest day, and be prepared to admit to those periods which are spent 'pottering' or 'relaxing'.

Depending upon your typical day, it may already be possible to see gaps or activities which might be shifted or eliminated to create some free time for study.

We don't expect miracles from just one day, however, and part of the purpose of this unit on 'Making the most of your time' is to get you used to the idea of *regular* periods of study.

20 minutes   STOP

Next, here is a timetable for a whole week. Just as a preliminary exercise you might like to shade in *with a pencil* those periods which at the moment are definitely spoken for by family or work commitments. Leave all the rest blank.

	7a.m. 8 9 10 11 12 1p.m. 2 3 4 5 6 7 8 9 10 11 12 1a.m.
Mon	
Tue	
Wed	
Thu	
Fri	
Sat	
Sun	

Where are the largest blank spaces? For most people the evenings   *Discussion*
and the weekends will leave most time free. But even so, you may
have shaded in periods which *at the moment* you feel are spoken
for but which with a little more self-sacrifice and discipline could
be made free for time in which to study.

Because most adults develop their patterns of living over a
number of years they tend to believe that what they do is *necessary*
– and of course many people assume that they are busier than
their friends, relatives, and neighbours. For the next part of the
exercise therefore you could perhaps try to imagine that you are
saving or creating free time for *someone else*.

                                            10 minutes   STOP

Make a list of those common everyday activities which our imagi-
nary student might
(a) Do more quickly and efficiently.
(b) Do *less* of.
(c) Sacrifice or eliminate.
(It is much easier to be critical of someone else's practice than
your own, but you should realise by now that the purpose of this
exercise is to encourage you to be more critical and self-
disciplined about your own use of time.)

Discussion Here are some of the more common you may have listed:
(a) Watching television.
(b) Housework.
(c) Reading newspapers and magazines.
(d) 'Pottering'.
(e) Shopping.
(f) Socialising.

(a) *Watching television*

The average person in Britain watches television for 24 hours per week. We are not saying that this is somehow sinful or wrong, but if you wish to find time for study isn't this an activity in which savings could be made? Be prepared to:

(i) Plan your viewing in advance. Select only those programmes you feel you really *must* see. (For instance, those which might help or complement your studies.)

(ii) Switch the set off after your programme has finished.

(iii) Leave the room if others wish to continue viewing.

(b) *Housework*

We have already touched on this problem when discussing Gaynor's typical day. It is a subject about which volumes could be written. In general, women often feel themselves overburdened with the petty tasks of running a household, cooking, cleaning, and washing. These can often be the most thankless yet time-consuming tasks. The solution to this problem touches on very personal considerations of 'standards' and our relations with others, but

(i) Perhaps you could ask other members of the household to help you.

(ii) More cold meals instead of elaborate hot ones?

(iii) Couldn't you teach children aged ten and above to make their own meals?

(c) *Reading newspapers and magazines*

People in Britain read more newspapers per head than any other country in the world. There is nothing wrong with that *necessarily*, but is all the time we spend poring over details of accidents, court reports, and gossip from the world of entertainment *really* time well spent?

Couldn't we

(i) Read them more rapidly, more efficiently?

(ii) Save the odd five or ten-minute gaps or breaks for reading them rather than the long periods saved for study?

(iii) Save them for reading when we are tired, and use our freshest periods for study?

As you become used to studying and thinking more *critically* about what you read you will probably realise that *much* of what is printed in newspapers and magazines is relatively trivial, of transitory significance, or entertainment value.

(d) *'Pottering'*

We *all* do it! From idle moments spent snipping at hedges, clearing out a drawer, or taking the dog for a walk, to looking through old letters or searching for something which we suddenly remembered we have lost: the possible list is endless. Many of the activities might in fact be useful, but we tend to just use up available time if we are not doing them consciously.

(i) If the small activities/tasks are necessary do them quickly and efficiently.

(ii) You could group them together, set them aside, or do them in conjunction with something else.

(iii) But if it is a case of 'filling in the odd hour' why not use it instead on a study task – revising notes, for example.

(e) *Shopping*

Another contentious issue! It is naturally a necessary activity, but tends to be time-consuming – often because

(i) It can be an attractive alternative to being alone in the house all day.

(ii) We are often distracted into window-shopping.

(iii) We often don't do it efficiently.
This is another activity in which your relations with others can be important in saving time and performing the task more efficiently.

(iv) Many families make a mammoth once-a-week shopping expedition instead of the more common daily outing.

(v) Does the whole family need to go? It might be easier and quicker if some members stayed at home.

(vi) Frequency. Maybe you could reduce the number of trips by careful planning.

(f) *Socialising*

A perfectly normal form of human interaction – but is *all* of it as fruitful as we might wish? And isn't it all too easy to while away an hour or two (even though very pleasantly) gossiping over a cup of tea, calling in on some neighbour or friend, or staying behind for a chat after a meeting. You can often save time by:

(i) Resisting the temptation to call on someone unexpectedly.

(ii) Limiting the time you make available (keep a lunch-hour appointment to exactly sixty minutes).

(iii) Get used to the idea that study will involve more isolation and solitude than usual.

The purpose of all this is not to turn every student into an unspontaneous robot. Remember the objective – *to find/create more time which might be used for study.* You should *not* imagine that the sharpening of your study skills and the pursuit of knowledge will result in your becoming a humourless killjoy. On the contrary, you will probably discover that a more active and purposeful life will give you a greater sense of satisfaction. At first you may indeed regret the sense of pleasant relaxation and idleness which it is all-too-human to enjoy, but with steady work at your studies you will discover the compensation of other satisfactions – a sense of progress, of self-improvement, and movement towards your goal. Many students discover that they feel happier when they are doing more purposeful work and it is often observed that the people who are most likely to take on extra work successfully are those who are *already* working hard. They have simply become used to being *busy* and working efficiently.

STOP **Here** Let's just recap on the *three* ways an adult student can combine study with everyday life. Can you remember what they are?

Discussion (a) Create more free time.
(b) Make more efficient use of existing time.
(c) Combine study with other activities.
We have been dealing so far with the first, the question of more free time. Now let's look at the second possibility – the *efficient* use of existing time.

2 *Making more efficient use of existing time*

Like many other techniques of study this is largely a question of bringing sound common sense to the question – and then having the self-discipline to apply the results to ourselves.
Efficiency in your use of time can generally be improved by:
● planning what you do
● creating the right conditions for study
● pacing yourself
● being an 'active' student
Let's consider each of these in turn.

Planning what you do
We have already mentioned the idea of a weekly timetable which will *show* you the periods you have free for study. This planning can be extended to *what* you study.

Let's say you have an essay to write, with two weeks in which to complete the task. What are the advantages and disadvantages of the following approaches? Don't just 'think about' your answers. Write them down on a sheet of paper.

(a)   You save up all your spare time and write the essay the day before it must be handed in, working late into the night to complete it.
(b)   You start work on the essay, then leave it for a while to think about it, and then complete it when the two weeks are up.
(c)   You set aside regular periods of time over the two weeks, working at the essay in stages.

---

10 minutes   STOP

(a)   This approach is the classic 'last-minute panic', which has all sorts of *disadvantages:*   *Discussion*
● you work in a state of anxiety
● only the thoughts of that one day are brought to the task
● you put a strain on your concentration
● you are likely to be tired
● there is no time left for revising ideas

(b)   This looks better, because you start off with good intentions, and there is a period of reflection on what you are doing, but a long gap between the start and finish of the task means that this advantage will be lost. You will have to pick up the threads of your argument all over again. And the last-minute finish will involve some of the disadvantages of the first approach.
(c)   This is obviously more sensible. You have more chance of completing the task comfortably. You can change your argument or add new ideas as you go along. You will not be working in a state of anxiety. And you may even have a chance to produce a second draft of the essay. The only possible 'disadvantage' here is that you will need to be far more self-disciplined – which at first may seem very difficult. But it is a study skill you will need if you wish to make any serious progress.

The lesson is obvious. The conclusion would be the same even if your task were something as simple as reading a set book. Regular periods of time set aside in which you decide in advance what to do will make you more aware of what you are doing.

Most courses of study will prescribe for you a minimum amount of work which must be completed (books read, essays written) but you should get into the habit of planning ahead the order of your work and the periods when you will do it.

Creating the right conditions for study

Not every student can create the ideal conditions for the most efficient use of study time, but it is a great help if you know what these conditions *are*. Some will seem obvious – others less so. Let's start with the most important.

Make a list of those physical, practical conditions you will need around you in order to study most efficiently and produce your best work.

(Remember that for most subjects this will mean a great deal of reading and writing).

STOP   **10 minutes**

Discussion   Answers may vary, but they should include the following important conditions:
- isolation
- no distractions or interruptions
- comfort
- study materials to hand

Each of these warrants further explanation.

Isolation This may seem utopian to those students living amongst large, busy families – and you may need the help and co-operating of other family members to create it – but you will work more efficiently when you are on your own. This may mean working in a 'spare room', working in a room not currently in use (say, a bedroom during the daytime), getting up in the morning before others, or waiting until they have gone to bed. Other possibilities exist however. If it is convenient you could work in your local library: many have an area or a room set aside for reference or research.

The ideal would be to have your own study, but this is not possible for everybody. It is important to remember however that you will *not* be able to work efficiently if you are surrounded by other people – which brings us to the second condition.

No distractions or interruptions The most common example of this is the busy young mother-housewife whose attention is repeatedly distracted by children. (Many women, for this reason, wait until their children are at school before they take up serious study.) But distractions exist in other forms: working near a television set, a ringing telephone, or even near the front door of a busy household will interrupt your concentration and prevent you from working efficiently. Each time your concentration is broken you will find it necessary to take a 'step back' to regain your momentum.

Some people find it relaxing to have the radio playing quietly in the background whilst they work. If you do, make sure it is music and not the spoken word. If friends insist upon telephoning you keep the conversation short and if necessary take the phone off the hook. If friends call when you are studying you needn't be rude and turn them away, but you can explain your wish to study for a decent period and perhaps usher them away after a quick cup of tea and a chat. After a while family and friends will come to terms with your study needs and – if they are good friends and an understanding family – come to respect them.

Cutting yourself off from contact with other people is one way of avoiding interruptions and distractions, but there exists another major source of them – *oneself*. It is all too easy, especially when engaged in a difficult or boring task to make *another* cup of coffee, to drift into daydreams or reading the newspaper, go for a walk, or find some task which seems so much more interesting. And *anything* seems more interesting, on occasions, than embarking on study. Guard against this. Split your study periods into small units if necessary, but *stick to them*, and *avoid distracting yourself*.

Comfort Don't try working in cramped corners in some freezing cold attic room, or any conditions which put you under physical strain. But BEWARE! Too much 'comfort' can be just as dangerous. Working in rooms which are overheated or reading sprawled out on a settee or in bed will almost inevitably make you feel very drowsy. A chair drawn up to a desk or table is the basic condition here – one which has well served thousands of students over many generations.

Study materials to hand It should be obvious that you will study more efficiently if all the materials you require are close at hand. Since these are most likely to be books, paper, pens, and your files, the desk or table-top is a convenient place to put them. You will not work well if you need to keep going in search of a pencil, the book you need, or your notes on a particular topic. Either *keep* all the materials you need close together in the room where you work, or *take* them all to it when you do.

Now for some 'conditions' which may not seem so obvious.

Lighting Don't read or write in gloomy conditions. This will cause eye strain, headaches and drowsiness. Have a good source of light directed on to the page.

Use 'standard' materials Most educational (and business) materials are now produced on international standard A4 paper size (8¼″ × 11¾″). Whatever your preference for lined or unlined paper – use this size. Don't write on scrappy little notepads or use letter-sized paper. Your notes and essays will be easier to keep in order (along with any handouts you receive) if they are all the same size.

The same sort of thing applies to pens and pencils. Whilst you may find it useful to employ coloured pens for note-making, write your essays in black (or blue–black) ink with a fountain or ballpoint pen.

Keeping a simple filing system As your studies develop you will need to retrieve notes made a long time ago. Keep them stored and sorted in a manner which groups them together logically and makes them easy to find. Use pocket files for each separate subject. Keep the notes in the order you made them. Number pages. Use colour-coding.

Whatever you do – don't just let your papers pile up together in one miscellaneous mass. You will be wasting time and effort every time you need to find one item amongst them.

Use plenty of paper Many students think they can economise by cramming as much information as possible on to one sheet of paper. This is not a good idea. If you do this you cannot find information quickly, you cannot add any new information to the notes at a later date, and your notes will not be as easy to read. Clean 'scrap' paper is usually easy enough to come by, and if not student notepads are cheap enough. Cramped and crowded writing is a false economy. Get into the habit of using plenty of paper.

Pacing yourself This idea of increasing your efficiency by pacing your efforts can be broken down into two sub-categories:
(a)   Arranging your time in manageable units.
(b)   Working at a time and speed which suits *you* best.

Most people's concentration begins to flag after a while, so even if you have a long period for study available, don't work non-stop thinking you'll get more done. Two separate study periods of two hours each would probably be more profitable than just one of four hours' continuous work. And even those two hours could be broken up into two sessions with a short break in between. There is nothing wrong with this – provided the break isn't prolonged until it has eaten up most of your second session!

So parcel your time out into discrete, manageable units. Organise *short* breaks for a drink, a change of scene, or just a breath of fresh air. This will keep you mentally fresh, you can look forward to the next break as a 'reward', and you can deal with your study task in stages.

Some people work better in the morning, some later at night. Try to recognise which is best for you and which fits in best with your other commitments. If you feel your freshest in the early morning, for instance, it might be possible to get up an hour or two earlier than usual and take advantage of the relative peace and quiet before either other people get up or you have to go to work.

Similarly, provided you don't feel too tired, it might be possible to work late at night when other people have gone to bed.

If you have the capacity to do a lot of work at one sitting you might organise your time in a series of large blocks. On the other hand, if you find you can only concentrate for short periods (see Chapter 3), you will do better to arrange a regular and more frequent series of study sessions in order to get the best out of yourself.

The key to this is – recognise how and at what pace you work best, then organise your periods of study to suit.

Being an active student Try to get into the habit of being more critically and actively engaged with the subject you are studying.
(a) Make notes on what you read.
(b) Be prepared to summarise arguments as you go along.
(c) Look up the meaning of any words or technical expressions you don't understand.
(d) If you don't agree with a point, make a note of your counter-argument.
(e) Make a checklist of important names, dates or events.
(f) Try to relate what you are studying to other work you have done on the subject.

Combining study with other activities 3

We have already come across the example of Ray Abbot who had two hours available to him if he was prepared to combine study with travelling to work on the bus. It should be obvious that the same opportunity exists for those travelling by train or as a passenger in someone else's car. But even the driver of a car needn't waste time. Those who have cassette players fitted can listen to instructional tapes or radio programmes they have recorded. (N.B. This is *not* illegal if it is just for your own individual use. Only playing them back for *public* use breaks the copyright laws.)

If you think about it carefully and are prepared to change your normal patterns of behaviour you will realise that *many* routine tasks can be performed without intense concentration – and can therefore be combined with some form of study activity. And remember that studying can include listening and thinking, as well as the more active reading and writing. For instance:

Housework Most forms of cleaning and tidying can be done whilst listening to the radio. This is a chance to listen to broadcasts relevant to your subject or to pre-recorded tapes. But it would also be possible to have some notes nearby and to check your memory of them whilst you were working. Alternatively, you could mentally rehearse the main outlines of a topic you were studying. All these activities will be good for mental discipline as well as for their own sakes. The same activity could take place whilst you were gardening, washing the car, painting a door, and so on. Just try to get used to the idea that whilst your hands are occupied with one thing, your brain can be busy with something else.

Leisure time Many people can read (or listen) whilst they are knitting, and there is no reason why, whilst listening to your favourite radio programme, you shouldn't be able to check through your notes – or even re-write them more neatly if necessary. One of the authors of these chapters once reorganised his teaching notes into separate files during an hour spent listening to a radio play. However – on this topic, A WORD OF WARNING.

Many people claim that they can read or write whilst watching television. *We would strongly warn you against trying to do this.* It is almost impossible to concentrate properly on anything serious or complex when subject to the distraction of both sound *and* vision. If other people are watching television when you wish to study – go into another room to do so.

4 *Conclusions*

The suggestions we have made in this chapter will help you to organise, plan, and make the most efficient use of your time. However, we recognise that not everybody can achieve a saint-like level of control and self-discipline – and some people's circumstances may make it difficult to implement some of the suggestions. What you should aim to do is—

Put as many of these suggestions as possible into effect.
Keep a watch on yourself and don't allow your own standards to 'slip'.
Get used to living with the feeling that you are not doing 'enough'.
The more you learn, the more you realise how much there is to learn. Let this be the spur to greater application rather than despair. Nobody can know *everything*. Just apply yourself to the *steady and systematic* process of learning and you will be surprised how much progress you can make in only a relatively short time.

Self-assessment exercises

Exercise 1
Without looking back in the book, can you list the topics we have covered in this chapter?

Exercise 2
I recently spoke to a Mrs Dorothy Griffiths on the telephone. She was interested in beginning some serious part-time study and so I explained the various possibilities to her. She said she was going to think about it and get in touch with me again. Shortly afterwards I received the following letter.
Read the letter carefully, then make notes for suggestions how Mrs Griffiths could reorganise her daily activity to leave more time for private study. How many possibilities can you spot?

❝ Dear Mr Johnson,
Many thanks for explaining the various study opportunities to me so clearly over the telephone. I have now had time to think about things and can confirm that I am very interested in beginning some serious systematic study. I was always reckoned to be promising at school but when I left at the age of 16 I had to say goodbye to thoughts of further study. I have always felt regretful about this however and for years have promised myself that when my children have grown up I would get back to my books again. However, following your suggestion I have worked out the way in which I use my time at present and there just seems to be no possibility of creating the kind of space which you say is necessary for worthwhile study. Let me run through a typical day for you and I think you will see what I mean.

I get up every day at 6.30 a.m. and begin making breakfast for my husband and three teenage sons aged 18, 16 and 13. I always think that you should start the day with a good breakfast and give them cereal, bacon and eggs, toast and marmalade and more if they ask for it. At 7.30 a.m. everyone comes down and we have a family breakfast. By the time everyone has gone off to work or school and I have done the washing up it's 9 o'clock.

I then treat myself to an hour's reading of the *Daily Mail* and at 10 o'clock usually go out to do an hour shopping in the local shops. At 11 a.m. I put in an hour washing and ironing.

My husband and sons are *very* particular about having well ironed freshly laundered clothes and I do like to see them going out well presented. At 12 o'clock I usually take the dog out for a run in the park; I hate to think of him being cooped up all day and he gets so much pleasure out of this daily outing. At one o'clock I treat myself to lunch and watch the one o'clock news on the television. This has become an important little oasis of calm in the day when I catch up with the world events.

After that, at about 2.30 p.m., I go swimming with some friends of mine. We started doing this a couple of years ago and now make it a regular occurrence. It's so important to take advantage of local facilities and the exercise does us all good. After a chat and a cup of coffee I come back about 4.00 p.m. to prepare the evening meal. My boys return from school between 4.00–5.00 p.m. and I normally have a chat to them about their school work, problems with girlfriends and all the usual things which I'm sure you can imagine.

At 7.00 p.m. we all sit down for our evening meal. At 8.00 p.m. I wash up and then find I always have to do important household jobs like vacuuming, cleaning, dusting and so forth, often until 10.30 p.m.! My family always complain when I do this but when else can I do it? Finally I watch an hour's television and then collapse into bed, usually pretty tired after what you can see is a very full day.

I must say that this exercise has caused me to despair. How can I think of serious study when I have to spend so much time doing housework in the evenings? I am very reluctant to give up an ambition which I have cherished for over twenty years but it really seems on the basis of my present commitments that I have no other option. I would welcome your further advice however.

Yours sincerely,
Dorothy Griffiths **〞**

Exercise 3
This is one of the first of many exercises designed to encourage clear thinking.
Below are four definitions of the word 'work'. Write down which you think are the strengths and weaknesses of each one.
(a)   An onerous or unpleasant activity.
(b)   What people do in order to earn money.
(c)   Paid employment in a specific area.
(d)   Effort towards a given end.

Exercise 4
Write 500 words or more on the problems you feel face the adult student.

3 *Concentration and memory*

Nothing in education is so astonishing as the amount of
ignorance it accumulates in the form of inert facts   *Henry Adams*

Just as eating against one's will is injurious to health, so study
without a liking for it spoils the memory, and it retains nothing it
takes in   *Leonardo Da Vinci*

Contents

Introduction

In this chapter we deal with concentration and memory together
because the two are so closely related. By concentration we mean
the focusing of the mind upon specific subjects for a sustained
period: it has relevance to all aspects of study. By memory, we
mean the ability to recall accurately what has been read or heard.

It is almost too obvious to point out that poor concentration when
learning leads to poor recollection of what has been learnt. Good
concentration and good memory also go together as the following
examples illustrate.
- Chess grandmasters can play thirty or forty games simultaneously whilst blindfolded and win all but a few of them.
- C. P. Snow's novels on Whitehall (e.g. *The Corridors of Power*)
  recorded his central figure, Lewis Elliott's admiration of top
  civil servants who could recall every item covered in a three-
  hour meeting without any reference to notes. When I was
  briefly a civil servant I discovered that such highly-trained
  minds could indeed be found in Whitehall.
- Sir Stafford Cripps, a post-war Labour Chancellor, was

formerly a brilliant barrister: colleagues attested to his ability to absorb highly complicated briefs within a matter of minutes.

- Daniel Moynihan, the American politician, once wrote that he believed himself the equal of Henry Kissinger in most intellectual respects except for the latter's ability to sustain his concentration at work for up to twenty hours a day compared with Moynihan's twelve.
- Finally an amusing anecdote. A Danish acquaintance of mine once spent twelve hours in a library absorbed in such complete concentration that when, at long last, he tried to move he found his muscles had locked in the position he had obliviously sustained throughout. To his alarm and subsequent embarrassment he had to be transported to hospital before his condition was diagnosed and treated with relaxing drugs!

The above examples relate to unusual feats of concentration and/or memory by unusually gifted people. Many of you are no doubt shaking your heads in wonder and thinking that by comparison your own abilities are virtually non-existent. A typical list of complaints would read as follows:

- 'I can only concentrate for about five minutes – after that my mind wanders and I can think of anything under the sun rather than the subject I am studying.'
- 'I can sit reading a book for thirty minutes and then realise that nothing has been understood and nothing retained: my eyes have been following the text but my mind has not taken anything in.'
- 'I might sit down to study with great resolution but after a few minutes remember some household chores which really *must* be done and then spend two hours doing them before dragging myself back to my study feeling hopeless.'
- 'When studying I leap upon distractions with delight: it might be someone calling, a phone call or even a television programme which I would not normally watch – anything to get away from the books and the need to use my brain.'
- 'I get discouraged so easily. Just a few words or an idea which I cannot understand and my concentration goes.'
- 'My memory is useless – recently I was reading something for ten minutes before I realised I had read the same passage a week previously.'

This litany of complaint is no doubt familiar. But it should be no reason for despair. Every successful student has had to negotiate the early stages when the subject is relatively unknown and the role of being a student unfamiliar. Moreover, all these complaints are made from time to time by most successful academics, journalists and authors. A friend of mine, who himself is a prolific writer wrote down his thoughts on the subject in this way:

It is extraordinary how seductive the charms of the washing up can appear when the alternative is facing a blank sheet of paper on my desk, or how carefully one finds oneself clipping the hated grass verges in the garden. I sometimes think my efforts of concentration are like a sheepdog (and a none too energetic one at that) rounding up unruly thoughts with great difficulty and striving to lead them somewhere, though I am not always sure where. It's a love-hate relationship I have with my work, especially when beginning something new: but now I am familiar with the contest and know that in the end my piece will get written.

Elusive or non-existent concentration and acute vulnerability to distractions are part of the condition of being a serious student; they can never be wholly eradicated but they can be reduced to manageable proportions. I hope that what follows will help the process along.

1   *Factors affecting concentration: three exercises*

Factors affecting concentration

Let's put your powers of concentration to the test in a way which will illustrate some of the factors which affect it. Read the following three passages and answer the questions at the end of each. Take as long as you like with your reading but answer the questions without referring back to the text. Memory or recall here will be used as an indication of how well you have concentrated on the texts.

Exercise 1

Brian Barratt's story

❝ I was born in Stepney 35 years ago. So far during my life I have spent nine years in prison and – though I will do my best to avoid it – there is a chance I'll spend a fair bit more before I am through. I am a professional criminal, or 'villain', as the media insists on calling us. I have tended to specialise in armed hold-ups – Securicor vans, that sort of thing – but I have done the occasional bank job at different times in my 20-odd-year career.

I am calling it a career because to me that's what it is. Other people get up early, put on their suit, catch the bus and sit in their offices all day – working. When I work it might only be for a few hours once a month or, depending upon the sums involved, once every three months. But don't think I am addicted to a life of doing nothing between jobs, staying up late in clubs, gambling and that sort of thing. Not many of us do that but we don't make good stories for papers or crime dramas on the telly when we don't. In fact I get up pretty early every day, spend a lot of time with my wife and two kids and with the families of my four brothers and two sisters. If I lived next door to you you would think I was a good neighbour and a friendly sort of chap – that's because I am both of these things. But it is not just leisure – when I am kicking a ball around the park with my two kids my mind is often working away on the next job.

You read a lot about the need for efficiency and good planning in this country: well no one has to be more so than me. If I make a mistake in the planning or execution of the job (not all of us call them 'blaggings' or 'heists' by the way) the result could be several years in prison, not just for me but for the rest of the team, with not much to keep our wives and families whilst we are there.

Do I feel guilty about stealing? It is hard to explain my attitude here: I know it is wrong according to the rest of society but my father was a criminal, our family and friends are involved in crime of some sort. It is a way of life, *my* way of surviving and providing for my wife and kids. It's funny really, if I had been born into a different family I'd be with everyone else on the bus. If I had been *really* lucky I'd have been in pinstripes with lots of plums in my mouth and been one of those really big 'on the level' villains working for Lloyds or some dodgy bank.

Do I use violence? Well, I threaten it – you have to. And if banging someone on the head stands between me, several thousand pounds and five years inside then yes, look out! But I am no head case. I only do it if I have to. I weigh up the risks and plan to the last detail and I am always in control. As I said before, I am a professional. **,,**

Questions
1 Where was Brian born? How old is he?
2 In what kind of criminal activities does he specialise?
3 Does he feel guilty about stealing?
4 What kind of a person does he think he might have been if born into a different family?
5 Is Brian a violent criminal?
(See end of chapter for answers.)

Exercise 2
The case for and against public school education

The case for
Those in favour of public school education argue along the following lines.
(a) **Quality of teaching.** Public schools provide a high-quality

academic education utilising the best facilities, teaching materials and teachers in the country in small-size classes. GCE results are testimony to this as are the high percentage of public school boys and girls who go on to university, especially the prestigious Oxford and Cambridge.

(b) **Choice.** The existence of public schools gives parents a valuable freedom to choose: they do not *have* to use the state schools but, if they are willing to pay extra, can give their children the best available education.

(c) **Less of a burden on the state.** Because they are financed by parental fees, public schools relieve the state of a considerable financial burden.

(d) **Tradition.** The history of public schools goes back to medieval times and pupils are given the sense of belonging to something lasting and important to the life of the nation.

(e) **Character.** Public schools stress values like loyalty, physical and moral courage, duty, responsibility, leadership, respect for authority and the easy exercise of it. Such values are instilled in pupils through teaching, the ethos of the school and the wide range of extracurricular activities, especially sport. The quality of this character training is evidenced by the dominance of public schoolboys in positions of authority: business, the civil service, the media, the armed forces, the church, politics.

The case against
Those opposed to public schools deploy the following arguments.

(a) **Academic results.** Many state schools outperform public schools academically and the latter's share of places at Oxford and Cambridge is partly explained by the considerable number of places which are reserved for them.

(b) **Finance.** It is not true that public schools relieve the state of financial burdens: most of their teachers have been trained by the state and their tax-exempted charitable status enables them to receive what is in effect a considerable state subsidy.

(c) **Choice.** The 'choice' is a false one in that it only exists for the 6% of the population rich enough to pay the £3–6,000 (approx.) per pupil per annum school fees. The 94% of the population who cannot afford such fees have no choice.

(d) **Equality.** Public school education gives an unfair advantage to a small, already privileged elite. Public schoolboys are able to dominate positions of power, often selecting fellow public schoolboys to join or replace them: the so-called 'old boy' network. This helps produce a self-perpetuating ruling elite of the richest group which inevitably tends to rule in its own interests rather than those of the rest of society.

(e) **Social unity.** The snobbish, superior attitudes produced by

public schools with distinctive accents and styles help produce a pervasive sense of 'us' and 'them' which is divisive
and sustains class divisions.

Questions
1 Name the five categories of argument in favour of public school
   education.
2 Name the five categories against.
3 What percentage of the population send their children to
   public schools?
4 Why are public schools said to be divisive?
5 In what way do the existence of public schools give parents the
   right to choose?

Exercise 3
The 'mother of parliaments'
" Britain's parliament is usually held to originate with the Witan,
the council of Saxon kings. Its further development was
sustained by the Curia Regis, the Norman Royal Court, which
embodied the judicial executive and legislative functions of
government. During medieval times the right of kings to rule in
arbitrary fashion was gradually checked – most importantly by
the 'Magna Carta' which King John was forced by his barons to
sign in 1215 – and by the emergence of two kinds of regular
meetings.

The first comprised the nobles and senior churchmen and
became known in the sixteenth century as 'The House of Lords'.
The second was the House of 'Communities' or 'Commons'
which developed as a non-aristocratic gathering summoned by
the King to raise taxes. Slowly these chambers established rights
and conventions which the King found difficult to deny,
especially if he wanted to ensure regular financial support.

In the seventeenth century, Charles I tried to rule without Parliament and provoked a major confrontation which ended for him
on 30 January 1649 with his head on the execution block. After the
Interregnum during which the Monarchy and House of Lords
was abolished, the House of Commons dismissed, and Oliver
Cromwell made Lord Protector, the monarchy was restored in
the person of Charles II following his acceptance of the Declaration of Breda in 1660.

Parliament was now sufficiently strong to resist a king who tried
to ignore or overrule it and in 1688 King William of the Nether-
lands was invited by seven leading politicians to depose the
unpopular James II. What followed was the Glorious Revolution
when William and Mary, in agreeing the Bill of Rights (1689),

virtually accepted the supremacy of Parliament.

After a century and a half in which Parliament gradually increased its powers the 1832 Reform Act made popular elections the ultimate determinant of a government's political complexion rather than the King. Now it became important to influence voters' choices and ensure a regular majority in Parliament with the consequent emergence of disciplined political parties. In 1867 and 1884 two more major reform acts extended the franchise; in 1918 women over 30 were given the vote and in 1928 all women over 21. In 1911 the supremacy of the House of Commons was confirmed when the power of the House of Lords was reduced to one of delay of legislation for a period of two years – later reduced to one year in 1949. In 1969 the finishing touch to our present system was provided when all voters over the age of 18 were given a vote. **"**

Questions
1 Name the royal court of the Norman kings and the functions it embodied.
2 What happened during the interregnum?
3 What did Charles II sign in 1660?
4 When were the reform acts in the nineteenth century?
5 When and how were the powers of the House of Lords limited?

Now check the answers at the end of the chapter.

How did you get on? Were you able to concentrate on the text and answer, say, half of the questions correctly? If so, you didn't do so badly and it proves you *can* concentrate, understand and retain information. If you were unable to concentrate even upon the short passage, if, for example, your mind went blank, then you still obviously suffer from considerable anxiety and psychological barriers to study. You should carry on working through the unit and then go back and try again.

STOP   **5 minutes**   If I am right you found the exercises became more difficult as you progressed through them. This was designed to happen – but how? Try and think for three to four minutes why it became harder to concentrate and to recall content.

Discussion   (a)   The first exercise is direct, tells a story, is unusual; the thinking of those who reject or even ignore conventional morality usually captures our interest.
(b)   The second is more difficult in that it is much more analytical and complex but the points are clearly signposted and the language is clear.

(c) The third exercise is very difficult in that it is densely factual, deals with a specialised subject and is written in a rather dry style using technical terms. Quite possibly your concentration was flagging a bit in any case by the time you reached this last exercise.

A number of factors therefore normally influence your concentration.

(a) Your attitude towards and interest in the topic.

(b) The way in which the topic is presented: the language used and the organisation of the material.

(c) The length of time you have previously spent studying.

How to help your concentration   2

Now I want to consider the various ways in which you can help improve your concentration – your ability to work efficiently for sustained periods. As with all study skills there is no magic wand to wave; it requires applied common sense and good organisation.

Concentration, as you have probably realised, is something which is affected by a whole range of factors dealt with elsewhere in this course. This section will only focus on two aspects of the subject: the first part will remind you – to the extent that they have an influence – of the study habits already learnt which help improve concentration; the second will deal with the physical and psychological barriers to concentration.

STUDY HABITS
From the earlier chapters studied, what study habits would you say are especially helpful to your concentration?

---

10 minutes   **STOP**

I would pick out the following: *Discussion*

(a) **Good conditions of study.** As you learnt in Chapter 2 it is very difficult to concentrate if you are trying to work on the kitchen table with the television going full blast and children playing cowboys and Indians underneath it. Unless you are one of those rare people who can switch off totally from their environment or one of those who genuinely benefit as opposed to those who mistakenly think they benefit – from a noisy background, you need a quiet, adequately heated place to study, preferably with bookshelves, a good-sized desk, a table lamp, pens, paper, rulers, and so forth.

(b) **No distractions.** You need to 'educate' family and friends about the need for longish periods of uninterrupted study. If friends do call unexpectedly, try explaining that you can spare them ten minutes for a cup of tea and a chat but no more. And try taking the phone off the hook; if people hear the engaged signal they will ring back later. (Again, see Chapter 2).

(c) **Study route.** This depends on your own preferences and commitments but try to develop regular study habits: for instance, every Tuesday and Wednesday evenings, or Monday, Tuesday and Thursday mornings for one and a half hours before breakfast. This regularity helps you acquire the right frame of mind which itself is an aid to concentration (once again see Chapter 2).

(d) **Self-knowledge.** You have already learnt something of your strengths and weaknesses as a student from Chapter 1 but you should pay particular attention to your ability to concentrate: For instance, do you work better in the morning or late at night? Can you only concentrate when the time to hand in your work is upon you? Clarifying your mind in this way will help you work at the most productive times.

(e) **Confidence: a positive attitude.** Apprehension, as we saw in Chapter 1, is inevitable when you start studying, but as this reduces you need to work on developing a positive attitude: the belief that you *can* do it and do it passably well. This approach helps focus your mind quickly on the task in hand and might even put a spring in your step on your way to your books!

(f) **Good planning and anticipation.** A good study strategy will help you establish clear achievable goals before you begin: this kind of awareness greatly aids concentration. It is a good idea also to anticipate your next task; on the bus travelling home, for example, or for the few minutes before you sit down to study. Though you may suspect otherwise the fact is that your brain does not *dislike* study – on the contrary it can come to relish it, even to need it. But it is often reluctant to start: you have to help make starting easier by weakening your resistance. A little device I use might also help you. I always try to finish a stint of studying by 'setting up' something specially interesting or easy to begin with next time. I might even write a few notes from a book or write a couple of sentences of the letter or article I must write next time. This helps me engage with my studies straight away and helps reduce the 'dead' time when the brain is reluctantly orientating itself towards the new task.

(g) **Discussion with your tutor and other students.** On any advanced course of study you should always consult your tutor if in doubt, and this goes for concentration problems too. Other students whom you will meet at seminars or informally will also be struggling against the same familiar enemies of apprehension, distraction and slothfulness: discussion with them will give comfort and reassurance and you will maybe be able to borrow some of the techniques they have developed.

Psychological aspects of concentration

Interest in topic. The best guarantee of effective concentration is a genuine interest and curiosity in your subject. Your reaction to this might well be to think that it is easier said than done. But there are ways in which you can help your interest to germinate, bud and then flower.

(a) **Starting up.** This is when concentration problems can be at their most acute: many students complain that they just cannot 'break into' a new topic. This could be explained in terms of unhappy memories from school or an off-putting initial impression of a subject. More often, however, it is the initial disinclination of the mind to adapt to new ways of thinking and the fact that the mind has not yet had time to establish a network of ideas and information in this area which will help integrate and give significance to the new material coming in. A new subject in this respect is like one of those long novels you have to work hard to 'get into'; maybe the first hundred pages are hard going but once over this hurdle the book becomes rapidly more and more absorbing. You have to persevere therefore when you begin a new topic and give your interest a chance to become aroused.

(b) **Try different approaches.** Try to stimulate your interest in a new topic through activities related to it. For example, suppose you were studying sociology and were finding the textbooks incomprehensible (a not infrequent occurrence, given the way many sociology books are written) you might try a number of different approaches.
  ● Read novels which give you an original perspective on the subject: for instance, Charles Dickens's *Hard Times* is a marvellous book and gives keen insight into nineteenth-century British society; or Robert Roberts's *The Classic Slum*, a fascinating analysis of Salford city life in the thirties.
  ● Read newspaper articles and journals which analyse society and give up-to-date information.
  ● Watch television programmes which deal with social problems.
  ● Discuss the topic with your friends and members of your family (who might prove more interested than you imagine).

61

This 'indirect' approach helps to stimulate interest which might otherwise be slow to arouse, producing poor concentration, poor learning and poor study satisfaction. Academic texts are usually very analytical and deal in specialised terms; it is not surprising that many students experience initial resistance to them. Indirect approaches are no less relevant and help make many subjects more meaningful whilst the language of the discipline is being learnt. Once well-versed in your new subject you will find your interest extends to these other areas quite naturally *from* your studies – but it is worth realising that they can help you find the way *into* them at an early stage.

(c) **Vocational interest.** A connection between your study and your work is not always necessary. A friend of mine deliberately chooses subjects to study which are wholly unrelated to his job as a solicitor; the last time I saw him he was learning to play the cello and to speak Swedish! Others find a connection sharpens their interest; the prospect of gaining greater competence and insight into one's work and perhaps advancement within it makes study seem more relevant. For others the vocational interest might originate in a dislike of their present job and a desire to move on into another area. This course of study may well fall into this category in that it aims to provide the skills needed to study other subjects more efficiently.

Physical aspects
Your physical condition. It goes without saying that study is difficult if not impossible when you are unwell, suffering pain or considerable discomfort. The mind cannot concentrate properly on such occasions. The ability to concentrate declines sharply with fatigue and the law of diminishing returns is soon displayed if you persist in trying to study when overtired. In such conditions sleep is the best answer, combined with good organisation of your hours of alertness.

(a) **Sleep.** Sleep is obviously the most important form of relaxation we experience: it is the time when the body recuperates and gathers its strength for the next day. Regular and proper sleep is an essential requirement for good concentration and all other intellectual activities. The majority of us need six to nine hours sleep every night. Some people (mostly teenagers in my experience) claim they need more, but this is unusual, and oversleeping can become a bad habit which itself can cause a near-permanent state of drowsiness. Others claim they get by with only three to five hours: Mrs Thatcher, for example, regularly works until 2.00 or 3.00 a.m. and rises at 6.00 a.m. Whilst this is unusual, and even successful high achievers insist on their eight hours' beauty sleep, it does seem as if it is possible to function efficiently with less sleep.

Recent experiments at Loughborough University involved a group of people whose sleep was limited to only five hours a night. Most of them adapted easily and reported considerable benefits in terms of what they were able to do with their extra time and the depth and relaxing nature of what sleep they got. Students who have to get up early to study or watch OU programmes may have to develop such a routine but if they find it difficult they can try to 'top up' their sleep with short siestas at other times of the day. A short 15-minute sleep – a practice much used by long-distance lorry drivers – can greatly refresh you and release new energy.

To help ensure your sleep is effective you should avoid:

● Too much tea or coffee late at night. These beverages are useful stimulants for students but two cups or more late at night will keep you up and damage your sleep.

● Alcohol: it will help you sleep but like all drugs even a little impairs its quality (see below).

● Intense study late at night; if the brain is overstimulated at this time it can keep you awake turning over problems into the small hours. Better to stop work an hour before going to bed and allow yourself to slow down gradually with some light background reading.

(b) **Overindulgence. Alcohol** is a powerful depressant which induces a feeling of wellbeing by inhibiting the various control mechanisms which make us appear sane and respectable people. The fact that it can cause dangerous behaviour and have disastrous effects on the liver and other bodily organs does not deter millions of people from consuming vast quantities of it daily. On the other hand, alcohol can perform vital social functions, encouraging togetherness, relaxation and good humour: all necessary requirements if we are to survive the demands of study, let alone all the other problems life puts in our way.

In fact, alcohol and study have always been closely associated largely through the efforts of a dedicated group of students through the years who have presented the process of study as an extended Bacchanalian binge. The reality is rather different.

Maddox (*How to Study*, Pan) cites American research showing that on average only 10–20% of university students drink alcohol more than once a week. The sober fact is that students who drink too much, too often, fail. Alcohol, even in small quantities, reduces the efficiency of the brain and can seriously interfere with concentration. And unless you are used to it and your body has developed resistance, substantial intake of alcohol causes hangovers; concentration is impossible when competing with headaches and nausea.

If you are intending to study seriously you need to adapt your social habits accordingly: do not, for example, plan to work the morning after a big night out at a party or in the pub – it will probably not be worth the effort.

(c) **Diet.** It is not my purpose or my place to advise you on a healthy diet. All that needs to be said is that too much food tends to induce drowsiness and indigestion – both of which harm concentration. Remember, too, that a big meal the night before can produce a 'food hangover' the next morning, when you might not feel like studying or indeed doing anything at all. Some people, I think of Mrs Thatcher here again, argue that they work more efficiently on a light diet. Certainly most of us eat too much and of the wrong kinds of foods; my own experience is that my afternoons are less productive after a heavy lunch than after a salad or a sandwich. Get to know your own metabolism; try to see how food affects your concentration and adapt your study habits accordingly.

This section reads a little as if I am a killjoy, which I am not. It would be wrong and foolish to ask you to transform your social habits for the purpose of study – rather, I am asking you to consider if they interfere unacceptably with your study ambitions and if so to adjust them so that there is less conflict. Overindulge by all means, but not when you want to study; moderation or even abstinence should be your watchword on these occasions.

(d) **The need for exercise.** Unless you are studying geology or some similar outdoor subject, study is mostly a sedentary activity. This can be a problem because it helps to be in reasonable physical condition when you study. This is because:

(i) The brain uses up to 25% of the oxygen taken in by the lungs and requires more oxygen when active. Stuffy rooms, therefore, can adversely affect concentration and fresh air really does help to clear the mind.

(ii) Exercise imparts a sense of wellbeing, of being at ease with yourself, which helps to compose the mind in preparation for concentrated study.

(iii) Vigorous exercise – jogging, aerobics, team sports, tennis – relieve the body of stress; this is especially true for highly-strung people.

(iv) Exercise builds up fitness and stamina, which is always necessary for sustained study and particularly so for adults trying maybe to help run a family, hold down a job and keep up their studies at the same time.

(v) Exercise relieves lethargy – often mistaken for tiredness. I speak from personal experience here. When returning from work I often slump in an armchair in a state of what I am convinced is near-exhaustion. However, when the flame of my willpower burns bright, or more likely when necessity insists that it does, I don my tracksuit and hit the pavement – returning twenty minutes later feeling very self-righteous, but fresh and full of energy for the rest of the evening.

If you still need convincing, there is evidence that physical fitness amongst students correlates with high academic marks. And don't be put off by the difficulty of booking courts or finding playing partners: running shoes are relatively cheap and an exercise scheme – like the famous 'Canadian Air Force' one – can be practised at home and takes up only three ten-minute sessions every week.

How to relax 3

Stress

It is well known that nothing so concentrates the mind as the thought of imminent death. This sounds logical in theory but I doubt whether many of us could summon the composure of Sir Walter Raleigh who was moved to write a passably good poem on the evening before his execution. In practice I suspect most of us would find it difficult to concentrate on anything at all in such circumstances. Most people suffer stress of some kind, if not regularly, then in response to certain situations or events. Stress is about as useful to concentration as are hangovers; it breaks up concentration and can make study of any kind impossible. Stress invariably has a number of physical symptoms; try to think what yours are under conditions of stress.

---

5 minutes   STOP

Stress can cause feelings of dizziness, weakness, nausea, a 'sinking' feeling in the stomach, headaches, pain in the temples and back of the neck and a variety of muscle cramps, especially in the thighs, back, jaws and shoulders (indeed people prone to stress sometimes appear to have a 'hunched' appearance from

Discussion

the constant bunching of their shoulder muscles).

Relaxing and managing stress

It would be foolish to think that stress can be eradicated, especially when it results from specific events like bereavements, but with good insight into your own chemistry you can reduce or manage stress through relaxation. Sleep – already mentioned – is obviously the most important form of relaxation, but there are a number of other conscious measures which can be taken.

(a) **Leisure pursuits.** One way to relax the mind is to tire the body. The praises of exercise have already been sung; the burning-up of physical energy can be important for easing tension and exercising muscles cramped by tension. But especially important is the absorption of the mind by a wholly different activity. Anything will suffice: watching football, gardening, reading, the cinema, television, theatre or social activity like going to the pub, chatting with friends, entertaining friends, and so forth. The point is that the mind should be engaged elsewhere, away from the sources of worry and stress.

(b) **Breath control.** The secret of most methods of relaxation lies in your breathing. When stressed, breathing is tight, rapid and shallow. When relaxed we breathe deeply and slowly, but the process works the other way too: by breathing in this way we become relaxed and the effects of stress melt away.

(c) **Counting down to zero.** This is an exercise to help your breathing. First take a deep breath, then try counting down from ten, exhaling totally as you internally say the numbers; as you approach zero you will find your breathing is easier and slower. Try doing this four or five times when stressed and you will find it helps a lot. The National Childbirth Trust recommends this method for women in labour but they advise counting down from 100!

(d) **Meditation.** This is the internal repetition of a sound time and time again. Try this with the word 'One'. You will find the word slowly elongating and expanding in your mind along with the gradual slowing of your breathing. Try doing this for a full twenty minutes morning and evening and you may find it helps you a great deal. Followers of certain Eastern philosophies, who practice meditation very seriously, can achieve states of trance-like inner peace through this technique.

(e) **Muscle relaxation.** Another much-used technique is systematic relaxation of each part of the body, especially those parts particularly vulnerable to stress. If you have never heard of this technique, lie on your back and take some moments to become comfortable, breathing deeply and slowly. Then direct your mind to your foot – all of it that is:

toes, heel, instep and sole. Lift it slowly a few inches and then let it fall completely limp. In this fashion proceed around all the limbs of the body – with the face, try tensing the muscles in a tight frown before relaxing – and within a few minutes you will feel quite relaxed. A variation on this technique is to tense your muscles first for five or ten seconds before allowing them to relax. Massage is also very relaxing but you need someone skilled to assist you.

Remember when relaxing not to overdo it. The aim is not to go to sleep but to prepare your mind for study, and for this you need to be relaxed but alert. Study requires sharpness and on occasions a sense of excitement, especially when you need to think creatively and generate ideas.
To find out more read James Hewitt, *Relaxation* (Teach Yourself Books, Hodder & Stoughton), 1985.

How to build up your concentration   **4**

So far in this chapter we have tested your powers of concentration, discussed how they can be helped, talked about the need for physical health and relaxation. We now move on to consider some practical ways in which you can help improve the quality and duration of your attention.
(a) **The incremental approach**
The idea here is to increase gradually the amount of time you can spend studying effectively. Those people who say they cannot manage more than five minutes at a time should start with this basic unit of time. Study for five minutes, then have a break for, say, three minutes before studying again for another five. Then extend the period to six minutes before you have a break and so on until the amount of time you have available for study is exhausted. Continue this the next time you sit down to study and try to build up your study units to about forty minutes. If you have a collapse of concentration, or find it especially hard to make progress in a particular subject, go back to the five-minute unit and build up again. The best work is done during substantial slabs of study (two to three hours) so try to move away eventually from the tendency to do ten minutes here or thirty minutes there: avoid isolated pecks at your study and go for sustained deeper bites instead.
(b) **Targets and rewards**
We all work better if we set ourselves targets. It helps

concentration a great deal if work is well planned and we set ourselves a series of short, medium and long-term objectives. So you might set yourself the target of reading a chapter of a book within minutes, planning an essay in two 40-minute stints, writing an essay before the end of the week, finishing all outstanding work assignments by the end of the month, and so on. It also helps to vary your tasks; introduce variety into the order of subjects studied so that you don't get bored with any particular one.

As you fulfil your objectives you can allow yourself 'rewards' in proportion to what is achieved. I allow myself a walk around the room every twenty minutes (some reward! you say, but I find it relaxing), a ten-minute break in the hour maybe, a cup of tea after two hours, a visit to the pub after a whole evening's work. Beware your 'rewards' are not anticipated or overdone: ten minutes' television watching can easily become an hour or more.

(c) **Regular breaks**

You need to take regular breaks from your study, not just as a reward, but to enable you to recuperate. Concentration declines, sometimes rapidly after a certain point has been reached, and it is a good idea to try to anticipate this with a short break. It depends on you, the stage of the course and the topic being studied, but my own view is that in general a ten-minute break every 40–45 minutes is about right. However, if you seem to be making good progress, don't break just for the sake of it: keep going. Concentration is an elusive state of mind: you may find you spend quite some time getting into your task but once you have, things begin to flow easily. When this happens – which it will – allow yourself to swim with the tide for as long as it flows strongly.

(d) **Avoid last-minute rushes**

I have known many students who claim that they can only begin to concentrate on a task when the deadline looms near. Consequently their study habits resembled long hours of languor punctuated by orgies of near-hysterical effort, fuelled by endless cups of coffee. The results are seldom satisfactory, either to tutors receiving the work and least of all to the digestion of the students concerned. These are not the ideal conditions for good concentration and first-class results. Certainly it is hard to focus one's mind weeks or months before a piece of work is needed but if you *are* going to work up to the deadline, *do* give yourself enough time to finish the job properly and to your own satisfaction.

(e) **SATRA**

Finally, an aid to concentration which is really a system in itself. The idea is to approach each task according to a five-step process: Survey, Aim, Task, Review, Analyse: SATRA.

Survey – your task in advance. Spend a few moments or minutes on sizing up the dimensions of the task upon which you are about to embark, whether it be a lecture you are going to listen to, an essay plan you are going to construct or an essay you are going to write.

Aim – clarify in your own mind what you are aiming to do; ask yourself throughout the task, what is my purpose in reading this? What is the purpose of the essay? And so forth.

Task – perform the task, calmly and systematically, taking whatever time you need to do it effectively.

Review what you have done and try to recall the main elements of what you have achieved and learnt.

Analyse how you performed the task and consider how you might improve your approach and method in future.

If you follow this sequence then no matter what the task you are more likely to focus your mind effectively throughout, to give of your best and to improve your performance when next faced with a similar task.

Memory   5

How to help your memory
Adult students suffer from two major misconceptions regarding memory. Firstly, they imagine that all highly-educated successful people must have excellent memories. Secondly, they believe their own memory is so hopeless that it is beyond redemption. Both assumptions are invariably wrong. This is not to say that some people are not blessed with brilliant memories: a friend of mine who was once a star of University Challenge has an astonishing ability to remember facts on a whole range of topics years after learning them. Nor is it to say that certain people do not have highly-trained memories: senior civil servants, barristers, journalists, for example, as indicated in my introduction to this chapter. But you should take comfort from the fact that many people achieve success with very normal, fallible memories and that your own is almost certainly less 'sieve-like' than you suppose. The former point is illustrated by a short anecdote: the latter by a series of observations.

Two researchers once wrote to people who had attended a meeting of the British Psychological Society and asked them to recall what had been discussed. 'Upon analysis it is found that only about a tenth of the points that had been made were recalled in the reports. Of these, nearly half were "substantially incorrect" ' (Josephine Klein, *Working with Groups*, Hutchinson, 1968, p.14).

Regarding your own memory, think of an area in which you are or have been especially interested or involved: a pastime or a sport, popular music from when you were young, for instance, or a favourite television series. Try to recall to mind as much as you can about it. Probably you can recall quite a lot. The factor explaining memory here is *interest*. Think also about how much you know about things like prices in the shops, traffic laws and regulations, the details of your work. Again it will probably amount to quite a lot in a very short time. The common factor here is *necessity*. Interest and necessity thus enable you to recall large bodies of information relatively easily.

The same processes apply to study. If you are interested in a topic you will remember its details much more easily than one in which you have no interest; if you need to know a body of information for an examination or completion of a course then this incentive will help fix it in your mind. These points are obvious, of course, but you need to absorb them fully to help break down any conviction you might have that your memory is utterly and absolutely hopeless and will never be anything else. There are ways, of course, in which you can help your memory to help itself.

1 **Information storage**
   To use an everyday example, if you need some of your 3-inch screws for a particular job, you will waste time if they have not been stored away carefully. If you were careless and left them anywhere when you bought them you may not find them at all even after considerable searching. However, if they were stored away carefully next to other screws and nails in your tool and equipment box you will locate them quickly and easily. Effective information storage operates on similar principles. What has been learned properly and accurately and put into the context of other related facts and ideas can be more easily recalled. It follows that you should organise your studies systematically – as we have seen in Chapter 2 – and learn in the fashion suggested earlier in this chapter. But it helps to have some means whereby items of information can be given some meaning in relation to each other.
2 **Understand the principles or basic ideas**
   You will generally find it much easier to remember principles and ideas than facts. For example, the list of 16 numbers which follow: 2, 9, 7, 14, 12, 19, 17, 24, 22, 29 would be difficult to remember unless it were realised that they proceed on the basis of 7 being added to the last number and 2 subtracted. With this knowledge you could easily produce the list of figures possibly days or weeks afterwards. Try doing it now, starting from the number 2.

	STOP

Easy? Now try something else. Without looking back at the opening exercise of this chapter try remembering as much as you can about the **third** piece of writing, which was headed 'The mother of Parliaments'. Don't check it until you have completed the next exercise as well.

Discussion

10 minutes	STOP

Not so easy? Dates and facts disappear rapidly from our memories, but see how much you can remember now if three basic ideas or principles explaining the development of parliamentary power are borne in mind.

Discussion

(a) The control over tax revenue to the king from medieval times.

(b) The willingness and ability of Parliament to take up arms against the king as shown in seventeenth century.

(c) The gradual acceptance of the idea that the popular vote should determine the colour of government.

10 minutes	STOP

You probably found this easier. Principles often provide frameworks on which facts can hang and which provide an explanation of the relationships which exist between them. By remembering the principles, you remember the facts, and you also help unlock other ideas and facts which may be lying dormant in your memory waiting to be recalled. Fortunately we seem to find it easy to remember concepts and principles even after a month has elapsed since the initial learning, as the graph overleaf illustrates. Poetry and other items learned by rote slip away quickly but concepts and principles are retained to a remarkable degree.

Discussion

3 **Note-taking**

Taking notes (dealt with in Chapter 7) helps you record facts and helps you to retrieve them easily after, for example, the books from which you took them have been sent back to the library. By summarising material read in your own words you help to internalise it and lay down a strong memory trace which will help store the information efficiently.

4 **The need for constant review and revision**

Research into study skills reveals that memory is greatly aided

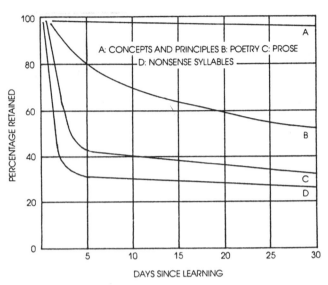

Curves of forgetting for different types of material

Source: Harry Maddox, *How to Study*, Pan, 1982, p. 56.

if what has been learned is constantly reviewed. Revision is something which many – possibly most – students leave until just before examinations (see Chapter 8). This should not be the case: you need to go back over your notes regularly to ensure that information does not slip away out of the *short-term memory*, but takes its place in the *long-term memory*. Medical students who need to use a great deal of their knowledge all the time are constantly tested on everything they have learnt. Language students too don't just learn new words once; they come to absorb them through constant use. The best time to revise is paradoxically just after you have learnt something; research shows that you can recall a great deal of a lecture just after you have heard it and brief revision of your notes at this time helps to fix the content in your mind. I know this is an unpopular idea because just after a piece of work or a lecture one's instinct is to relax after a protracted period of concentration, but try to get into the habit of briefly going through your notes. If you glance again through your notes every two to three weeks you will find you can easily remember a great deal more.

5 **Key words**
A useful revision trick is to use key words to help remember the important elements of what you have learnt. To practise this try to find key words to help you remember the three principles explaining the development of parliamentary power on p. 71.

---

5 minutes   STOP

What did you come up with? I used the following key words.
(a) Finance
(b) Military
(c) Democracy
Each word sums up the heart of the thing I want. Remember, the principles themselves were important: they help explain and consequently help to recall a great deal of other information. Key words, therefore, become like the tips of icebergs; remembering the key words gives you access to what lies beneath the surface. Just as an illustrated exercise try to find, say, six key words which help you to recall 'Brian's story' given at the beginning of this chapter.

---

10 minutes   STOP

How did you get on? I decided on the following: *Discussion*
'Villain, career, family, planning, stealing, violence'.

6 **Mnemonics**

This is a common memory aid whereby a pattern is applied to something which you wish to remember. For instance, the first letters of key words might be arranged in some kind of memorable fashion, perhaps to spell a word. The doctrine of nuclear deterrence is summed up frequently by the word MAD, which is short for 'Mutually Assured Destruction'. Try to formulate a similar mnemonic for the three key words I chose for the principles in 5 above.

---

5 minutes   STOP

I chose to extract the first letters of each word – FMD – and let   *Discussion*
them stand for three (literally) related words: 'Father, Mother, Daughter'. This device would certainly help me remember the letters FMD, which would help me recall 'Finance, Military and Democracy', which would help me remember the key principles, which would help me remember . . . etc.

7 **Association of ideas**

This is a device much loved by commercial publications which promises to give you a perfect memory. Whilst most of these publications are of little value in my view, you may find this particular technique useful. The idea is to let each number from, say, 1 to 20 stand for something unusual. Thus, '1' could be 'bear', 2, 'house', 3, 'mouse' and so on. The idea is then to relate your pre-learnt list of unusual items with the list of items you wish to recall. Thus to remember our three principles we might think of: a bear counting money; a house being crushed by a tank; a mouse casting a vote. In this way, you can remember long lists of key words, facts or whatever you like. In my view, however, it is better to rely upon genuine rather than artificial associations of this kind.

One final note is necessary. Some people worry lest the brain reaches saturation point, that there is only so much which it can take in. This is not the case. The brain's capacity for information is astonishing; most of us use only a small percentage of its full potential during the course of our lives.

For an original and useful book on memory, see Tony Buzan, *Use Your Memory* (BBC Publications, 1986).

Answers to the three exercises in Part 1

Exercise 1
1 Stepney; 35.
2 Armed hold-ups.
3 Not really: it's his way of surviving.
4 An insurance broker or banker.
5 He could be in certain situations.

Exercise 2
1 Quality of teaching, choice, less of a burden on the state, tradition, character.
2 Academic results, finance, choice, equality, social unity.
3 5%.
4 Create and perpetuate class divisions.
5 Only by offering places to those who can afford to pay.

Exercise 3
1 Curia Regis; judicial, legislative and executive.
2 Monarchy and House of Lords abolished.
3 Declaration of Breda.
4 1832, 1867, 1884.
5 1911; delay of two years. Reduced to one year in 1949.

Self-assessment exercises

Exercise 1
Without looking back, can you recall the main elements we have covered in this chapter?

Exercise 2
Below is an extract from an article by Lorraine Culley called 'Women and Politics' (from L. Robins, *Updating British Politics*, Politics Association, pp. 151–2). Read it through twice, carefully, and then answer the questions posed at the end.

" The sexual division of labour
An understanding of the experience of women in any sphere must take as a central issue the existing sexual division of labour in society generally, and particularly the role of women in the family. Marriage, motherhood and indeed daughterhood are crucial areas for women. Kinship and marriage structure most people's domestic arrangements for most of their lives. Most women are housewives whether or not they are in paid employment and are mothers all their adult lives. Several writers have stressed that the most serious and enduring obstacle to the political participation of women is their responsibility for children, and the major part of domestic labour in the home.

The 'caring' roles of women do not end when children are older. The traditional roles associated with women mean that they are expected to provide much of the regular support and care needed by the elderly and chronically sick living in the community. Half of all housewives can expect to look after an elderly, disabled or infirm person at some time in their lives.

> The impact of the domestic burden upon women and the cultural attitudes which support her continuing responsibility for servicing the family, although by now a truism, cannot be overestimated. Otherwise attractive activities such as those involved in commitment to political or trade union organisations are likely to be regarded as luxuries by all but the most determined of women.

This may at least in part, explain the extent of women's political activism in local politics, and in community based and single issue campaigns, where the time commitment is of a different level and nature than national politics. And it may partly explain the involvement of women in the organisations of the Women's Movement, where at least there is a basic understanding of the practical difficulties involved in being active politically as well as a possibly more welcoming atmosphere.

In addition to family responsibilities, women are increasingly involved in paid work outside the home. The proportion of women in paid work has increased dramatically in the last 30 years. In 1981 71.6% of women of working age (16–59) and 59.2% of married women of working age were in the labour force. There is considerable evidence to show that the kind of work women do is affected by their domestic responsibilities. The presence of children and other home responsibilities affects the likelihood that a woman will work outside the home, whether or not the work is part-time, and the type of work she feels able to undertake. Seventy per cent of working mothers, for example, work part-time. Employment has to be fitted in with household duties and childcare arrangements which many women and their families regard unquestionably as women's responsibility.

Employment is particularly and positively related to grassroots political activity. But,

> On the other hand employment outside the home does contribute to women's dual work burden and that is why, at the intermediate level of political participation, housewives without outside work commitments predominate, often together with women in part-time work.

At the top end of politics, however, it is employment of a specific kind which correlates with political success and it is a kind of employment less likely to characterise women's work experience, being largely professional in nature. In the House of Commons company directors, doctors, lawyers, journalists, lecturers, and former trade union officers hold sway.

In a society where women are seen as being primarily responsible for domestic labour, childcare and care of the elderly, as well as playing an increasingly active role in paid work outside the home, there is often simply little time or energy left for political activity in union or party politics. **"**

Would you say the following statements correctly reflect the sense of the article? If they do, give evidence from within the article. If they do not, say why. (Please note, you are *not* being asked for *your own opinions* in response to the questions.)
1 Women tend not to become involved in politics because they are happy to leave this sort of thing to men.
2 It is natural for women to care for children and old people.
3 Most women have no problems in combining domestic responsibilities and full-time work outside the home.
4 Women who work outside the home tend to be more politically aware.
5 All the domestic responsibilities which women have to bear, reinforced by social attitudes suggesting that such burdens *ought* to be borne, explain why so many escape into part or full-time work.

Exercise 3

This is the first of a number of what we are going to call word-power exercises. They are designed to help you extend the range of your vocabulary. You should get used to doing two things as far as words are concerned. Make sure you use them correctly, and look up the meanings of ones you don't understand in a good dictionary. In the following exercise, only *one* of the four possible words will make grammatical sense in the sentence.

1 The department has put a 5% . . . on the importation of foreign goods. (embargo/prohibition/limit/reduction)
2 The librarians are taking an . . . of their existing stock. (invention/expansion/inventory/assessment)
3 Running about so wildly, he will . . . all his energy. (dissolve/dissolute/disrupt/dissipate)
4 The inventor took out a . . . on his work. (patient/pattern/patron/patent)
5 He was a man of very . . . disposition. (Saturation/satiate/saturnine/scapular)
6 Because of the importance of his testimony, the witness was given . . . from prosecution. (immutable/immunity/imply/impropriety)

4 *Studying alone and in groups*

That is the happiest conversation where there is no competition, no vanity, but a calm quiet interchange of sentiments

Samuel Johnson

Contents

Introduction

As you come to this chapter – presumably reading it on your own – the subject of studying in groups may not seem immediately relevant. After all, a great deal of our study time is spent alone. But if you are planning to enter further or higher education you will have to prepare yourself for the fact that a great deal of study at this level is conducted in groups of one kind or another.

In higher education most students, at the undergraduate level at least, learn as group members of some sort. Most typically, they are part of a particular year's intake and they proceed through their three-year degree courses in the company of their fellow students from that same year. Lectures are usually listened to passively (but they are now often concluded by question-and-answer sessions). Other teaching may take the form of seminars when a lecturer might introduce a topic and then conduct a discussion session around it. Tutorial groups will often meet to comment upon essays written or short presentations given by other members of the group. Finally, groups will often be set up – perhaps during a lecture or seminar session or perhaps on a longer-term basis – which are expected to fulfil certain tasks on their own. Such groups are often found in adult education, occasionally pursuing a complete course of study, perhaps with a 'study circle leader' rather than a specialist tutor. It is these **non-tutor-led groups** upon which I will tend to concentrate in this chapter, as they are the kind for which students most often need a little preparation.

This chapter aims to:
  (a) Discuss the uses and workings of group study, especially the non-tutor-led groups.
  (b) Develop the skills needed to make the most of this kind of study.
My own observations of adult students suggest that they generally enjoy group activities and take to them naturally and easily. However, there is a little more to effective group study than orthodox common sense: groups operate in complex and subtle ways, as I hope this chapter will illustrate.

Studying alone and in groups 1

We begin by asking you to consider some of the advantages of studying alone and, secondly, the advantages of studying in groups.

---

10 minutes STOP

The advantages of studying alone can be expressed as follows:
(a) The major part of one's study is ultimately performed alone and practice in independent study encourages habits of self-reliance and concentration. When you think about it the great scholars of the past did not sit around in circles discussing for long periods of time but established their own reputations through individual study – think of all those hours Karl Marx spent in the reading room of the British Museum. Those who come to depend on group support and interaction to study effectively are at a disadvantage compared with those who have learnt to study on their own.

(b)   Personal study is much more flexible; you can study when and where you choose.

(c)   Certain study tasks can only be efficiently performed by you alone, most importantly, reading and writing essays.

(d)   For people who are a little shy, working in groups can be an ordeal which they would prefer to avoid by working quietly on their own. Groups which do not work efficiently waste a great deal of time; private study precludes this.

The advantages of working in groups, on the other hand, would include the following:

(a)   It provides an opportunity to interact with people who are studying in the same subject and facing the same problems. Most people enjoy social contact and find studying with other people to be fun as well as reassuring.

(b)   On occasions, group members can help each other psychologically. Personal study can produce feelings of isolation and adversely affect morale. Group learning often enables members to support each other and provide encouragement through the black days when study seems to be a waste of time.

(c)   It provides a chance for students to try out their ideas and test the validity of these ideas with the help of fellow students.

(d)   It provides students with the chance of benefiting from the wide range of different information and ideas which they will encounter in groups of fellow students. This will encourage them to alter or enlarge their own views and stimulate them to develop their own ideas.

(e)   Group study can be a useful approach for certain tasks like problem-solving, clarifying complex issues, generating ideas and subjecting them to critical investigation.

(f)   It provides practice in developing communication skills. Study can certainly be an enjoyable end in itself but it is also important to be able to communicate what you have learned verbally. These skills will stand you in good stead should you choose to go on to apply your studies, for instance as a teacher, a trade union official, a lawyer or a member of some other profession.

(g)   Group work gives students a chance to develop a co-operative approach, an ability to work as part of a team rather than as an individual.

The proper place of group work

2

Private and group study then, both have their pros and cons and both have their champions. The tradition in British schools puts the emphasis on individual study and achievement; excellent opportunities to use group work were mostly ignored in the school which I attended. On the other hand, some teachers, especially in higher education and especially in social science subjects, seem to think all education should be conducted via group work. I recall one lecturer in education who divided up the participants in a conference which I attended into small groups and set us talking about nothing in particular for an hour and a half. I subsequently overheard him asking one of his helpers how her group had gone. 'Well . . .' she replied doubtfully. 'Did they keep talking?' he prompted. When she confirmed this (we had been far **too** co-operative) he answered, 'Oh well, that's fine – as long as they kept talking.' In my view it was most definitely **not** all right; I had gone to the conference with certain expectations and objectives and found much of it little better than casual conversation. As you gather, I believe this kind of non-tutor-led group work should be used carefully and strategically by tutors and course organisers. Ultimately, it is true that most study is done privately, and I know of no group that has ever managed to write a decent paragraph collectively, let alone an essay. But group work is valuable in sustaining study morale, in developing social and communication skills and in performing those tasks where two heads are better than one.

Good tutors ensure that:
- Groups have a definite objective upon which all members are absolutely clear.
- They have been sufficiently briefed with information.
- They have adequate time to complete their task.
- They should not be too large or too small; about 4 to 8 is the ideal size.

Students should not be inhibited from pointing out to tutors if they feel any of the above points have been neglected. When used properly, group work of all kinds is a marvellous aid to study; when misused it can be an utter waste of time.

To help illustrate these points, read the following fictional discussion between six people. They have been asked by their course tutor to discuss and make some observations on the subject 'Children need discipline'. After 30 minutes' discussion they will be called upon to make a short verbal report to all course members. What you will read is obviously only an extract, but try to

make notes of:
(a) What you think is good about the discussion.
(b) What you think reflects poor group work.

3   *Two group discussions*

Extract from group discussion A on 'Children need discipline'

Brian: Right, well, this is a bit of a stupid question if you ask me. Of course kids need discipline. I suggest we decide to say 'Yes' and slip out for a cup of tea. What do you say?

Sue: Come on Brian, be a bit more positive. It's how much discipline and what kind of discipline we have to discuss. Now what about your own kids, how do you keep them in line?

Brian: Look, kids need to know who's in charge. That's obvious. If you let them think otherwise you'll never hear the last of it. You must be firm, say what's going to happen if they misbehave and crack 'em one if they do. As long as they know it's you who's boss, then there is no trouble. Take my next-door neighbour. Very nice woman, she's a social worker. Never heard her raise her voice to her kids, lets them do whatever they like. Result? They are both impossible to deal with, run around like young savages. I told her myself that if they were my kids I'd . . .

Pamela: Oh Sue, didn't you tell me your eldest had made it into York University?

Sue: Yes he did. We were very pleased. He's studying History.

Pamela: History? Oh my husband studied History, what a coincidence! But he went to Bristol. At least I think it was History. My niece is a Biochemist now. No! I mean a Marine Biologist, anyway, something like . . .

Brian: She refuses to take responsibility. Kids don't thank you for it. They need a clip round the ear now and again. Helps them to feel secure. Now *my* dad kept his belt hanging behind the door . . .

Sue: Didn't that mean his trousers were always falling down, Brian?

Pamela: My father went to Northampton University – he wrote Theology I think.

Sue: But there isn't a university at Northampton, Pam, is there?

Pamela: Isn't there? Oh well, perhaps it was Nottingham . . . or

Southampton perhaps?

Brian: I thought we were supposed to be discussing discipline – this is more like University Challenge! What do you think about kids and discipline, Dave? Do you reckon you should give 'em a whack now and again?

Dave: What? Oh, I don't know. I'm not sure whether it works, it depends on the child and I . . .

Sue: Brian, you are quite right. We mustn't stray off the subject, it's very naughty of us. Now, I think to strike your own child is awful and I won't do it. I am sorry Brian, I won't. *Mind you*, I did once give my youngest a whack. I was going to cross Market Street when he suddenly ran out into the traffic. I managed to grab hold of him and before I realised what I was doing I'd slapped his legs quite hard. It was the shock, I suppose.

Graham: Shouldn't we . . .

Brian: If you'd whacked him a few more times when he was younger, Sue, he wouldn't have run into the road like he did.

Sue: But that's absurd, Brian! How could beating him as a child have given him traffic sense? If that's the way you bring up your children I am sorry for them.

Brian: Look, there's nothing wrong with the way I bring up my kids and I don't beat them either – an occasional clout round the ear isn't a beating. Just because no one in my family's been to university doesn't mean we don't know how to bring up our kids. And having seen some of the chinless wonders that come out of these places I'm not so sure they're much use to anyone anyway. That social worker next door, for example, she's . . .

Rachel: Well *I* think universities are wonderful places!

Pamela: Oh yes they are! Last year we went on what they call a summer campus holiday in Loughborough University, or was it Exeter? And we had a lovely time studying Antiques.

Sue: They certainly encourage a more courteous, intelligent and enlightened attitude towards so many things.

Brian: Yes, I suppose you mean like spraying paint over ministers and chucking eggs at the Prime Minister. What kind of courtesy do you call that, Sue?

Sue: Oh Brian really! You know what an awfully small minority of extremists do that kind of thing.

Brian: Look, I'm sorry, but I think it's all part of this topic we are *supposed* to be discussing and which I tried to drag us back to. A lot of the rot has started in these places with Marxist professors telling our young people they don't have to obey rules, that our society isn't worth the trouble. Our schoolteachers take their lead from them and don't control our kids, with the result that they end up like little anarchists throwing stones at the cops and burning cars and shops.

Sue: I've never heard such drivel.

It is probably just as well that the discussion stopped here as it clearly was not going to get any better. Now write up your notes on the good and bad points regarding this discussion.

STOP **5 minutes**

Discussion **Good points**
1 In her first contribution Sue tried to correct the unfortunate tone which had been set by Brian and succeeded in involving him in the discussion.
2 Brian did try to address the topic a number of times and raise some important issues, after his own fashion.
3 A number of indications were made that other group members might have contributed usefully, given the chance.

Bad points
1 The discussion was dominated by two people, Brian and Sue. Rachel and Dave only made one contribution each and one person said nothing at all. Apart from Sue in the beginning and Brian on one occasion, no one made any real effort to involve other members of the group.
2 Most of the contributions were irrelevant, Pamela's especially so, and no real effort was made, apart from Brian's, to return to the subject.
3 There were frequent interruptions – one one occasion when Dave, during his single utterance, might have had something interesting to say.
4 There was no evidence of preparation or considered thought: merely the airing of prejudices. Virtually no evidence was brought to bear apart from personal experience, and several sweeping unsupported statements were made.
5 On one occasion Sue and Brian's exchanges developed into a quarrel; it was obvious that there was some tension between them throughout.

On balance, the discussion was pretty useless. It meandered shapelessly and purposelessly and was mostly a waste of everyone's time.

Now read a discussion which takes place in one of the other groups looking at the same topic.

Extract from Discussion B on 'Children need discipline'

Linda: I've done these group discussion things before so could I suggest that we arrange our chairs in a circle and, as we have only 30 minutes, someone acts as an informal chairman or chairwoman to keep us on the right track? It's also a good idea if someone keeps a record of the points for the report-back session. I'll write things down if someone else will take the chair.

Jane: Fine, why don't you be in the chair, Carol?

Carol: Oh, all right, if I have to . . .

Keith: Well . . . Go on then, set us off . . .

Carol: Oh I see, well; I suppose we ought to be clear what we are talking about. 'Children need discipline'. I suppose we have to decide upon the degree of firmness which children need in order to grow up properly. Does that seem reasonable? Or why don't we go round the table for some very quick initial comments from everyone in the group.

Keith: Leave me until last as I've got a book here which I thought I'd mention.

Carol: Okay. John?

John: I tend to be a bit authoritarian with my kids, which worries me a little, but kids who get no parental control at all can end up being impossible.

Alice: The important thing is surely to try to understand how our kids are perceiving us and what they are feeling. If we can do that and it *is* difficult, we are in a better position to know what to do.

Jane: I don't feel able to say much about this. My little boy is 2½ and is virtually impossible to control. I would try and discipline him if I knew how but he is totally defiant and throws terrible tantrums. Last week in the supermarket . . .

Carol: Can I stop you there, Jane, I wonder? Because these points should be very brief . . . Linda?

Linda: Yes, well, I think each child needs to be treated individually. I reckon there is no general rule upon how they can be turned into civilised beings, except of course that they need lots of love and care.

Carol: Well that's quite a wide range of reactions so far. Keith, you've done a bit of homework, haven't you?

Keith: When I heard we would be discussing this topic I picked up a recent book which seemed useful. It's this one here. *Happy Children* by Dreikurs and Solz. If I can summarise this approach: it is based on the assumption that children more than anything else need security, need to feel they belong, especially to the family group. When they behave badly therefore they shouldn't be rejected or excluded as this is likely to make things worse. We should recognise also – according to the authors – that children are struggling to assert their identity and will fight us if they feel this is threatened. We shouldn't therefore get involved in power struggles in which our will is pitted against theirs. The book suggests that in such situations we should withdraw from the field of battle, even to the extent of locking ourselves in the bathroom and the child, robbed of its adversary, will usually calm down and become co-operative. Another approach is to let the child learn through consequences: if she won't eat breakfast let her go hungry to school for a couple of mornings – she'll soon learn that eating is for *her*, not merely something designed to please her parents. They also suggest children respond well when offered a choice: for example, 'Either you are quiet in this room or you can be noisy in the next: which do you prefer?' This democratic kind of approach – letting the child choose – develops a sense of responsibility. Finally, they stress the need for reinforcing good behaviour with lots of encouragement. I've not done anything like justice to the authors but is this enough for us to discuss, I wonder?

Jane: It sounds all right, but my child Roger would be hopeless if I locked myself in the bathroom: he can't be trusted not to hurt himself, and what if I let him suffer the consequences of running on to the road? He is not old enough to reason with either or offer choices to: he wants both or all the choices and howls blue murder if he doesn't get them.

Linda: I don't know, I think there's a lot in this approach. My little girl sounds like yours, Jane, until she was a bit older, when I found she could easily accept the idea of 'either/or': 'Either you have a piece of chocolate, or a toffee, but not both.'

Carol: Yes, the 'withdrawal' idea does work sometimes, I think. I remember my little girl when she was about three used to kick up the most awful row about putting on her clothes in the morning. Then one morning I just left her in her bedroom in desperation and when I came back she had dressed herself.

John: My problem is I just don't have the time. I couldn't afford to wait around until a 3-year-old deigned to get dressed or not. I have to show them that when I say something I mean it and no messing. I would like to be more patient but I haven't got the time to be – if you see what I mean.

STOP   **5 minutes**   Now write up your notes on the good and bad points of discussion B.

This discussion is, of course, a little idealised and everyone   *Discussion*
sounds a little *too* polite, articulate and sensible, but it does
illustrate, I hope, some of the features of good discussion.

1 Someone agreed to take the chair and keep the discussion on
  the right track; Carol tactfully pre-empted a possibly long anecdote from Jane and ensured that everyone was invited to say
  something.
2 Linda, who had obviously suffered from poorly organised
  group work in the past, took on the useful job of firstly defining
  clearly what had to be discussed and recording points for the
  report back.
3 There seemed to be an atmosphere of mutual respect and
  openness without interruptions, personality clashes, rivalry or
  people showing off.
4 Keith had prepared something to feed into the discussion and
  one felt after he had spoken that the discussion now had
  something to bite on and somewhere to go. Personal views are
  of value only up to a point (though in this case one felt they
  might also have a therapeutic function), and it's helpful to feed
  in the views of someone who has studied the topic in greater
  depth and in systematic fashion.

How do groups work?   4

The two examples you have just read and considered illustrate
some of the quite complicated things which go on within groups.
The first example showed how certain aspects of group
behaviour can prevent it from achieving its objectives, can make
discussion diffuse, repetitive and sterile. The second showed a
group functioning well, sharing information, investigating a
problem and helping to create new insights into it. Josephine
Klein, a psychologist who has studied group behaviour in great
depth, identifies some characteristic roles which people play in
properly functioning groups.

Experts
Some people perform the role of information-givers. They offer
facts and ideas for other people to discuss. Keith took on this role
in the second discussion.

Facilitators
These people may lack information but are aware of what is
needed and try to encourage other members to provide it or
express their points of view. 'It is never to be supposed that
quieter members are less important or less knowledgeable'

(Josephine Klein, *Working with Groups*, Heinemann, 1968, p. 50). Carol performed this task through her role as chairperson.

Co-ordinators

Others are blessed with the subtle skills of being able to marry and reconcile different points of view to help produce agreement if, as is usually the case, agreement is the goal. They are often the people who make explicit proposals in meetings.

Morale-builders

These people help to create the right atmosphere, maybe making occasionally irrelevant remarks which might amuse or otherwise help people to remain relaxed and content.

Other students of group behaviour (often involved in management studies) have identified other roles which people perform, for example:

Innovators

Some people specialise in making proposals, coming up with new ideas or original insights.

Evaluators

These people tend to analyse and summarise what has been achieved so far.

Completers

These are rather dynamic people who help energise the group to achieve its objectives.

What goes on in groups which are working well is therefore quite complex. Naturally, the roles mentioned above are not performed exclusively by different people. You may find you take on several roles in one meeting and a different set of roles in another. Try to think about your own behaviour in groups and give a view upon the roles which you tend to fulfil. Jot down your observations.

STOP   10 minutes

---

5   *Guidelines for working in groups*

From your consideration of good and bad discussion practices and the roles which people play in groups, can you now construct a set of guidelines which you think studying in non tutor-led groups should follow?

---

20 minutes

STOP

My list of guidelines works out as follows. You will notice that all the elements of SATRA (Survey, Aim, Task, Review, Analyse) are included.

1 **Seating arrangements** – Try to arrange your chairs in a circle or horseshoe shape; this greatly aids communication.
2 **Prepare** – Where possible prepare for the group work or at the very least think about it a little in advance.
3 **Clarify your aims** – Be clear as to your objectives before you begin your discussions.
4 **Don't dominate** – If you realise you have been talking for most of the time then take a back seat for a while and let others contribute.
5 **Don't be too negative** – Even if you are shy or lacking in confidence try to say something in your group: don't sit there being silent throughout.
6 **Listening** – Listen carefully to what others are saying and try not to interrupt (see note on active listening below).
7 **Encourage quieter members** – Try to encourage the quieter members of the group to say something: often that is all they are waiting for and virtually everyone has something to say on most topics.
8 **Don't deviate** – Try to keep your comments to the point and direct others back to it when they stray from it. Irrelevant remarks may be necessary from time to time, however – jokes, for example – to create the right atmosphere (see next point).
9 **Atmosphere** – Try to create a good atmosphere for discussion, e.g. relax tension with humour, smooth overheated disagreements between group members.
10 **Be polite** – If you disagree with someone don't do so in a way which riducules or diminishes someone. Speak calmly and avoid emotive language or personal comments when debating.
11 **Open mind** – Don't reject other points of view before you have tried to see what merit they might have.
12 **Chairperson** – Appointing someone to the 'chair' to keep order, allocate tasks, ensure objectives are achieved, calm down heated tempers and involve all members of the group is usually a good idea. If no chairperson is appointed then try to perform some of these tasks yourself: don't rely on others to do it for you.
13 **Roles** – Be aware of the helpful roles which you can play and try to adopt those which seem necessary at particular times: for instance, defining, informing, summarising, encouraging.
14 **Analyse performance** – You should go back over your

Discussion

89

participation in group work and try to judge whether your performance could have been better.

15 **Review what you have learnt** – Don't leave it just to the group's 'scribe' to do all the writing. Keep some notes yourself and try to recall afterwards what you have learnt in the group work session. It may not be very much but it may be a great deal of new information or original insights.

Group study habits in tutor-led groups

Similar rules regarding your participation in tutor-led groups apply. Here you will find your tutor taking the lead in such roles as expert, facilitator, evaluator and completer but you should not leave it all to him or her. The purpose of seminars is to provide an exchange of views, to promote discussion, debate and new learning. You should not assume a negative or passive role but should try to involve yourself centrally in what is going on. Tutors, of course, should follow the guidelines for group participation themselves. This will vary according to the topic being discussed and the personality of the tutor concerned, but good tutors will promote discussion, not dominate it themselves. Tutors are not perfect, however, and you may need to help them with their roles, for example as facilitators or morale-builders. If you are dissatisfied with the way a seminar is conducted then you should have a word with your tutor. Most of us are only too aware that we don't always succeed and welcome student feedback and suggestions as to how group work, seminars or any aspect of our courses can be improved.

6 *Active listening*

In any group work or seminars, but especially in lectures, it is necessary to listen properly. This topic harks back to the subject of concentration covered in Chapter 3 but a few extra words of advice are necessary in this particular context.

Just as when you are reading without really concentrating, it is possible to convince yourself that you were listening properly whilst virtually nothing is going in. During a lecture this is often because:

(a) Your mind has wandered off after ten minutes or so to think about something else.

(b) You feel that you are not especially interested in the subject being dealt with.

(c) You find the lecturer uninspiring to listen to – for instance, if it is delivered in a humourless, monotonous voice.

(d) You are being distracted by whispered conversations with your neighbour or giggles about your lecturer's dress or mannerisms.
(e) You are sleepy because of insufficient sleep or poor physical condition.

Active listening can be difficult but it helps you if you:

(a) Ask yourself precisely what the lecturer is talking about. Good tutors give you an outline of their talk so that you can gain an idea of the strategy they are following; others state clearly what they are going to do at the beginning of their lecture.
(b) Adopt a questioning attitude throughout. Absorb what the lecturer is saying and consider whether you agree with it. In this way make listening into a kind of dialogue with your lecturer.
(c) Take notes of the main points: note-taking keeps the mind alert and helps you to remember what you have learnt.
(d) Try to ignore what shortcomings the lecturer might have as a communicator and concentrate upon the ideas and information he is giving.
(e) If you have missed an important fact, don't be afraid to interrupt; this often helps other people who may have missed the point and a short respite from listening sometimes helps concentration when you resume.
(f) Try to look at the lecturer as you would anyone with whom you are holding a conversation; watch the face and especially the eyes. Lecturers often use expressions and other kinds of body language to help convey their ideas.

It is always possible when lecturing to spot those who have 'switched off'; I always try to address my remarks especially to such people in an effort to win back their attention – not always with success, I might add. Good listeners are easy to identify also. Their eyes are alert and their faces clearly register their reactions to the different points you are making. You notice, with pleasure, that they are taking notes and that their whole person seems to convey interest. Almost invariably these are the most active and productive members in seminars and small group work and – no surprise here either – those who perform best in tests and exams. If you become one of these active, positive people in your studies rather than a passive learner, you will make progress rapidly, and, I can assure you, become extremely popular with your tutors and lecturers!

Self-assessment exercises

Exercise 1
Without looking back, can you recall the main topics we have
covered in this chapter? (You will need six headings.)

Exercise 2
(This exercise will be of most use to those going through this
course with the aid of a tutor who can comment on what you
write.)
Analysing discussions
No doubt you regularly have informal discussions with friends
on a number of topics; just for the sake of the course try to study
how such discussions work over the next week or so. If you like
you can subtly initiate the discussions yourself. When they are
over make some notes straightaway and write them up into a
little report.
Look in particular for the following things:
(a) How much do you and your other discussants listen to each
    other?
(b) Do you think that you personally tend to interrupt too much;
    or do you feel that you are too negative in discussion?
(c) Are you able to direct discussion and introduce new topics
    and lines of argument?
(d) Do people tend to make assertions on the basis of no
    knowledge, prejudice or personal experience, rather than on
    deeper knowledge? How well informed are you and the
    others on the topics you discussed?
(e) Do you notice that you tend to become impatient and lose
    your temper in discussions? If so, what are the symptoms?
(f) What role or roles do you think you play in such informal
    discussions? Try to identify the roles played by other
    participants.
When you have written your report, show it to the tutor for
comment.

Exercise 3
Have a go at writing the dialogue for a good group discussion on
one of the following topics:
(a) 'Private education is a vital part of our educational system'.
(b) 'Soap operas are a waste of time'.
(c) 'The owners of dogs who foul the pavement should be
    heavily fined'.
(d) Any other topic of interest to you.

Exercise 4
Here is another word-power exercise. Only one of the four possible words will make grammatical sense in the following sentences:

1 After a long period of . . . the animal was born.
  (gesticulation/gesture/gestation/injection)
2 The . . . of the pendulum helps regulate the clock.
  (osculation/ossification/oscillation/Scintillation)
3 Pollution from car exhaust fumes is at its most densely concentrated in the . . . environment.
  (rural/arable/geographic/urban)
4 A student who only makes . . . use of her notes before the exam may find that she remembers little.
  (cursive/curative/cursory/cursorial)
5 Whilst speaking on one poet, he made a brief . . . to another.
  (illusion/allusion/elusive/effusion)
6 Arriving late, he made a . . . entrance on to the stage.
  (beleaguered/belated/beneficial/beneath)

5 *Verbal communication*

All the great speakers were bad speakers at first   *Emerson*

Eloquence lies as much in the tone of the voice, in the eyes, and in the speaker's manner as in his choice of words   *La Rochefoucauld*

Contents

Introduction

Many of the study skills we will deal with later concentrate on the problems of coping with the written word, of expressing yourself on paper. But in any course of higher education, there will be times when you have to speak, to convey your ideas and thoughts through the medium of *verbal communication*. For many students and people generally this is a terrifying thought as soon as it is anticipated within a more formal or academic context, instead of within an 'everyday' or casual situation. But *communication* is something that we are all very good at, from birth; it means our ability to get in touch with others (in a variety of ways, some more unconscious), and thus convey information, including our feelings and needs. Communication is the transmission of information between people, and in most cases we learn to do it instinctively and efficiently. What makes us tense is the need to do it more formally, in a context where our 'performance' may be judged, either in written or spoken English. (If speaking in public holds few or no fears for you, this chapter may be superfluous, but you are advised to work through it anyway for the self-analysis and practice it will provide.

In higher study, inevitably, there will be times when you will have to communicate *orally* (and not just by written exam or essay) and in a more academic and official context. How many sorts of possible situations of this kind can you think of, for example, if you were taking a university degree?

---

5 minutes   **STOP**

Some of these overlap, but I would think that you would certainly   *Discussion*
have to cope with most of the following at some point in your
student career:

● Formal interview with your tutor, professor or head of department: defending your choice of a project or short thesis to any
  of the above people.
● Answering questions or arguing your point of view in a tutorial or discussion or seminar group.
● A seminar paper (talk) given to a small group or tutorial class.
● An oral exam (often called a *viva*, from the Latin phrase *viva
  voce*, with living voice).
● A more formal lecture given to a larger group of students and
  staff.

The importance of being able to communicate verbally, in a clear and effective way, is now more recognised at all levels of study. Not only is a GCSE exam in oral communication planned, but many O-level exams in English language have included a spoken element: the student has to give a talk, between 5 and 8 minutes in length, on any subject, to an audience of classmates and a teacher from the school or college who acts as examiner. The student is assessed on preparation and structure of the talk, clear delivery and effective communication with audience, variety and interest of delivery and tone. All these areas are, of course, crucial in any verbal communication you take part in, and we will try to cover them in this chapter.

Practice
Wise proverbs like 'The skill to *do* comes from doing' (Cicero) seem to apply more than usual to the particular problems of verbal communication. Only *practice*, and forcing yourself to do something which initially might terrify you, will give you the success and confidence which makes an effective speaker. But, paradoxically, this is one of the hardest areas in which to get practice and experience on your own, as the final test *must* be in front of some sort of 'live' audience. It is possible to do this much

more easily in study skills classes, where students can 'work up' slowly from talking to one person (not usually an inhibiting experience!), to speaking within a group of four, then to half the class, and only finally delivering a short prepared talk to the class as a whole. At the end of a course, many students say that this was by far the worst thing they were asked to do, but, with hindsight, the one from which they learnt most about themselves and gained the most confidence.

Confidence is a key word in verbal communication. It seems to be an intangible quality compounded of several aspects: sound preparation, genuine knowledge of and interest in your subject, and experience gained from practice. Knowledge and interest will depend upon your own personal motivation and depth of study; as Socrates said, 'Everyone is eloquent enough in what they know.' Remember this, and how naturally fluent you can be on, say, the intricacies of your job, the problems of bringing up children, or your favourite hobby. If you can talk about these things which deeply interest you, to one person, there is no reason why you cannot adapt and enlarge that ability in order to speak to a larger group on other subjects as well. The following ways of practising on your own are designed to break down some of our very natural inhibitions at hearing the sound of our own voice in a formal context, and to give you the confidence necessary to tackle various sorts of more public speaking in the future.

As many books on the art of verbal communication point out, 'public' speaking to more than one person is only an expanded form of your side of a conversation with a single listener. If you can properly explain your point to one person, you can do it to two or four – or to twenty. So start by asking yourself, critically, about *your* side of your everyday conversations: Is your verbal expression limited to sentence fragments and monosyllables, or do you follow something through in one or more completed sentences? Do you find yourself at a loss for words, or do you use a variety of vocabulary and an interesting range of words in what you say? Do you peter out almost at once on a given topic, or do you try to expand your, and your listener's, ideas upon it in an interesting way?

As you can see, many of these skills link in with your ability in written expression. It does not mean that you must sound stilted and formal, or like someone reading a book, every time you open your mouth, but that you can *use* your knowledge of increased reading confidence and word-power, or of the rhythm and structure of a complex sentence, or of how to create variety and force in an essay argument, in order to make your *spoken* expression more fluent, forceful and interesting. Consciously practise this the next time you have an extended conversation with an acquaintance, or meet new people in a formal context – not forgetting that a true conversation is a matter of give and take, and that the other person has to be given a chance as well. Even at this level, a little thought and preparation can help your confidence too; consider the other person's interests or qualities, or how you might discuss topics of controversial or general interest, or how you could develop and sustain the conversation (if appropriate) in a more absorbing way. Keep in mind, too, that this can also be practised over the telephone, where one is even more dependent on *verbal* (rather than visual) skills to convey one's interest and information. If, as many say, the art of conversation is dying because of television, try consciously to revive it with those you meet in the near future.

If talking at any deeper or more extended level than our usual everyday colloquial 'shorthand' is difficult for you, try *asking questions* more formally, as well as initiating longer conversations. Many of us have opportunities in our daily lives to say *something*, if only a sensible and probing question, in a public setting. If you go to any sort of general meeting or gathering – at work (committee or union meetings), at a club, at church, at school (PTA members, for example), in local government or politics, in any sort of organisation – try to stand up and make a pertinent comment or ask a relevant question. As in a larger speech, think carefully about the content and point of what you want to say, and the most fluent, clear and effective way of saying it. If it's only a few words, it is still a practising of your verbal skills – and it will be *easier* the next time.

For many people, the sheer sound of their own voice, heard formally in what seems an awesome silence, is in itself an inhibiting prospect. Practise this by *reading aloud* to yourself in private: take a longish paragraph from a serious book (or a poem, if you like poetry), and read it aloud at a normal pace, with variation of tone, expression and interest in your voice. If you know any verse or prose by heart, or even the words of popular songs, you can try this while driving on your own, in the bath or anywhere private. After doing this a few times, try to practise a formal reading with a tape-recorder – a very useful tool for critical self-analysis in speaking. Play back and listen to your reading carefully, and give yourself points for audibility, variety of pitch and expression, clarity in handling the sense and rhythm of the sentences, warmth and interest of your tone, and (if you can be at all objective about it) the actual attractiveness of the sound of your voice. Think carefully about which features could be improved, and then try this again as many times as you can, until you are happier with the actual *sound* of your reading. There are a number of books on the skill of elocution and speech training, which you could look up in your local library if necessary.

Having got used to the sound of your own voice in a vacuum, as it were, and to using a tape-recorder to monitor your progress, let's start some exercises which develop the *content* and meaning of what you are saying. After some initial preparation and thought, all these exercises are really better also done with a listener (in person, or even on the end of the telephone), so do ask a friend or a member of your family if they can be a silent (and non-critical) audience for a few minutes occasionally; if that is not possible, practise with a tape-recorder only and listen to yourself after-wards, as well as when you are delivering your words.

Exercise 1
Prepare, write out and deliver a **1-minute announcement**.
Subjects:
● selling your car
● a small child, or an object, lost at a fairground
● arrangements for a cultural outing, or for a political or PTA meeting to be held next week

This should be no more than about 150 words, but needs to be logical, clear and very detailed in order to communicate efficiently. Write out and read every word at this stage, if you need to, but try to structure the announcement around *main* points (headings), to which you can add the smaller details.

Exercise 2
Prepare, make *notes* on, and deliver a **1½-minute explanation**.
Subjects:
● why you were late to work (to your boss)
● how to get from your house to your work, or the centre of town, or the nearest hospital

This should be no longer than about 150–200 words – perhaps only four or five sentences – but try to make every sentence a proper and complete one which says something important. By thinking carefully, and jotting down your main points in a logical order (perhaps one point per sentence), you should be able to expand each one into an interesting and sensible statement, *without* writing down and reading out every single word from the page. Try not to repeat yourself or 'dry up' before the end of each sentence. If you found this very difficult the first time, try it again, with a new subject from this or the next exercise.

Exercise 3
Prepare, make notes on, and deliver a **2-minute description**
Subjects:
● the most precious thing you own

● describe your own house to an absent friend who has never seen it
● take a picture postcard view and describe it in detail to any member of your family, or a friend

In all these subjects, try to draw a visual and mental picture for your listener which is accurate, detailed, vivid. As in the previous section try to work from a series of *notes* (incorporating key words) which will remind you of the details of what you want to say – rather than writing out every single word and then reading it. Keep trying to complete all your sentences, and to use a variety of vocabulary and sentence patterns. Remember, as in your writing, that the exact and concrete are much more memorable than the vague and abstract. If you feel that you could speak fluently and happily on these topics for much longer, do so (up to five minutes, say); but, if not, keep practising on a slightly different description until the words begin to come more easily to you, and you can more confidently convey your ideas without reading every word from the page.

How to prepare a short talk   1

I hope by now, if you've worked through some of the previous exercises, you feel more confident in delivering a couple of minutes of speech on a given topic, by expanding on a few, well-chosen key points and notes. This sort of *balance*, between a very carefully prepared and structured *plan*, and the ability to 'talk from' its main points in a more spontaneous and flexible way, is the same skill you will need for giving a good academic talk or seminar paper – though of course you will then need to go into much more scholarly depth. A short talk on a general subject is a good bridge between these two levels of speaking: it involves the skills you have been practising so far, but brings in the more careful preparation necessary for a scholarly paper.

A short talk of this kind can be of various lengths, and it is important that you know *how long* a talk is expected of you, so you can plan and pace yourself accordingly. At the end of this section I will ask you to practise by preparing a talk of about 8–10 minutes in length, so do your planning at this point with that in mind. It is also important that you know exactly the sort of *audience* you have, so that you can focus and aim your information at the right level – neither too general (and therefore not superficial or boring), nor too specialised (and therefore not obscure). At college or university, your audience would normally consist of your own tutorial group or classmates, or members of your own department (a very specialised audience), though sometimes people from other departments might be there as well (a broader audience). It is a good rule to assume that your audience, as interested individuals, know a lot about a lot of things *except* your topic. By assuming this you compliment and flatter your listeners, by appealing to their own varied knowledge (and thus avoiding 'talking down' to them in a condescending way), and also challenge and intrigue them by your confidence that *you* also have some specialist expertise and information to offer.

Having thought initially about your topic, the length of your talk, and your audience, the actual preparation method you follow should be very similar to that of the early stages of planning a written essay. If you are at first short of ideas, start with a 'brainstorming' session: take a large sheet of paper, and immediately jot down all and any ideas, thoughts, connections, examples and quotations which come into your mind. Keep adding to it, and even go back to it later if you have other inspirations. Then begin to group and categorise your information and ideas: which go together logically, which overlap or repeat each other, which need to be added to, which are, on reflection, off the point or useless and therefore must be omitted altogether. As you would for a formal essay, begin to pull your ideas into coherent and unified headings, as if you were going to write complete paragraphs.

At this point, you may need to stop and think about the necessary accuracy, detail and depth of your subject, and thus how much background study and *research* is required. If you are talking on a topic about which you already know a great deal, you may need to do little more than verify a fact or a name, or add a precise statistic or an accurate quotation. If the subject is rather more out of your normal field, or requires a lot of extra detail and material, now is the time to go to the library, or dig out your texts on the subject, in order to fill in the gaps and give substance and authority to your comments. Take as many notes as you feel you need, in your normal way. Nothing gives you confidence more than really *knowing* what you are talking about, and, if you become a student, knowing the details of various fields will be your *job* and part of what you are learning every day.

Having sorted out your ideas a little, and done the necessary reading and research to fill in your knowledge of the background, you need to start *planning* your talk in earnest. Work as you would when preparing an essay: group your notes into a logical and coherent sequence, which flows through a series of main points (equivalent to paragraphs), and has an overall *structure* (argument) and a clear beginning, middle and end.

To make sure of absolute precision and effect at the key points of your talk (start and finish), you might want to write out, in full, just the initial sentence(s), and one or two which give a satisfying conclusion. Remember that, like an essay, your first words need to both announce a subject and your approach to it and also arouse interest and catch your audience's attention, while your final words need to summarise your argument neatly and remind your listeners of the whole point of your discussion. But, unlike an essay, do not write out a full draft for the body of your talk, but only *key words* (which remind you of main ideas) and as many *supporting ideas* as are necessary to jog your memory for the details. You are aiming here for a structured but spontaneous effect, in which you can *talk* and elaborate clearly around a planned series of points – *not* formally read a rigid, set text.

For a short general talk of this type, your notes are probably best put on numbered file-cards (which you use as 'cue-cards'), on one side only and with no more than one or two main points per card. Think of each major point as equivalent to a paragraph in your writing: it ideally needs a clear initial statement (key sentence), minor points which illustrate or add to it and fill it out (supporting sentences), and a summarising sentence which repeats its main purpose and possibly links it to the following main idea. Keep in mind that a *listener*, as opposed to a reader, cannot turn back the page if he has missed a point or connection, so much *more* obvious repetition and indication of the structure and plan of your talk (i.e., where you are in your argument) is necessary.

In practice, of course, in actual speaking, we are rarely so neat or logical; ideas and extra inspirations strike us and carry us away – which is usually fine, as long as you can rapidly return to cover the rest of the planned points on your card. How much detail you actually put down on the card to jog your memory is an individual choice, and must depend on your experience, your real knowledge of the subject and the level of your material. At first, you may feel you need to put down a note or a word on almost everything you want to mention, and trust nothing to your memory or your ability to extemporise; as long as these are still notes, and not proper written-out sentences (i.e., you do not have to read every word), your talk will still have a feeling of directness and of flexible *speech* (rather than the rigidity of a read sermon, which you are trying to avoid).

The main exception to the note-form of your talk will be any quotations, statistics, exact illustrations which you wish to include. Few of us carry such details totally accurately in our heads, so a moment of actual reading of a quotation or an exact piece of information will sometimes be necessary. It is important to write down such material precisely, read it out word for word, and get it right, in order to give authority and conviction to what you are saying. This is even more critical in a more scholarly or higher-level academic paper or lecture, where your whole analysis and argument may turn upon the accuracy of the details.

If you are having trouble in a general short talk, however, in finding enough to say or in filling out the details, do again remember some of the writing techniques already covered in this course. Fewer, but well developed, *main* points – challenging and interesting ones which you have thought up – are better than a whole jumble of smaller ones, merely touched on but not explored in any depth. Your audience can easily get confused by this sort of loose list, whereas if you announce at the beginning that you have, say, four main angles on your topic which you are going to cover, and then treat each one in detail (and with variety and interest), they are much clearer where you are going and what they have to look out for. Remember to remind your audience, each time you move to a new main point, where you are in your argument, and where this section of your talk stands within the overall structure.

As practice for this section, will you now follow these methods of planning, and *prepare and write out* your notes for two short talks from the following lists of subjects. Take one topic from the first list, which contains rather more general and easy subjects, and for which you might have to do little or no research; and then one from the second list, which contains rather more challenging and argumentative topics, and for which you may well need to look up some background information. You should plan the talk to be about 8–10 minutes in length, and assume that your audience is a general, but well-read one.

List A:
● Fireworks should be banned.
● The worst day of the week.
● Which three famous people would you like to have dinner with, and why?
● Your pet hates.
● It is always right to tell the truth.
● What will the world be like in a hundred years' time?

List B:
● All public transport should be free.
● The pros and cons of co-education.
● Smoking should be banned in all public places.
● All families should be limited to two children.

● Education is wasted on the young.
● Should animals ever be used in scientific research?

                                        30 minutes   STOP

How to deliver a short talk   2

Most people, I would think, are infinitely happier working at the preparation of a talk than actually giving it! At the thought of standing up and (even possibly) making fools of ourselves in public, we *all* suffer agonies of nerves and severe crises of confidence. Everybody, I am told (and I find this comforting), goes through this to some extent – excellent speakers as well as less experienced ones. So one fundamental thing to remember is: you are not alone, as everybody with sensitivity will be aware of, and sympathize with, your quite normal fears and nervousness. Good speakers, though, find ways of controlling and diverting their tension, and even of making it work *for* them instead of against them. After all, feelings of fear or nervousness are primitive, and very necessary, reactions to an unusual situation that demands a response, and in which we *must* be alert and 'on our toes'. The adrenalin in our body which gives us 'stage fright' also charges us with extra energy and heightened reactions to deal with this situation. Perhaps you have had the experience of listening to a speaker who had clearly churned out his talk hundreds of times before. It is a routine job, a stale duty; he has clearly no fears, nor adrenalin, nor tension – and it shows, in the lack of sparkle and interest in his presentation. So try to welcome your nervousness and extra tension as totally normal, and something that can be made to work positively to your advantage.

As I said earlier, confidence comes from a combination of knowing your subject, sound preparation, and some practice and experience in actually *doing* some proper and formal verbal communication. At this point, let's assume you have dealt with the first two, and are now ready to get on with giving your talk. Think hard for a moment, though, about the good and bad points of the delivery in talks that you yourself have heard, as you can learn a lot from observation and from your own experience as a listener. Can you make a list, first, of the good points, the features which helped the speaker to communicate; and, secondly, of those things which distinctly worked against him, and which put you off or sent you to sleep in the audience?

STOP   **15 minutes**

Discussion   Under your list of *good points*, you may have noticed some of the
following:

- the speaker *looked at* his audience, he addressed you directly.
- he used a *variety* of tone and pitch in his voice.
- he used a *range* of gestures and facial expressions.
- he used some *visual aids* (blackboard, slides, pictures, objects, demonstrations) to break up his talk.
- his *interest* and enthusiasm communicated itself to you.
- he spoke *clearly*, and at a reasonable pace.
- his talk was obviously carefully *structured* and left you in no doubt as to where it was going.
- he *lightened* the atmosphere by making you smile or laugh at times.
- he made you *think, personally*, about his subject in relation to you when he had clearly covered all relevant aspects of his topic.
- he *stopped* before his audience got restless.

Under your list of qualities which put you off a speaker, you may
have included some of the following points – many of which are
the reverse of the previous list. Perhaps you said that the speaker
was just plain boring, but think further about some of the probably reasons *why* this was so:

- He rarely moved his body or face.
- His voice hardly ever altered in pitch or tone: it was monotonous throughout.
- The talk was 'heavy' and formal from beginning to end, with no attempt to include humour, wit or intimacy.
- His examples were always 'dry' facts and statistics, which he never made you feel had any relevance to you personally.
- His language was too often vague and general, rather than concrete, specific, vivid, detailed, visual.
- He kept his head down and read his text from start to finish, never looking at you and establishing a feeling of rapport or communication with his audience.
- He never varied his delivery, or broke it up by using visual aids of any kind.
- The talk appeared to have little clear plan, so that you lost the thread, and became confused and uninterested.
- He repeated himself unnecessarily.
- He didn't communicate any of his own enthusiasm for the subject, and therefore it never sparked yours.

On the other hand, you might have been put off a speaker not just because he was dull, but because some aspects of his delivery immensely annoyed you:

● You couldn't always hear what he said – he spoke too softly, mumbled, gabbled too fast, or artificially slowed down his speech to a dreary snail's pace.
● He misjudged the level and expertise of his audience – he either 'talked down' to you, or else lapsed into obscure jargon which he didn't explain.
● He had irritating mannerisms, which distracted you from what he was saying (for instance, he sniffed, he fidgeted, he said 'er' or 'um' or some pet phrase in almost every sentence, he hesitated for an inordinately long time before pronouncing some words).
● He told a couple of not particularly appropriate 'set' jokes, which were not relevant to his theme and appeared very forced.
● He went on far too long!

These two lists of good and bad points provide sound basic guidelines as to the 'dos' and 'don'ts' of effective verbal communication, so do consider them carefully. Listen to your own performance on the tape-recorder: think positively about your own particular strengths, and try to develop them, and look critically at your possible weaknesses, and try to eradicate and correct them.

There are also several other aspects of your presentation worth considering (some of which overlap with the preceding points, but should be mentioned again) before you embark on a trial of your full speech.

1 Don't worry *too* much about the 'ums' and 'ers' in your speaking. Some of them are natural and unavoidable, especially at first; they only become irritating if they are really intrusive or occur several times a sentence. Try substituting a pause instead, if you are hesitating or lost for a word, rather than making a meaningless noise. The best way of assessing this is again to work with a tape-recorder (as it is very hard to hear our own personal mannerisms objectively). Try to speak for 60 seconds, without an 'er' or 'um', on either the pattern of your typical day, or exactly what you are wearing at this moment, or what you can see out of the window. If you are producing more than one 'waffly' noise per sentence, go back and try it again, and see if you can consciously cut down this habit.

2 Because it gives an immediate visual impression when you stand up to speak in public, be sure you *look good*, to yourself – which in turn helps to give you confidence. Perhaps wrongly, we all tend to judge people by appearances, so if you *look* relaxed, comfortable and elegant, you will start off by giving

that impression, even if you know you feel *very* different inside.

3 *Attention-winning devices* can help to keep your speech lively and your audience alert. Anything which breaks the expected pattern of your talk, and shifts people's focus or interest into another direction, will help to keep your listeners awake and responsive, especially during a longer presentation. I have mentioned *visual aids* as a means of adding variety and concrete examples to what you are saying; and also the device of challenging your audience by pulling in their personal experiences or reactions, and thus involving them more with your subject. A *humorous* approach to your topic, through which you can win a smile or a laugh, also wins attention, as well as getting your audience in a more friendly and relaxed mood. A relevant introductory anecdote, a witty or wry appeal to common feelings or experiences we all share, a topical or local reference, a funny comment against or about yourself (perhaps even playing on the idea of your own nervousness or inexperience) can all help to lighten the atmosphere and create a feeling of *rapport* and warmth. It makes *you* seem, to your listeners, more human, natural and friendly, and establishes a bond of intimacy and sympathy.

Remember, though, that the purpose of humour is not to prove yourself the Comedian of the Year, but merely to break the ice and catch – or perhaps, later on, jolt – people's attention.

4 *Pace and timing* are crucial to your delivery. If you have no idea how fast or slowly you speak, test yourself with the tape-recorder, by counting up, during one of the exercises, roughly the number of words you typically speak in a minute. The average should be between 120 and 150 words per minute, which will give you a speed which is neither confusingly fast, nor funereally slow. Within this norm, though, you also want to aim for variety. *Emphasise* your really important points, or your culminating argument, by slowing down considerably in your delivery, and giving extra weight and seriousness to the crucial ideas. Try to *stress*, or even occasionally repeat or give a synonym for, words which are *key* words of your topic, and which you want your audience not to forget. A careful and deliberate use of *pauses* can also be very effective, particularly before or after a vital phrase or concept. If your timing is good and your delivery confident, your listeners won't think that you have merely forgotten your place or your words, but realise that you are giving dramatic effect to an important point, or time for them to catch up mentally and ponder the implications of what you are saying.

5 Remember the importance of *eye-contact*, and of trying to speak, not read, your talk. It helps you to realise that you are

not talking to yourself, but *communicating* something of importance to you. Pick out some friendly faces in the audience, and
focus on them in turn (for not more than a few seconds each) by
looking at them directly or talking to them as known individuals. Don't just talk to people in the front row, or very close to
you, as it makes more distant listeners feel excluded; when you
look up from your notes move your gaze around and try to
include as many of your audience as you can within as wide a
range as possible. If you are really embarrassed at establishing
eye-contact with strangers, don't focus on any one person for
more than a couple of seconds; you can even look at their
foreheads, rather than directly into their eyes. What you need
to avoid is either addressing the ceiling or a distant corner of
the room, or never raising your eyes from the text to establish a
genuine rapport and communication at all.

Delivering a talk in the privacy of your own home, even to a
member of your family or a friend, is of course a very different
thing from doing it to a 'proper' audience. This is where practice
within a class can be much more like the real thing. But do now
take your short prepared talk, and deliver it formally, as you
would like it to be heard in public – either to your tape-recorder or
to your private home audience (or both at once). Play back your
talk, and listen to yourself fairly and critically, for problems you
can correct or improve; get your live home audience to offer
friendly and constructive criticism – and see if you agree with
them! You might have several practices or 'rehearsals' at this
point, in which the structure and content of your talk remain
exactly the same, but the words come out slightly differently each
time. This is excellent practice to give you increased fluency and
confidence. Don't be afraid to alter things quite drastically, either
in content or delivery, if you are not happy with it – but don't be
unrealistic and expect perfection. Few of us are superb and
naturally golden-tongued orators, who can immediately charm
with their force and fluency; what you are aiming for is a clear,
sensible and interesting exposition, and an increased confidence
that you have something to say and can express it effectively.

Relaxation
If you still feel, even with the confidence of sound knowledge and
preparation behind you, that tension or panic is going to fatally
inhibit your performance, you might try some deliberate physical
relaxation exercises to calm your nerves. One important area is
breathing. Many of us, when nervous, tend to breathe more
rapidly and shallowly than usual, which actually adds to our
problems, as it can tighten our chest muscles and make us feel
dizzy. If you feel this happening to you, try the technique of
deliberate slow breathing: breathe in to the count of five, and
then out again equally slowly. Repeat this several times, at a

point well before you expect to speak, and, if necessary, once or twice in pauses during your talk. If you are really getting breathless when talking, you certainly need to either slow down your pace and rate of words, or to take several deeper and longer breaths (between sentences or even while speaking) in order to relax your chest muscles and give your lungs the fuel they need for clear delivery. You might need to do *both*, very deliberately, in order to gain necessary control over your speaking.

If you feel too much tension building up while you are waiting to speak, try a basic yoga relaxation technique. Unobtrusively clench one hand really hard for a count of five, then let it go totally limp and relaxed for another similar count. Repeat this with the other hand, with your toes and foot and calf muscles, with your jaw muscles (particularly subject to tension), and any other muscles in any other parts of your body which you can tense and relax in this way, unnoticed. This can very much help to loosen and relax your muscles and prevent you 'tightening up' too much, especially just before a talk. For most people, the first half-minute of the presentation is by far the worst, but if you are well prepared and genuinely interested in your subject, and keen to communicate this to your audience, your adrenalin combined with the momentum of the occasion should carry you along, once you have got started. The secret is to be absorbed in what you want to say about your *subject*, rather than in worries about *yourself*.

3   *Other types of talks*

All these previous points about verbal communication have been applied to giving a short general talk, but in university or college study you will sometimes be called on to give a much narrower and more academic presentation. All these points – on preparation, practice and delivery – still very much apply to whatever sort of talk you are giving, however. But you also need to think more specifically about the sort of scholarly 'papers' or talks which you might have to cope with during degree study; these would probably be either a *seminar paper* or a more *formal lecture* (though the latter might never occur).

Seminar paper
Definitions of exactly what a seminar implies tend to vary, often from department to department or within different large faculties of a university. Within the arts or social sciences, for example, giving a seminar paper usually implies delivering a semi-formal talk on an academic subject (often a very narrow and specialised

topic) to a small or medium-sized group, normally of one's peers or fellow-members of a department, followed by a discussion in which you defend your argument and answer questions about it. It could even mean a very informal presentation, where interruptions and discussions are invited throughout, to the half-dozen members of your own tutorial group (and your own class tutor); or perhaps only preparing carefully enough to *lead* the group in structured discussion on a pre-agreed problem or area of study. Within the sciences, a seminar paper often indicates a much larger and more formal presentation – closer to a lecture – and often with a wider audience.

Lectures
A lecture certainly implies on even greater degree of formality, though even here your delivery might be adapted to suit the audience, the depth of the topic – and your own confidence. A lecture is usually a more 'set' and rigid occasion, where a speaker delivers – and often completely *reads* – a longish paper on a given topic for a set time, without interruptions (although a period is frequently allocated at the end for questions, comments and alternative viewpoints). Here, yet again, the same methods of preparation and planning hold good, even though the final result might be a much larger and more dense piece of work in its depth, length and detail.

Many lecturers, even with a large and mixed audience, are experienced and confident enough to work from notes, albeit much more detailed ones which might cover a great many cards or sheets of paper, and to talk through their ideas in a way that comes across as spontaneous, fresh and direct. Others feel that the more formal occasion demands a more formal approach, and deliver their lecture, word for word, as a totally read paper, where almost every line is polished and perfect and worked out for its most impressive effect. This latter method, especially if the lecturer can still establish frequent eye-contact and a direct sense of rapport by not reading, but speaking, many of the ends of the his sentences, has considerable advantages: the speaker says *exactly* what he wants to say, in its most persuasive and effective form, and can also thus work into his well-rehearsed sentences such rhetorical devices as balance, rhythm, dramatic repetition, alliteration – all of which can add considerably to the convincing emotional effectiveness of a performance. (It is also often absolutely necessary for speakers such as politicians, who cannot afford to get a single word wrong, or to ad-lib, in case it later gets them into trouble or is turned against them). But, as was mentioned earlier, the dangers of a rigidly prepared and read speech are that it can all too easily come across as stilted, insincere or stale, and lose that all-important sense of intimacy and personal contact which a good speaker always tries to establish.

Whichever method, or combination, you feel will suit you for giving a more official lecture, remember that all the earlier 'rules' for a good short talk still apply – even if the final result is more detailed and lengthy and takes much more elaborate preparation and delivery. Do remember, too, that verbal communication is one skill that only improves by doing it, as frequently as possible, in order to gain experience and confidence. However unhappy and critical you are about your initial 'public' attempts (and you may well be pleasantly surprised!) you will certainly get better at it, in time, the more you practise.

Further reading
There are many books on the shelves of public libraries on the arts of public speaking in general, or on training the voice. One of the most comprehensive is *The art of Speaking Made Simple*, by William R. Gondin and Edward W. Mammen (Heinemann, London, 2nd edn, 1980). Many of the study skills books already mentioned include a brief section on giving a talk, but few go into it in any detail or apply it in depth to the particular problems of verbal communication for the mature student in the academic world.

Self-assessment exercises

Exercise 1
Prepare a 10-minute talk on any of the following topics and either
(a) write it down as closely to the spoken form as possible (it should be 1,500 to 1,800 words long); or
(b) deliver your talk into a tape recorder and analyse your own performance when you play it back.
1 The threats to our environment.
2 You can't choose your relations.
3 My favourite actor.
4 The best film I've ever seen.
5 The problems facing policemen.
6 Where I would like to live when I retire.
7 My best friend.
8 A successful holiday.

Exercise 2
Channel Four television used to offer a 5-minute evening 'Comment' slot for people who wished to express their views on a

particular subject – and sometimes the 'Video-Box' is used for the same purpose. Imagine that you were given five minutes to speak on a subject you feel strongly about. Script the statement you would like to make, or alternatively record your statement on a tape-recorder and analyse your own performance on playback.

Exercise 3
This is a letter-drafting exercise. Imagine that you are the parent of a young child who has been sent home from school for refusing to eat school dinners. Your child never eats meat, and you object to this course of action. Draft the letter you would send to the head teacher – then compare it with the one we print in the Guidance notes.

Exercise 4
Below is a short essay written by a former student. Make notes on what you think about it, then compare them with the observations we offer in the Guidance notes.

Friday the 13th
It is Friday the 13th again, with all its associations of bad luck, but to me it is a memorable anniversary of a very special Friday the 13th a long time ago.

It was towards the end of the war. My father's business had been 'blitzed' in 1940 although by then he had managed to re-start in a small way making Utility furniture which was sold to the public through a very strict rationing system. My brother was a glider pilot and we were anxiously awaiting news of him after the Arnhem Operation.

Despite the miseries of perpetually gloomy news from the various battlefronts, food shortages, clothing coupons and the blackout, young people seized every possible opportunity to have fun. A very select dancing academy was our venue where the proprietor who always smoked cigars kept a fatherly eye on the proceedings – strict tempo dancing, no jiving, and positively no pass-outs for ladies during the interval! Even now, the mingled aroma of coffee and cigar smoke brings instant recall of the discreet manoeuvres to secure the best-looking partner for the refreshment interval. With luck he might turn out to be a candidate for the last waltz and then who knew what further delights might ensue! I remember with especial glee the clumsy compliment made by one bashful young fellow who commented on my nice teeth and asked whether they were my own!

I was taken aback one evening when a slim blond young man, with a distinct resemblance to the film star Leslie Howard, suggested I might like to use a spare ticket he had for a performance of 'Hamlet' at the Palace Theatre in Manchester on the following Friday – the 13th. Such an outlandish suggestion was a far cry from the usual seat in the ninepennies at the local 'flicks', or even the one-and-sixpennies if the swain was determined to make an impression, and I accepted his invitation with some trepidation.

At that time I was on 'work of national importance' as a typist in an engineering factory in Trafford Park – a dull and dreary job often involving long hours in poor conditions. That evening it was raining heavily and I well remember negotiating the puddles between the railway lines which criss-crossed the roads in that industrial wilderness. I had donned the best finery I could muster for the occasion and arrived breathless and damp at the theatre, just in time for curtain-up.

The atmosphere in the theatre was charged with excited anticipation as the war-time audience settled down to escape for a few hours from the real-life horrors of the war outside. This was my first experience of 'Hamlet' and I was much impressed by the acting, although I felt the plethora of dead bodies in the final scene to be somewhat excessive. The spellbound attention of that audience was in marked contrast to my only other experience of Shakespeare in the theatre. This had been a Donald Wolfit production for a schools matinée of the School Certificate set play 'Richard II'; during the scene in Act IV where in despair King Richard flings down the mirror it bounced instead of shattering 'in a hundred shivers', and the already restive audience dissolved into hysterical giggles.

After the performance my escort suggested going for a meal. This was indeed high living in those austere times, and overwhelmed by shyness and the aura of menace emanating from the swarthy waiters in the Greek restaurant, I pleaded lack of appetite and ordered the simplest item on the menu.

This had been a very unusual and memorable evening for me, but when I arrived home my europhoria was quickly dissipated. A War Office telegram had arrived during the day announcing officially that my brother had been posted 'Missing' at Arnhem. The pleasant companion of my evening's entertainment was destined to share my family's sorrow; he joined with us in the fruitless search for possible leads as to my brother's fate, and was a source of great comfort to my parents when Holland was finally liberated – a make-shift grave in a garden of the small Dutch town of Oosterbeek finally revealed my brother's last resting place.

The young man eventually became my husband and helped to fill the gap in my parents' lives left by the brother-in-law he never met. Through all the vicissitudes of our subsequent life together since that fateful Friday the 13th I can claim, as Winston Churchill did when writing of his marriage to his beloved Clemmie, that 'we lived happily ever after'. **99**

Exercise 5
Without looking back over this chapter, can you list the main points we have covered in it?

6 *Efficient reading*

The reading of all good books is like conversation with the finest men of past centuries   *Descartes*

Contents

Introduction

Reading seems in many ways, for an adult, one of the most 'natural' abilities we have, a skill which we have taken for granted since the age of six or seven. Yet when students contemplate the amount of material they have to cope with in higher education, it can seem daunting because of the sheer volume of books to 'cover'. There is a world of difference between the casual and unpressured reading of everyday life (taking in necessary documents and letters, glancing at a magazine or newspaper, relaxing with a novel), and the disciplined absorption of a great deal of written material for the purposes of a college degree or producing a scholarly essay. It has been estimated that a typical arts or social sciences student will be reading hard for at least 1,000 hours per year; in academic study, reading lists of set books are often very long and 'suggested' reading lists even longer!

Greater efficiency in reading therefore becomes crucial. Not necessarily greater speed, but an increased awareness of your purposes and your methods can help to build up better habits of efficiency, which will pay off as the amount and type of reading you do vastly increases. There is no magic about efficient reading, but constant *practice* and *flexibility* will certainly increase your confidence and your ability, and save wasted time and effort.

Types of books 1

Imagine first that you are in a library or bookshop looking for books for an essay or project. What kinds of books might you need? Think about the great range of written material which you might be asked to look at as part of academic study. How many types can you jot down?

---

5 minutes **STOP**

My own list (in no particular order and with a lot of overlapping) would include: *Discussion*

- Textbooks – both introductory and specialised
- Reference books
- Information books
- Standard works/texts
- Critical works
- Journals, magazines, periodicals
- Newspapers (perhaps)
- Books about books
- Books of readings, essays

There is a great range of different sorts of books and materials here but you would not want to read them all in the same way, or in the same depth – or even for the same purpose. So a crucial skill at this point is a rapid judgement of what the book is about and whether or not it will even be any use to you. The next section suggests some ways of doing this.

2 *Previewing the book*

As a student, you're often told 'You don't have to read all of this book – just have a quick look at it!' This is not an easy thing to do without practice and experience. You need to be able to judge rapidly which books you need, or even whether a book will be any use to you at all, so that you don't waste time on unnecessary reading. One way of practising this skill is called the 'book-in-a-minute exercise'.

Again, let's suppose you have to write an essay or project on a particular topic. Go to a library, or perhaps a friend's bookcase, and pick a book you don't know; it helps if it is a reasonably structured book, with a coherent theme (i.e., not a collection of readings, but a book on a single topic). Give yourself exactly *60 seconds* to find out all you can about the book, especially what its main theme and angle is, its level and approach, and therefore whether it might be useful for your purpose. After one minute, STOP, and then try to do two things:

1 can you suggest roughly what the book is about?
2 can you jot down what you did in order to elicit this information?

STOP   **1 minute**

Discussion   This might seem an impossible exercise, given so short a time, and your answer to 1 might be rather vague, but you should have gained *some* idea of the book's theme and content. What is more important is 2 – *how* you did it. Things that you could have surveyed rapidly might include:

- the title (and sub-title)
- the author
- date of publication
- the dust-cover and the 'blurb' information on the back of the book
- the contents page or chapter headings
- the index
- any illustrations, tables, graphs, pictures
- the preface or introduction

Notice that looking at all these areas involves moving *rapidly* through the whole book, with very little continuous reading at all. You should be trying to gain an overall impression of what the book is about; the traditional method of starting with the first word on page 1 and ploughing through solid reading for your 60 seconds is *not* the best way to get a rapid image of the book as a whole, or its use to you.

On the other hand, you will have to learn to judge the relative worth of some of the information on the above list. Title, sub-title, and the contents page or list of chapter headings are always vital, as is the date of publication (usually on the back of the title-page); if you are looking for information on, say, discoveries in genetics, and the book you have picked up happens to be published in 1930, you know that you can close it and stop right there, however apparently relevant its title. Information on the dust-cover or back cover always has to be treated with caution, as it can range from a valuable synopsis of content and theme which tells you at once all you want to know, to background biography on the author (possibly not very useful at this point), or to outright propaganda, in the form of persuasive advertising or the best bits of critical reviews, which might help to sell the book but is very little use to a discriminating and selective reader, like you!

In the same way, a glance at the preface or introduction may immediately reveal the author's theme and purpose, or it may only offer background material or a list of sources and acknowledgements (a waste of your time at this point). The index can usually give you an idea of the scope and range of the book, but here you might have to know the subject quite well in order for many entries to make sense. The same qualification might also apply to your rapid assessment of any graphs or pictures.

This exercise can also be taken to a second stage with the same book: give yourself *five minutes* this time, and see how much more information you can glean now. Where did you turn this time to get more detailed knowledge?

---

5 minutes   STOP

Given more time, you might have done a little more continuous reading of the introduction or the first chapter – but remember that your job is still to gain a useful impression of the book as a whole. Don't get 'bogged down' in solid reading of large chunks of it, especially if you realise that the book is not what you want, is irrelevant to your purpose or at too high or low a level. One more thing you might have done here was to read the *first and last sentences* in each chapter, or look at the *concluding chapter* in a little more detail. If the book seems to be proving useful and interesting, a longer preview (say, ten or fifteen minutes) might allow you to read initial and concluding paragraphs in each chapter, or even the whole first chapter if it is a short one. Remember, though, that your efficiency in previewing or surveying a book in this way depends to a large extent on the clarity and efficiency of the author; if he structures his book logically, with coherent

Discussion

statements of purpose and theme at the places you expect to find them, your job will be a lot easier and quicker. If the book itself is less logical in its planning, or the author buries his main points deep in the chapters, it might well take you a lot longer to extract relevant information, or even to judge whether the book is of use to you at all.

So, try practising this exercise, in two stages, in the ways suggested on a variety of different books, all at different levels. You will soon realise, by experience, which aspects of a book are most useful to preview for really rapid assessment.

This technique of *previewing the book* should become a necessary part of any of your handling of written material from now on, whether you dismiss the book in a few minutes as not for you, or whether you eventually decide that this is a volume you will need to study and absorb in complete detail. A habit of rapidly surveying your task before settling down to read is a crucial one for efficient study. It also forms part of a total method for handling written material in a more thorough way – the first stage in comprehensive study of a book. This system, which is found in a number of manuals on study skills, is called the *SQ3R method*.

3 *SQ3R*

These initials stand for:
Survey Question Read Recall Review

Survey
This is the initial previewing of a book which you have already practised, in order to get a rapid and general idea of its content, plan and approach. It is a *sampling* stage, as crucial for a short article as for a full-length book. It should give you an overview, a general sense of perspective and anticipation of what the author is able to offer you. This stage gives you a chance to get an idea of the book *ahead* of your reading, to consider and *anticipate* the content. Remember that we anticipate all the time, in smaller ways, in any reading of written language – by deciding between different meanings of words, by using our familiarity with the actual pattern of sentences.
Question
Thoughtful anticipation of what you might expect in a given book should lead you to ask questions about it. These should ideally give you a sense of purpose in what you read, and also develop a generally enquiring mind, an alert attitude, as you absorb

material. The questions may at first be rather general ones: 'What is the author trying to say here? What is the most crucial point in this chapter? Do I know anything about the subject already?' But as you get more into the text, they may be much more detailed and specific: 'Why does the author approach this topic in this particular way? Has he supported his argument? Does it develop in a logical way? Do I agree with his assertions or conclusions?' This sort of alert and questioning attitude creates a sense of dialogue with the text, which should begin by a purposeful anticipation of what the book can offer, and then continue right through your closer study of the material.

Read

If the first two stages indicate that the book might be important or useful in your study, you can now start careful and in-depth reading of the text. Notice, though, that this is the *third* stage in using a book – and not the first and only one, as many people would think. Keeping in mind the sort of questions raised by stage two, read actively and critically through the material, at a speed which allows you to understand and grasp the content. Some people claim that, even at this stage of 'reading proper', a rapid *skimming* type of reading (which we will return to later) to gain a general grasp of ideas, followed by a slower and more thorough reading is a much more valuable method than a slow once only working-through from beginning to end. This may very well depend upon the difficulty of the text, and how easy you find it to grasp the content and understand the main ideas.

As a practice here, try testing yourself with a short newspaper article (for example, the 'leader' in a serious newspaper, or a more general discussion piece on a social or political problem). Read *very rapidly* once – no more than ten seconds – for a sense of what the piece is about; and then, a second time and more carefully, for a detailed understanding of its content. Can you now summarise the key ideas of the piece in a few sentences of your own? We will return to methods of skimming, and of improving overall reading efficiency, later on in the chapter.

5–10 minutes   **STOP**

Recall

Putting down, in your own written form, what you have gained from your reading, is one crucial way of indicating whether you have understood it fully. Another is to have someone test you on the content, by asking you specific questions about it. Just *thinking*, as a method of recalling what you have learnt, is rarely enough, as you need to focus your ideas by putting them down on paper – usually in the form of brief notes. This is the hardest part of the process, yet the most important. Some people, with their own books, like to help recall by marking the text – underlining or checking crucial passages, key concepts or words, or even jotting brief notes in the margins.

How often you pause to *recall* your reading also seems to be a question of personal choice and experience. To do it too frequently (say, after every paragraph) would almost certainly break up the flow of your reading, and make your grasp of the author's ideas too fragmentary and disjointed. But to read a whole book, right through, without stopping for any conscious attempt at recall, would probably leave you with too broad and vague a concept of what the book is about. The end of a chapter, or of a long section within a chapter, are logical places to spot, and jot down, what you can recall. If the material is particularly dense or difficult, you may need to do it more frequently.

Review
This is the last stage of thorough study of a written text. It involves going back over the article, section or chapter you have just tried to recall, and checking that you have done so accurately and thoroughly. Re-read rapidly to see if you have left out anything important, and then complete your recall by filling in any gaps or making any necessary corrections in your notes. Reviewing is best done as soon as possible, in order to impress the recall stage on your mind; but it might also form part of a general revision of the material at a much later stage (say, for an exam).

4 *Types of reading*

The SQ3R method of tackling a book can be a very useful and thorough one, but even this system involves several different types of reading. Thinking of the different sorts of reading that you yourself might do, can you identify and jot down various ways in which we take in written material?

STOP   **5 minutes**

Discussion   Your answer might include:
- surveying rapidly (as in the previewing method above)
- sampling, or exploratory reading (essentially the same thing)
- reading rapidly for entertainment (to find out 'what happens next')
- selective reading (focusing only on parts of a text)

- skimming (to keep in touch with a text, but rather superficially)
- scanning or search-reading (watching for particular ideas or facts)
- close and detailed reading (for comprehensive understanding of the content)

Some of these ways of reading certainly overlap, and some of the terms for describing them can be confusing because they can mean almost the same thing. But the crucial point here is the *variation* in reading speeds and purposes which you might want to use. There should be no one 'set' speed or type of reading: being *flexible* in your reading, and switching from one type of speed of reading to another, when necessary, is a vital step towards greater efficiency. After all, you would expect a vast difference in reading between a rapid glancing down the page (for example, to find your name on a list), and the sort of painstaking thoroughness needed for proof-reading or a piece of close literary analysis. One problem for students is to break down the feeling that because something is actually printed, and in black and white, it must therefore necessarily be important and worth giving your whole attention to. Don't feel guilty if you only read selectively, or skip over chunks of text instead of reading every word. By being flexible in your reading and using your judgement you are certainly handling books more efficiently, and helping to concentrate your effort where it is *needed*. Adapting rapidly to different sorts and speeds of reading will certainly save you time and effort, and make you a more sensible and efficient reader in the long run.

Three general sorts of reading can be grouped together from the above list. These are:

- skim-reading or skimming
- scanning and search-reading
- detailed and in-depth reading

Skim-reading

Skimming involves moving rapidly and selectively through a text, to gain an overview and a rough idea of what the material is about. It uses some of the techniques of previewing, which we have already discussed, such as focusing on important areas of the book and not being afraid to skip over others. Skimming should be a questioning and exploratory kind of reading, which surveys the text as a whole, and tries to get a sense of perspective about it. There is no set speed for skim-reading; your own personal rate might vary a lot from book to book, and even within one text. It is not speed *in itself* which matters, but a sufficient grasp of the general meaning gained as rapidly as possible. Remember you must concentrate your effort only where needed.

This, particularly, is a skill which needs practice. As an exercise, which you might try frequently, pick a book from your library and spend five minutes skim-reading it, using the techniques of the second stage of previewing. Or give yourself only twenty seconds a short newspaper or magazine article. Try to record briefly what you have taken in. Don't be worried if, at first, you seem to gain a rather confused impression of the text. Slow down *a little*, so that you can grasp the overall meaning in a bit more detail and keep practising!

Scanning and search-reading
These terms, which are often used interchangeably, imply a much more *selective* sort of reading than general skimming. This is reading with a specific quest and purpose in mind, to discover and isolate a particular piece of information. Until you find what you want, you are doing no more than running your eye down a page, as when you check a list of prices in a shop for one particular item, or scan a recipe for the amount of one specific ingredient. When you think you have discovered your information, then your reading can immediately slow down, to focus and digest the meaning in detail.

As an exercise, here is part of the introduction to a nineteenth-century essay by the biologist and geologist Thomas Huxley, on the history of chalk. Your purpose here is to *scan* these five paragraphs (skim-reading as fast as possible) for two facts only, and then jot them down:
1 How long is the layer of chalk which runs across England?
2 What happens to the lime in chalk when dropped into vinegar?

" If a well were sunk at our feet in the midst of the city of Norwich, the diggers would very soon find themselves at work in that white substance almost too soft to be called rock, with which we are all familiar as 'chalk'.
Not only here, but over the whole county of Norfolk, the well-sinker might carry his shaft down many hundred feet without coming to an end of the chalk; and, on the seacoast, where the waves have pared away the face of the land which breasts them, the scarped faces of the high cliffs are often wholly formed of the same material. Northward, the chalk may be followed as far as Yorkshire; on the south coast it appears abruptly in the picturesque western bays of Dorset, and breaks into the Needles of the Isle of Wight; while on the shores of Kent it supplies that long line of white cliffs to which England owes her name of Albion.
Were the thin soil which covers it all washed away, a curved band of white chalk, here broader, and there narrower, might be followed diagonally across England from Lulworth in Dorset, to

Flamborough Head in Yorkshire – a distance of over 280 miles as the crow flies. From this band to the North Sea, on the east, and the Channel, on the south, the chalk is largely hidden by other deposits; but, except in the Weald of Kent and Sussex, it enters into the very foundation of all the southeastern counties.

Attaining, as it does in some places, a thickness of more than a thousand feet, the English chalk must be admitted to be a mass of considerable magnitude. Nevertheless, it covers but an insignificant portion of the whole area occupied by the chalk formation of the globe, much of which has the same general characters as ours, and is found in detached patches, some less, and others more extensive, than the English. Chalk occurs in northwest Ireland; it stretches over a large part of France, – the chalk which underlies Paris being, in fact, a continuation of that of the London basin; it runs through Denmark and Central Europe, and extends southward to North Africa; while eastward, it appears in the Crimea and in Syria, and may be traced as far as the shores of the Sea of Aral, in Central Asia. If all the points at which true chalk occurs were circumscribed, they would lie within an irregular oval about three thousand miles in long diameter – the area of which would be as great as that of Europe, and would many times exceed that of the largest existing inland sea – the Mediterranean.

We all know that if we 'burn' chalk the result is quicklime. Chalk, in fact, is a compound of carbonic acid gas, and lime, and when you make it very hot the carbonic acid flies away and the lime is left. By this method of procedure we see the lime, but we do not see the carbonic acid. If, on the other hand, you were to powder a little chalk and drop it into a good deal of strong vinegar, there would be a great bubbling and fizzing, and, finally, a clear liquid, in which no sign of chalk would appear. Here you see the carbonic acid in the bubbles; the lime, dissolved in the vinegar, vanishes from sight. There are a great many other ways of showing that chalk is essentially nothing but carbonic acid and quicklime. Chemists enunciate the result of all the experiements which prove this, by stating that chalk is almost wholly composed of 'carbonate of lime'. **"**

---

                                                    5 minutes STOP

I expect you found the answer to 1 quite quickly in your scanning, *Discussion*
as '280 miles' stands out in the text (in paragraph three) and involves little more than a visual matching task. But to find the answer to 2 was more difficult, partly because you had to search–read for a description of a process, and not just a simple fact, and partly because the terms may have been less familiar and therefore needed more careful reading. After scanning rapidly on

through paragraph four, which is clearly all about geographical rather than chemical features, I hope you would have slowed down and focused more carefully when you got to paragraph five. Here, by narrowing your attention and searching purposefully, you should have discovered (about two-thirds of the way through the paragraph), that the lime in chalk dissolves and vanishes when put into vinegar. If you became sidetracked into reading all the passage equally slowly (and took much longer than about thirty seconds over it), or in trying to understand all you read and take in all the proper names, you were not really scanning very efficiently or for the right purpose. You might try this again, with a short newspaper piece in which you would expect to find specific and simple facts; or, if you can, get a friend to help you by looking first at a short passage, and then asking you to search as rapidly as possible for some very limited information.

Detailed reading

This is the level of 'reading proper', where you are reading for efficient *understanding* – which is the main objective of developing your reading skills. There is little point in training yourself to read faster, if you have a corresponding loss of comprehension. Efficiency in reading seems to us more important than sheer speed, and knowledge of your purposes in reading as vital as improving the 'mechanics'. Genuinely *better* reading is a product not only of time expended (i.e., speed), but of the purpose and result of the work (i.e., what you have learnt and understood). It is here that a positive and questioning attitude – *thinking* about your purposes, as in the SQ3R method – can help to redirect your effort more efficiently in the most fruitful direction, and can be more important than sheer 'mind*less*' speed-reading. But this means that you cannot leave the point and purpose of your reading to someone else. You need constantly to exercise your judgement in reading; as a mature student you've learnt to do that in everyday life, and there is no reason why you cannot apply this to texts and material which at first seem strange.

Detailed reading test

Many students, nevertheless, do worry about the actual speed at which they read. If you want to test yourself at this point, here is a short but typical reading exercise, followed by some comprehension questions to which you can jot brief answers. Read it through at your usual speed for 'close' reading, trying to combine maximum speed with an efficient level of comprehension. Have a watch with a second hand beside you, and note down your starting and finishing times.

The article is a short and amusing piece which was written for a newsletter – but it also contains some factual information on which we will pose a few questions when you have finished reading it. So check your speed, but pay attention as well!

" *A funny thing happened to me at the forum*
When I was first asked to contribute an amusing piece to this newsletter, culled from my working life, I didn't really know where to start. As a tutor I have found that 'all human life' is represented in extra-mural classes and being Director for the past two years has afforded moments of hilarity too. But after only a cursory search of my mental archives one incident positively sat up and begged to be chosen: Saddleworth Forum, 1975.

This body, comprising a fair proportion of retired and elderly folk, was in the habit of inviting guest speakers to address chosen topics. Some eighty people turned up to hear my biographical analysis of the then Prime Minister, Harold Wilson. After being introduced by the chairman I began to hold forth on Hudders-field's favourite son. As I dilated upon his precocious scholastic achievements, I paced around, as I tend to, and noticed a wasp crawling slowly and drunkenly on the floor. 'What a terrible thing it would be,' a passive part of my mind mused 'if that wasp were somehow to crawl unnoticed up someone's leg.' How much more terrible it would be if it should sting them as well – especially if that "someone" happens to be me.' The simple solution was to include the wasp, apparently casually, in the path of my peregrinations, but something held me back. I realised that several elderly ladies in the front row had followed my gaze and had also spotted the wasp. At least one of them seemed to have divined my intentions and her stern look seemed to say that if I should dare to tread on this innocent wasp she was quite pre-pared to rise up before this congregation and denounce me as a heartless monster.

Smiling benignly at the lady I carefully avoided God's little creature and continued to expand happily upon how Harold Wilson had become an officer during the thirties in Oxford University's Liberal Society. However by the time I had reached his resignation from the Labour Cabinet with Nye Bevan in 1951, I began to feel a slight tickle. 'If it were not absolutely impossible,' my passive voice hissed, 'that tickle could be caused by a drunken wasp intent upon scaling the north face of your leg.' Dismissing the idea, I began a heavily ironic account of the 'White Heat of Revolution' – but the tickle persisted and became even more like . . . well, like a wasp crawling up my leg.

I was now a little alarmed. As I paced around, building up to the 1964 General Election victory, I began surreptitiously to flap my trouser leg to dislodge the putative wasp. I also bent my head to check the floor. No wasp. Whilst my head was down there I distinctly heard a buzzing noise from my trouser leg. With Wilson poised on the threshold of No. 10 – I panicked. The Saddleworth Forum was treated to the sight of their lecturer jack-knifing about, shouting incoherently and apparently rolling up his left trouser leg like some demented Freemason. The wasp dropped to the floor. 'There it is!' I cried, with shin and knobbly knee exposed. My septuagenarium chairman who had been sitting in a horrified trance during my cavortings now leapt into reasonably well co-ordinated action. Knocking aside a couple of card tables he descended heavily from the stage and stamped repeatedly upon the wasp until it was very dead.

The hall had fallen silent, breath suspended whilst the drama was enacted in front of them. My chairman stared at me triumphantly, secure in the knowledge that he had fulfilled any conceivable obligation to be found in Sir Walter Citrine's *ABC of Chairmanship*. I stared back. The silence was broken by a large lady who might well have been a district nurse. 'Are you all right, Dr Jones?', she boomed. 'Did it sting you?' 'No, perfectly OK,' I replied with forced cheerfulness. 'Got the little blighter too.' At this the audience broke into spontaneous and sustained applause. Hugely gratified, I returned with some difficulty to my task of re-electing Mr Wilson in 1966. But, once my adrenalin began to return to normal, I felt a sharp pain. It *had* stung me! If there were a medal for Extra-Mural Bravery, I would have qualified for it that afternoon. Gamely I yomped on through the 1970 defeat, the miners' strike, and return to power in 1974. At the end of the lecture several nice motherly ladies crowded around and when my – by now – swollen leg was revealed, a cry went up. The district nurse produced some ointment which she applied liberally. Whilst basking in all this sympathy, the little old lady to whom I had attributed a Buddhist concern for living creatures, approached me.
'You know, I saw the wasp earlier on, crawling around.'
'Yes,' I replied 'I noticed that you noticed.'
'But what I want to know is,' she went on, 'why didn't you step on it *then*?'
Why indeed. **,,**

STOP   **5–10 minutes**   Now without looking back at the piece, see how many of the following questions you can answer.

---

1 At what venue did the wasp-stinging incident take place?
2 In what year?

3 In which town was Harold Wilson raised?
4 Which university did he subsequently attend?
5 What was the year of his first general election victory?
6 Who wrote *The ABC of Chairmanship*?
(The answers to these questions are given at the end of this chapter.)

The passage you read was about 800 words long. At an average reading speed (of 250 words per minute), it should have taken you just over three minutes. Reasonable comprehension is considered to be about 75%; that is, being able to answer four out of six questions correctly. If you took much more than four minutes to read the passage, your speed was below 200 wpm, and there is certainly some room for improvement. If your speed was between 200–300 wpm, you are reading at an average rate for most people, but it is still well below what many educationalists feel is a possible and much more efficient level. Most students who work consistently at practising and speeding up their reading performance have been able to double their speed (typically to 500 wpm) without any loss of comprehension. Do remember, though that sheer speed alone does not make an effective or intelligent reader – it is understanding, purpose and thought which counts as well.

However, many people certainly do read more slowly than they need to, and even in your own detailed reading your speed can *vary* considerably. Can you suggest some reasons for this?

5–10 minutes   **STOP**

Reasons you could have suggested might include: *Discussion*
● physical ones, like eye-strain or tiredness
● lack of interest in the subject
● prejudices against the content or point of view of the author
● anxiety, lack of concentration, or other distractions
● lack of basic knowledge of the subject
● difficulty of vocabulary or concepts
● reading passively, rather than with a questioning sense of purpose
● 'bad' habits of slow or wasteful eye movements
Some of these factors can be improved or eliminated in relatively simple ways – by giving yourself a rest, dealing with distracting problems, doing exercises to improve your concentration. Others we have already mentioned when discussing the increased efficiency you achieve from purposeful reading, and from an alert and questioning attitude towards your material. Problems to do

with lack of knowledge or of particular terminology can best be tackled by:

1 Prior reading at a simpler level within the field.
2 Consciously pulling out, looking up and clarifying the main concepts and theories in the subject.
3 Making a glossary of necessary terms which you may not know, but which are important if you are going to study this subject further. It may be that your general *vocabulary* needs extending.

A good reader is aware of a *lot* of words, and does not constantly have to slow down and consider their meaning as he goes along. In order to increase your word-power, try to get the habit of using a dictionary more: look up, and write down, the meaning of words you don't know. Don't let yourself be satisfied until you have checked *every* word unknown to you. Reading more widely, and in a variety of fields, will also in itself broaden your vocabulary, especially if you can also consciously use new words in your own writing. Even playing scrabble, or doing crossword puzzles can help.

5 *Improving your reading speed*

The last reason I included on the previous list is a more fundamental one, a more 'mechanical' reason about which there has been a lot of research and discussion in recent years. Most writers on reading skills now feel that 'bad' habits in eye movements are the *result* of bad reading habits – and not the other way round. That is, bad eye movements are the symptoms, rather than the causes, of difficulties in reading. If you reconsider and think positively about the method and purpose of your reading, it will be much easier to retrain your eye movements, with practice, and change the 'bad' habits of a lifetime.

It is crucial here to realise the differences between reading and merely 'seeing'. We all apparently have phenomenal abilities to *see* words rapidly; it is the deeper comprehension, and registering of that information by the brain, which is more difficult. Tests have shown that we can all see groups of words in 1/100th of a second, but to relate and 'read' them by the brain takes nearer to 1/8th of a second. Although, in reading, our eyes have to move constantly across a page of print, it is only in the brief pauses, called *fixations*, that we actually register and read the text (as a sort of visual snapshot of a small group of words). It has been estimated that these fixations, these stops between the jumps, in which the eye actually absorbs the material, take about a quarter-second – for almost everybody. It is thus the *number* of pauses or fixations we make along a line of print, and how much they overlap, which tends to determine our reading speed.

You can test this out for yourself by very closely watching some-one else's eye movements when they read. Have someone hold up a book at eye level (or make a small hole through a newspaper) and watch carefully the rhythmic movement and the number of pauses the eyes make in travelling across the page.

It has been shown that faster and more efficient readers make fewer fixations or pauses, which overlap less, and that they less frequently 'regress' – that is, go back to repeat a fixation before moving forwards again. A diagram can illustrate the difference between a slow and an efficient reader:

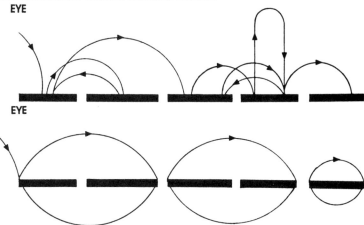

As you can see, the first reader (a slow one) reads much smaller groups of words with many more fixations (often only one word at a time), often goes back (regresses) to check or repeat his fixation on a word, and also lets his eyes drift off the line of print altogether. The second, more efficient, reader takes in a larger span of words, in fewer fixations or pauses, and does not back-skip or let his eyes wander. This can also be shown by marking off an actual sentence or line of print. Take a sentence from the previous speed-reading exercise (of 17 words):

'there is a bad tradition in English education that nothing is truly valued until it is assessed.' A good reader might make these fixations:

A poor reader might read the sentence thus:

The latter reader has made three times as many fixations; he has back-tracked three times, let his eye wander over a longer word (lack of confidence in vocabulary?) and read a number of words *singly*, instead of spanning them as a visual group. On the other hand, not all combinations of words *can* be grasped easily and in a single span. Whereas phrases like 'a bad tradition' or 'until it is assessed' can be (and *should* be, in efficient reading) taken as a whole, a phrase like 'the radically autonomous text' or 'Boltzmann's theory of entropy' would give almost all of us pause, unless we happened to be very well versed in the concepts and terminology of modern structuralist theory or of thermal physics!

If you feel that any of these problems with less-than-effective eye movements apply to you, there are several ways you can try to improve things.

1 Reduce the *number* of fixations you make in a line of print. In a normal line of text, with material that is reasonably easy to understand, three or four fixations should be enough to read the line. As an exercise, try to read a short passage *only* pausing at four set points across the page:

   x   x   x   x
   x   x   x   x

   To check this, get someone else to watch your eyes and count the fixations. If you can reduce them, and constantly practise forcing yourself to have fewer pauses, your speed will certainly improve. Getting into a rhythm of fixations across the page can help here, but remember that it should be a rhythm that is *flexible* and always quickly adapted to changes in difficulty and material.

2 *Widen* the visual span of each fixation you make, so that there is less overlapping. This clearly goes with the previous point, as in order to absorb the meaning with fewer fixations, you will have to 'take in' several words at a time (not just one or two). When you try the above exercise at first, you may feel that you are 'losing' words at the edge of each fixation, and thus some of the meaning; but with practice you will find that larger groups

of words (i.e., units of thought) will gradually stand out, and that not all words have to be read, in any case, to make perfect sense of the whole line.

3 Reduce *back-skipping* and regressions in normal (i.e., reasonably easy) reading. Here again, you need to practise by forcing yourself, for short passages, to keep moving along the line at a steady rate, and not letting your eyes slide backwards and thus waste time and effort. Remember, though, that this cannot be a rigid rule, as a good reader will occasionally *need* to glance backwards, as part of his alert and questioning approach to the meaning of the text. Again, it helps if you have someone else to watch your eyes, and correct your regressions, until it becomes more of a habit to you to only glance back *consciously*, when absolutely necessary – instead of wasting effort in the bad habit of doing it every line.

4 To help alter all these habits of slow or poor reading, many people feel that a *visual guide* can be useful. It can help to pull your eye smoothly along the page, and prevent you back-tracking or wandering. Something like a pencil or ruler is better than a solid card, because it allows you to see more widely at the edge of your vision (both up and down) and to focus on logical groups of words together. Move the guide smoothly along underneath the line being read, and make your eyes, and their fixations, keep up with it. If you want to push your speed even faster, try a short session in which you deliberately move the guide much more rapidly than you think you need in order to easily assimilate meaning. You will probably find that you can still understand a surprising amount, even when you approach the more general skimming techniques mentioned earlier. At even these very rapid and surveying speeds, your visual guide can still often help by zig-zagging smoothly down the page and keeping your eye moving steadily.

5 Finally, all these techniques and changes in reading habits will only happen with some consistent *practice*. Just ten minutes a day, consciously given to improving your reading methods and skills will certainly alter your patterns of reading within three or four weeks. Practice with short and easy material at first, but pushing yourself harder with, say, newspaper or magazine articles. Gradually try reading a greater variety of material, of increasing difficulty and length. Set yourself particular targets over a specified period; for example, try to increase your reading speed, on average, another 50 wpm every week, until you have stretched yourself to a much higher level of efficiency and comprehension. It isn't always easy to break the habits of a lifetime, but in the crucial area of better

reading, it pays immediate dividends in your increased confidence and efficiency and ability to absorb and handle a much greater volume of written material.

Summary
Improved reading skills come from:
1 Reading with a questioning sense of *purpose and understanding*.
2 Being highly *flexible* and adaptable in your speeds and methods.
3 Broadening your *vocabulary*.
4 Practising more efficient *eye movements*, to achieve a faster and more rhythmic pattern of reading with fewer fixations and regressions, and a broader grasp of whole groups of words.

Recommended reading
Read Better, Read Faster, Manya and Eric De Leeuw (Penguin Books, 1965). This is the most comprehensive guide, but most general study skills books include a chapter on reading.

Appendix on using libraries

1 *Introduction*

If you become a student, or begin to explore any academic subject seriously and consistently, you will rapidly need to extend the range of material you consult and work with. Few of us own a large enough collection of books and resources to satisfy our real curiosity about a subject. As a student in a particular discipline, you may certainly wish to buy and own many of the standard texts in the field, and regularly used works like set books or textbooks you should definitely try to acquire for yourself, if at all possible. But to use the resources and literature of your subject effectively, it is crucial that you are able to use *libraries* with efficiency and confidence. Knowing where information is to be found, and how to handle it, is a vital accompaniment to the process of thinking for yourself and expanding your abilities – in other words it's an integral part of your education.

This section is therefore a very brief, 'beginners' guide to using libraries, designed to give some pointers to the many people who are inhibited and confused by a large library (and therefore often give up exploring further because it doesn't seem worth the trouble!). If you feel you know 'where you are' and can always

find your way speedily and happily in a library, please skip this
section.

Kinds of libraries   2

It is difficult to generalise about library facilities, because the
types, sizes and even classification methods used vary tre-
mendously. But learning to become confident in your use of a
range of libraries with very different structures and systems is
part of becoming an independent learner and a sensible student. I
would assume that most of you are familiar with your own local
public library – which could be anything from the mobile trailer
unit arriving in the village once a week, to a large branch in a
major city. If you are not a member of your local public library, do
join soon, as it is a good place to familiarise yourself with the
system – and to get to know books more closely and practise your
reading. Your local branch library is part of a larger public system,
which will certainly have a Central Library at the heart of the
organisation in your area. Here you would find a much wider
range of books, for borrowing and for reference (not for loan) as
well as many other resources. If you still cannot find a book you
want here, you can request it via the inter-library loan system, as
all public libraries – large or small – are now linked as part of a vast
national complex, with the British Library in London at the
centre. Within the public library system, you can also often find
specialised collections of books, which you can use in person, or
also sometimes have access to via the inter-library lending
scheme.

As well as public libraries, which everyone can join, there are also
a number of other libraries, including those of private and business employers, of industrial and research organisations, and of
the many educational institutions like colleges of further education, polytechnics and universities. In some cases you may be
allowed to use these facilities, in others not. If you become an
official student at a college or university, you will of course be
able to use its library, but access is often restricted for general
members of the public. It is always worth *asking* if you could be
allowed access, and many institutions are happy to let serious
readers become special or temporary members – at least for
research and reference on the spot, if not for borrowing.

3 *Varieties of sources*

Libraries nowadays (and this is changing rapidly all the time) are no longer just a collection of standard *books* on shelves. In most libraries, this still makes up the bulk of the collection, but there are also many *other printed materials* such as journals, magazines, periodicals, pamphlets, newspapers and newspaper cuttings, charts and maps. A wide range of *audio-visual* communication material has also been created over recent years; thus you might also need to consult material in the form of video or cassette tapes, pictures or photographs, records or slides, films or film strips. Much material is now transmitted to libraries (often directly and solely) in *micro* forms, and you might need to use a special reading machine to consult either a *microfilm* (a continuous roll of reduced film) or an item on a *microfiche* (separate pages reproduced in micro form on a flat sheet). Many of these items have particular problems of storage or usage, and are therefore found in special collections within the library.

In many libraries, computer terminals are now used, by librarians, as part of a *Computerised Information Retrieval Service*. This is a rapid method of searching for material or data through hundreds of databases (electronic equivalents of printed information from periodicals, encyclopaedias, directories, newspapers, articles and so on) in many different subject areas. It can be expensive for the user, but can also save much valuable time within complex research.

More likely, as a student, you will need to consult the printed reference material (not for loan) which is available, in order to find the books or articles or references you need. It is impossible to list the great range of reference material here, so do find out for yourself what is available in the library you are using. But for this sort of literature search, the main information is usually found in:

bibliographies (= lists of books issued), of which the *British National Bibliography* and the *British Books in Print* are among the best known; library *catalogues*, such as the *British Library General Catalogue of Printed Books* or the *National Union Catalogue* (USA), or specialist library catalogues;
indexes or collections of *abstracts* (summaries) of the contents of periodicals or theses;
reference books, such as dictionaries and encyclopaedias, biography lists such as the *Dictionary of National Bibliography* or *Who's Who* and its offshoots, annual reviews or yearbooks of political, historical or statistical information.

To find out the range of sources available in any library (and how to make the best use of them) ask for and study the library's own information leaflet(s) – if they have any – or consult the Readers' or Information Desk, or any librarian. I think it is impossible to say too many times that if you have *any* problems or questions about the resources or uses of any part of a library, by far the best thing to do is to *ask the library staff to help you.* That is their job, and they will be happy to tell or show you anything if you have difficulty. Many large university libraries now employ specialist staff in some fields, to help with detailed queries about finding research material, references or specific printed items. Libraries and systems vary so greatly that no general written information (like this) can ever be as good as actually consulting the trained person on the spot who knows.

How libraries work 4

Although all libraries are run on the same general principles, within the cataloguing of books there are various systems and methods, so *start* by getting specific information from your own library, and carefully reading all notices and instructions. Almost all libraries are divided into *reference* sections (including the books and indexes and sources mentioned above), where you may sit and consult material but not remove it from the premises, and *borrowing* sections, where you have to find the book you want and then apply (using your personal library card) to take it out on loan – usually for a period of up to four weeks. Many university and college libraries, whose undergraduate students are constantly using the same basic books, also lend out copies under a *short loan* system (overnight or a few hours only), so that as many students as possible can get necessary access to their crucial texts.

When you want to borrow a book, you can of course (as most of us do when we just want 'something to read' from our local library) go and browse along the shelves until something catches your eye and looks interesting. But as a serious student you will certainly need to borrow and read very particular books; and you will therefore need to know how the classification system of the library works, how to use the catalogues yourself, and then how to find the books on the shelves. Most central or university libraries are large and complex places, often with many floors and areas, and even quite separate buildings; you can waste a great deal of time in fruitless hunting around, or constantly asking questions, unless you become confident and efficient in coping with the system.

Classification systems
Dewey Decimal and Library of Congress
There are at least two main systems of classifying books in use in British libraries at present, but many of them still use the older *Dewey Decimal Classification* (DDC), invented by an American in the 1870s, or some expansion or modification of it – of which the Universal Decimal Classification (UDC) is the commonest. Books are placed together on the shelves according their subject content (except for fiction, which is arranged alphabetically, and usually in a separate category) and classified by a notation of numbers and decimal points, which allows for a complex process of division and sub-division by tens. All knowledge is divided into ten main classes, and the numbers allocated to these ten major subject areas are:

000–099	General works (used for books covering the whole range of knowledge, such as encyclopaedias, or for subjects covering the entire field of knowledge, such as journalism, museum, essays, libraries themselves)
100–199	Philosophy and related disciplines
200–299	Religion
300–399	Social sciences
400–499	Philology (language and languages)
500–599	Pure sciences
600–699	Technology (applied sciences)
700–799	Arts (including recreation)
800–899	Literature
900–999	History, biography, geography

Each major subject area is then divided into ten main divisions. For example, the major area 800–899 (Literature) is divided into:

800–809	Literature – general
810–819	American
820–829	English
830–839	German
840–849	French
850–859	Italian
860–869	Spanish
870–879	Latin
880–889	Greek
890–899	Other

Each of these main divisions is then further divided into ten sub-divisions; for example, the category of English Literature (820–29) breaks down into:

820	English Literature – general
821	poetry

822	drama
823	fiction
824	essays
825	oratory
826	letters
827	satire and humour
828	miscellany
829	Anglo-Saxon

After this three-figure base, the decimal point is introduced to sub-divide categories further. Within English Literature – poetry (821), for example, it is sub-divided by period:

821.1	Early English (1066–1400)
821.2	Pre-Elizabethan (1400–1558)
821.3	Elizabethan (1558–1625)
821.4	Post-Elizabethan (1625–1702)
821.5	Queen Anne (1702–45)
821.6	Later 18th c.(1745–1800)
821.7	Early 19th c.(1800–37)
821.8	Victorian (1837–1900)
821.9	Early 20th c.(1901–)

In addition, further sub-divisions have been made for some individual poets, so that only Chaucer is found under 821.17, or Spenser under 821.31. In all subjects, further sub-division can be carried out in the same way until sufficient places have been made for every necessary subject – which sometimes creates quite a lengthy classification number in some complex fields.

A second common system (and not only in America) is the *Library of Congress Classification* system, which uses capital letters for its 26 main divisions, a second letter for initial sub-divisions, and then numbers for further categories. The main divisions here are:

A	Encyclopaedias and reference books
B	Philosophy, psychology, religion
C	Antiquities, biography
D	History
E–F	American history
G	Geography, anthropology
H	Social sciences, economics, sociology
I	Political science
L	Education
M	Music
N	Fine arts
P	Language and literature
Q	Science
R	Medicine

S	Agriculture and veterinary science
T	Technology
U	Military science
V	Naval science
Z	Books and libraries, bibliographies

A subject like Scottish history would thus be classified as DA 750–800, a number created by D (for history), DA (for the history of Great Britain), and 750–800 (for the sub-division of Scotland).

It would clearly be useful to familiarise yourself *generally* with the classification numbers of the area or subjects you work with a lot, and also the physical part of the library which holds the books (and the periodicals) in those subjects.

5   *Catalogues*

To find and borrow a book in any large library, you certainly also need to be able to use the *catalogue*, which is the key to all the books held in the library, as it tells you all their classification numbers and therefore (via a location guide) where to find them on the shelves. Catalogues can be physically in the form of a loose-leaf sheaf binder, a computer print-out or microfilm, or – still most common – the card-index system (housed in a number of narrow stacked drawers). There are two sorts of catalogue, both of which are necessary; which you use at any time depends on the amount of information you already have on your subject, and what you want to know. If you actually know the author (or editor, compiler, translator and so on) of a particular book you want, or the name of a person you are interested in (i.e., the subject of a biographical or critical work), you go to the *author/ name catalogue*, where all books are listed in alphabetical order under the author's or person's last name. This catalogue will thus tell you if the library has a *specific* book by a named author, and, in the same place, *all the other books by this same author* which are held. Make sure you also know the author's first name or exact initials, or else you can waste a lot of time in a large catalogue ploughing through all the 'Browns' or 'Smiths' to find the precise one you want. Libraries vary in the exact way they index their author names, so if you have any problems – again, ask a librarian. When you have identified the author or book you want, note the classifi-cation number on the card (also often called the press mark) and consult the library's own guide or plan or list of locations, in order to find the physical site where material with that number is shelved.

If, on the other hand, you are generally interested in a subject and want to know what books this library has on it (but know no authors or names in the field), you will have to consult the *subject catalogue*. This is also known as a classified catalogue, because items are filed in the same classification number order as the books are on the shelves, and thus it brings together all the related books classified under the same subject heading. Unless you already know the exact classification number of your subject, you first will have to consult the shorter *subject index*, and look up your subject under its obvious name, or as many other possible related terms as you need to identify your subject area. In large libraries, there may even be several separate subject indexes, covering science, or medicine, or humanities and social science independently. Each subject in this large index will have a classification number beside it, which directs you back to look up this same press number in the full subject catalogue; here you will find listed all the relevant books which the library has in this field. You can now browse through this part of the catalogue to see the range of material available, and then again note down the names and classification numbers of any books which interest you.

Some libraries do not have their own subject index, but depend on the Dewey Decimal Classification system's own *relative index*, which similarly lists and cross-references all the possible subjects in alphabetical order, and again gives the classification number of the subject area where they will be found. Finding your own way around the subject index or the relative index is not easy, especially in a large library, so, yet again, do ask library staff if you initially have problems. You often have to think very hard *around* the general subject you are interested in, or for alterntive ways of approaching it, in order to pin down exactly where are the books you need. For example, I recently wanted to look up anything under the subject of (English) church architecture in my local public library: the DDC Relative Index, under the heading 'church', listed no sub-heading for 'architecture', but only a minor sub-division under 'Church of Christ Scientist; archi-tecture' (726.589 5): not really what I wanted. But this led me to consider 'Church of England' as a sub-heading, where I was referred elsewhere to 'see Anglican church'. Under 'Anglican church' in the Index there was indeed a sub-heading for 'Build-ings' and yet another for 'Architecture' (*726.583*).

Approaching the same subject from another route, I first looked up 'Architecture' (720–30 under the major 700–800 class of 'Fine arts'), and identified the sub-heading 'Buildings for religious purposes' as 726. Further sub-divisions led me to 'Christian church buildings' (726.5) and to 'specific denominations' (726.58), and finally to the last sub-division of 'Protestant'

(726.583), where I realised my main interest in general English church architecture would lie.

If you have the time to familiarise yourself thoroughly with your local or central library system, try a similar exercise in tracing a single subject and its ramifications, via different routes, through the subject index (or relative index), the subject catalogue, the author/name catalogue, and finally to the physical location on the library shelves.

6 *References*

Finally, a word about *references*. If you become a student, you will spend quite a lot of time following up and tracking down academic references to other books and periodicals, and using them yourself. You will save much effort and wasted time if you get into the habit, right from the start, of being *totally accurate and complete* in any references you take or use. There is nothing more frustrating (and my own carelessness or lack of thought as a student often got me into this position!) than finding you have a useful source or reference (which you need – to follow up, or to cite as part of a necessary bibliography for an essay) which you then discover is incomplete or incorrect. You cannot now actually find it again easily, or quote the reference, or ask for that book or periodical under the inter-library loan system, without a possibly long and tedious tracing back to your original sources. Remember always to note down and reference your works in a comprehensive and standard form: for a book, you need name(s) of author(s), title, publisher, country of publication (usually), and date (and *exact* page references, if you are quoting from them); for a periodical, you need name(s) of author(s), title of article, name of periodical, volume number, year, and page numbers of the issue of the periodical in which the article appeared.

It is also worth taking the trouble, initially and properly, to understand the 'shorthand' of the standard academic system of referencing – much of it very traditional, and much of it based on Latin terms. In footnotes and references, you will frequently come across abbreviations which you need to be clear about, in order not to get misled or to waste time. Some common abbreviations here you probably know: p. or pp., I or II., ch. or chap. or chs., vol. or vols., ed. (editor or edition or edited by), rev. (revised) and tr. or trans. (translated by). Other English abbreviations include MS or MSS (manuscript, manuscripts), n.d. (no date given), n.p. (no place of publication), b. (born), d. (died) and fig. (figure). The commonest Latin abbreviations are *c.* or *ca.* (*circa* – about or around a certain time), *et al.* (*et alia* – and others), *ibid.* (*ibidem* – in the same place, referring to a work cited immediately before), *op. cit.* (*opere citato* – in an earlier work already referred to), and *passim* (here and there, found throughout). If these terms or others, which are frequently found at the foot of a page or in references, are not known to you, study an academic style sheet of abbreviations (in a dictionary or research manual or often posted in the library itself) and notice how formal footnoting is done. As a student, it is worth taking a little trouble over this to avoid awkard mistakes. Yet again, if you have any problems or queries about any aspect of the library system, don't be afraid to *ask* a member of the library staff, as this brief account here can in no way cover all aspects of library usage.

Further reading

All guides and leaflets issued by any libraries you use are always the first place to start.

Many study skills books, including those cited throughout by Maddox and Parsons, have a very brief section on using libraries.

Grateful thanks to D. Diana Leitch, Information Officer of the John Rylands University Library of Manchester, for help in checking this appendix.

Answers to reading exercise questions

1 Saddleworth Forum
2 1975
3 Huddersfield
4 Oxford University
5 1964
6 Sir Walter Citrine

Self-assessment exercises

Exercise 1
Below is another extract from the article by Lorraine Culley, 'Women in Politics', cited in the last chapter. This extract is slightly longer and contains a fair amount of factual information. Time yourself when reading it and then answer the questions posed at the end of the extract.

" Women in electoral office

Although the 1979 General Election in Britain led to Mrs Thatcher becoming the first woman British Prime Minister, the fewest number of women MPs since 1951 were returned with her to the House of Commons. In October 1974, 27 women were elected to the Commons, while in May 1979 only 19 women were returned, consisting of 11 Labour and 8 Conservative members. This figure increased to 23 by the end of the Parliament. In the General Election of June 1983, only 23 women were returned, 13 Conservative and 10 Labour.

In Britain then, over 96% of MPs are male. Women have a similarly low rate of participation in the USA. In 1977 women were only 4% of the House of Representatives and there were no women in the Senate. Advisors and officials appointed by Presidents are also predominantly male. Only 3 women had ever held Cabinet rank in a US Administration before 1977. President Carter was the first President to include 2 women Cabinet members. In the State legislatures, women do very slightly better overall, although this varies considerably from State to State. New Hampshire had 16% women in 1973, while Texas and Alabama had less than 1%. In Australia in 1980 there were 6 women Senators out of a total of 64 and no women members of the House of Representatives (127 members).

In France also, women have a low participation rate in political office. In 1980 only 4% of the 491 member National Assembly and 2.3% of the 295 member Senate were female. The 1979 elections to the regional assemblies (General Councils) returned only 2.3% women.

In Sweden, on the other hand, 30% of the membership of the country's elected assemblies are women. Between 1970 and 1973 there was a sharp increase of 50% in women's participation in the Swedish Parliament. A similar level is achieved in Finland, with a steady increase in the proportion of women MPs throughout this century, reaching 26% in 1979. In the Norwegian Storting 22.5% of members were female and there were five female members of the Cabinet.

To what can we attribute this apparent greater success of women in the Scandinavian countries? Is it that women are generally more powerful members of the community, or that the Women's Movement has had a greater impact here? Certainly in the Scandinavian countries there is a legal and institutional framework and an ideology which is more favourable to women than in many European countries. While this is of distinct advantage to women in many ways, it does not in fact lead to significantly greater equality between the sexes in terms of, for example, employment or education. Women are still predominant in low-paid, low status jobs, with few women in professional occupations. Women's pay is still only 80% or so of men's pay in the Scandinavian countries. Moreover, in the USA the Women's Movement is alleged to be particularly strong, but this is not reflected in a greater presence in political office. A much stronger correlation in fact exists between the numbers of women in electoral office and the nature of the electoral system. Generally speaking, women tend to do better in those countries where some form of proportional representation is operative. All the Scandinavian countries operate a Party List system. The Irish Dail is elected using the Single Transferable Vote system and women have achieved a greater political presence than in Britain (approx. 5%). Few would regard the social, economic or ideological climate in the Republic of Ireland as more favourable to women than that of Britain or the USA. Further evidence for this relationship is provided by the West German case. Half the Bundestag is elected by the single member system and half by the Party List system and the great majority of women enter by the lists (over 6% compared with 1%).

It would be wrong to suggest, however, that proportional representation or a particular form of it, would in and of itself increase women's participation in political office. To ensure a greater number of women in office under any system, political parties must be committed to promoting women as candidates and there must be a supply of women coming forward. The reasons for the under-representation of women and strategies to increase participation are discussed in more detail later.

In terms of representation in *local* government women do rather better than in national legislatures. This is the case for most European countries and for Australia, though it is less marked in the US. In Britain the proportion of women councillors increased from 12 to 16% between 1964 and 1976. Few women councillors, however, take the Chairs of local authority committees.

In Western Europe and the USA, then, despite formally egalitarian political systems, women are virtually absent from certain political arenas. The gap between official ideology and actual political practice is perhaps widest of all, however, in the non-capitalist countries of Eastern Europe and the USSR Marxist–Leninism specifically insists upon the full and equal status of women in all areas of life, including of course politics, yet there are many similarities between the Eastern Bloc countries and the West in the political behaviour and representation of women.

Women in the Communist Bloc countries are more prominent in national legislative bodies than in the West, but these bodies play a more limited role in the formation of policy. In the powerful elites of the various Communist Parties, women are virtually absent from top positions. In 1978 women accounted for 8 out of 199 full or candidate members of Politburos in all East European countries. In 1976 24.3% of all CPSU members were women.

As Sharon Wolchik has argued, in Eastern Europe as elsewhere,

> Women's representation in political elites conforms to the 'law of increasing disproportion' . . . which characterises the political representation of minorities and women in other societies, i.e., as the importance of the office increases the number of women declines.

In all countries, of course, 'politics' is not confined to electoral bodies and political parties, a point which will be expanded upon later. Legislative institutions and apparatuses are not the sole *loci* of public decision-making. The following sections will discuss briefly two other important political arenas where there are considerably less women than men in positions of authority; on public bodies and in trade unions. **"**

1,100 words approximately: if it took you five minutes you managed 225 words per minute. Now check your comprehension by answering the following questions; you should aim to get five or six right.

Questions

1 How many women were elected to the Commons in October 1974 and May 1979?
2 How many women members were there in the Australian House of Representatives in 1980?
3 What percentage of Sweden's elected assemblies are female?
4 'Women's pay is equal to men's in the Scandinavian countries.' True or false?
5 What kind of electoral system helps increase female representation?
6 What form of electoral system operates in Ireland?
7 How many women were there in 1978 out of the full or candidate members of the East European Politburos?
8 Explain Sharon Wolchik's 'law of increasing disproportion'.

(Correct answers to these questions are given in the guidance notes to this chapter.)

Exercise 2
Here is another letter-drafting exercise.

Mrs Sibley has been cleaning your house for four hours a week for the past three years. In recent months it has become apparent that she has been doing virtually no cleaning at all. Draft a letter indicating that unless she does more work for the money received you will be forced to dispense with her services.

When you have done this, compare your letter with the one we have printed in the Guidance notes.

Exercise 3
Another word-power exercise.

1 His lengthy explanation became impossibly . . .
   (profound/prophetic/prolix/protean)
2 Eventually, the general discussion petered out to just a . . . between the two of them.
   (dialect/dialogue/dynamic/diorama)
3 My success gave me a sudden feeling of . . .
   (eulogy/euphony/euphoria/euphuism)
4 He then proceeded to . . . out of the room.
   (flourish/flout/flounder/flounce)
5 Rats, mice, and shrews are all of the rodent . . .
   (genre/gentian/genus/genuine)
6 She thought relaxation and wine-drinking were . . .
   (hedonistic/hegemony/heinous/helical)
7 The strong opposition will . . . his ambition to progress
   (impeach/impede/impend/imperil)
8 His crafty scheme was an . . . manner of proceeding.
   (ingenious/ingenuous/indulgent/indignant)

Exercise 4
Preview two or three books from a library or from your own shelves. Write not more than half a page on each, striving to record the essence of what the book contains. Then compare what you have written with the example we give in the Guidance notes.

Exercise 5
Without looking back over this chapter, can you list the main points we have covered in it?

7 *Making good notes*

To learn is a natural pleasure not confined to philosophers but
common to all men   *Aristotle*

Contents

Introduction

Throughout any course of study in further or higher education
you will need to take notes from lectures, class discussions, radio
and TV programmes and, of course, books. It is something that
we all do in one way or another without thinking about it too
much, a task for which we all have our own personally patented
method. Indeed, some of us use different methods for different
assignments. The purpose of this chapter is not *necessarily* to get
you to change your own methods of taking notes. Its aim, rather,
is to *stimulate you to think about what you do* and to provoke you into
analysing your own practice so that you become more aware of its
strengths and its possible weaknesses. You can then, we hope,
develop the former and consider alternatives to the latter.

No one method of note-taking can be considered better than
another. It's a very personal matter. It's up to you to formulate
the technique that works best for you. But we hope that if you are
in any need of assistance on this matter, the chapter will offer you
some tips and guidance based upon the most tried and trusted
methods which have worked for many other students.

Purpose of note-taking   1

Before we look at some of the techniques of taking notes, briefly list some of the reasons why good notes are vital for the conscientious student.

---

                                          5 minutes   STOP

Most of us find note-taking essential: *Discussion*

(a) To involve us actively in a lecture or a book. Taking notes forces us to concentrate on what the speaker or writer is saying and stimulates a consideration of what is being said that creates an admittedly limited dialogue in our heads. When we are taking notes we are thinking, we are working. Of course many of those in the lecture room who are not taking notes are thinking as well. But all too often they are day-dreaming about members of the opposite sex, personal problems or what they will be consuming for their evening meal. They are wasting valuable study time.

In the same way, there is reading and there is reading. If, having read through an important chapter in a book we read through again with pen in hand, making notes, we will be more alert, our reading will be active, and more fruitful.

(b) To provide us with a *permanent record* of what happened in a class or lecture. Memory is fallible: if it is left unstimulated and unaided it fades away over time. Information essential to study may be lost forever and our revision and examination preparation inhibited and weakened.

(c) To provide us with a *personal record*. If you are making effective notes then, at the same time as receiving the transmission from the book or lecturer, you will be, in a limited way, entering into contention with some of their views and thus recording your own personal impressions. This is an invaluable means of retaining material and aiding understanding. The student who borrows another student's lecture notes often finds them hard going on every level. This is not simply because they are written in another's personal code. It is because to the borrower they are a record of *somebody else's* learning experience which is very difficult for an outsider to recapture. Right from the start of your course you should chalk up on your mental blackboard: *Efficient and comprehensive note-taking is absolutely essential to effective learning.*

Listen to a 10-minute news bulletin on Radio Four and make notes on it. Then assess how well you have done. Don't worry if you find it a struggle; news broadcasts are difficult to take notes from. If possible, record the broadcast, then check your own performance whilst listening to it for a second time.

STOP   **Here**   **10 minutes**

Discussion   How did you get on? Here are some of the problems we have found inexperienced students encounter.

Too much too soon Sometimes students try to take down *everything* the speaker says. That's not the point. What you want are the *main points*, the *important arguments*, the *essential examples*. Often new students do not *discriminate* sufficently.

For example, in any speech, lecture or report there will be *introductory comments*, scene-setting, sometimes *waffle*, intended to put the speaker at ease or establish rapport with the audience. There will be *examples* you do not need or multiple examples where you only need to note one or two. There will be *jokes* and *reflections, anecdotes* not essential to the message of the talk or lecture. Not only do you not need to note all these down. Too often, particularly if you are new to the game, you may end up with notes which consist of the byways but which miss the main highways. Or you may become so confused trying to take down too much detail that you become hopelessly mixed up and either miss vital points or, even worse, give up completely, putting yourself in a bad mood for your next note-taking session.

Note-taking is not about getting down *everything* that is said. If we tried to do that we would not be able to *critically* involve ourselves in the lectures. Effective note-making is above all an exercise in *selection* which requires you to develop the faculty of *discriminating* the major from the minor points.

It is, moreover, an experience which requires you to be wide awake and concentrating. A moment's lapse and you may lose the thread between the different points, the link between disparate information. When you are making notes you must be continually asking *yourself* questions. What is the overall theme? How does this point relate to the last point? This is an argument for, is there one against? Is this a minor or important point? Do I need this detail or is it insignificant? Do I understand without it?

The exercise has hopefully shown you some of the problems. Admittedly it was a little bit unfair. In your course you will have *advance notice* of what lectures and classes will cover and be able to *prepare*. If you need a radio or TV broadcast for study purposes we would advise you if possible to record it and then take notes. But perhaps the exercise has brought home to you

The need to *listen* attentively.

The need to *select* what is important.

The need to watch for *signals* for important points. For example, in a lecture, the speaker's entry into the real substance after introductory comments about administrative arrangements or a recapitulation of last week's lecture. 'Right (focus word), today I'm going to deal with . . .' or getting to the central point . . . 'Now (often focus word) I come to the main issue' . . . 'Let me emphasise . . .'

The need to key into the *speaker's structure* by observing his or her signals. 'Firstly, secondly . . . and finally' . . . 'At this point . . . I'd like to leave the subject of China and move on to . . .'

Note-making and précis writing   2

You will have observed that a central skill in note-making is the ability to précis and compress material and transform the spoken or written word into your own language. To help you with this skill read through the following passage and then try to express its basic ideas in four or five sentences. If necessary, read through it twice before writing anything down.

" The first permanently organised trade unions in Britain were small local societies of skilled craftsmen. You may know of a pub near you called 'The Carpenters' Arms', 'The Bricklayer's Arms', 'The Weavers' Arms'. Local workers belonging to particular trades would meet at such hostelries to relax, socialise and talk shop. Other workers from the same trade arriving from other areas would know where to find colleagues and discover what the local employment position was, what opportunities there were to work, what the terms and conditions of employment were.

Gradually these kinds of informal links between workers became formalised and regular meetings would be held to discuss matters of common interest. Eventually permanent societies or unions were established. It must be emphasised, however, that these 'unions' were small, local bodies, mirroring the fact that product and labour markets remained geographically restricted, whilst those seen as capable of organisation were not the majority of the workforce but only the highly skilled.

The development of the railways revolutionised this situation. The craft societies has used the method of tramping and unemployment benefit to deal with the problems of the local labour market. When there was unemployment surplus craftsmen would be given a sum of money and asked to tramp to the next area to see what the situation was there. The revolution in transport meant that there was a growth of *national* markets. This stimulated in turn a growth of national unions. They are sometimes referred to as New Model Unions and the most famous is the Amalgamated Society of Engineers established in 1851.

These new model unions were the first bodies to have permanent full-time officials and modern methods of administration. They attempted to organise *all* engineers, *all* carpenters, *all* bricklayers. They attempted to control entry to the trade and increase their bargaining strength with the employers through controlling the apprenticeship system and establishing a closed shop. They extended the system of relatively high benefits covering a range of eventualities from unemployment to death that their predecessors had established. These unions did not, as do their successors today, believe in *bargaining* with employers. They believe that the function of the union was to *unilaterally* lay down terms and conditions of employment. If an employer was not prepared to accept these then no 'society man' should work for him. The craft unions were particularly powerful in the engineering and building industries and there were big strikes in those industries in 1852 and 1859 respectively. Historians differ on the degree to which the New Model Unions represented novelty or continuity. The division between the society member and the labourer on a building site or in an engineering factory however remained a gaping and apparently fixed one.

This pattern was at least to some degree based upon the world economic situation and Britain's place in it. This period from the 1850s to the 1880s was not merely the period in which Britannia ruled the waves and world markets but a period in which her naval and economic supremacy was almost unchallenged. Some small portion of the benefits of this dominance could be passed on to the skilled workers who thus enjoyed reasonable prosperity. The twenty years to the turn of the century witnessed new developments as countries such as

Germany and the USA emerged as powerful competitors and as important new technological developments were set in train.

With new external pressures affecting the world of employment many labourers, hitherto regarded as unorganisable, joined trade unions. These new bodies were very different from the conservative craft societies and their leaders were very different from the 'top-hatted trade unionists' whose moderation had characterised the strategies of the older bodies. Socialism was now emerging as a coherent available credo. Members of the first British Marxist grouping, the Social Democratic Federation, such as Ben Tillett, Tom Mann and Eleanor Marx were involved as organisers with the new unions. Unlike the craft worker the general worker lacked a high level of *skill*. Employment was less permanent. Often it was seasonal. Dockers might work at the docks part of the year, in a gasworks for the rest. The socialist ideas of the organisers were often in tune with the organisational impetus of the new bodies; as many general workers as possible, regardless of the specific jobs that they did, should be organised. If they were not, then the pool of substitute labour available to an employer in the event of a strike was vast indeed. Whilst it might be difficult to import alternative skilled labour it was relatively easy to replace unskilled workers striking for better conditions.

By 1914, then, the labour force was covered by both craft unions and the general workers' unions, the forerunners of unions like today's Transport and General Workers Union. We also need to take note of a third development particularly marked in the last quarter of the nineteenth century. This was the growth of semi-industrial unions, organisations in the mines, on the railways and in the steel industry which sought albeit unsuccessfully to recruit all the workers in that particular industry regardless of job or grade. **99**

Your objective here was to boil this passage down to its central points cutting out examples and amplification. What were the central points? I recorded them as follows:

Discussion

(a) Early unions were local societies of craftsmen.
(b) Railways in the nineteenth century opened up a national market for skilled workers.
(c) New Model unions emerged in the nineteenth century which (i) had full-time officials and (ii) presented employers with the terms under which their members would accept employment.
(d) In the late nineteenth century non-skilled workers were organised in general unions.

151

(e)   In the early twentieth century attempts were made to set up 'industrial' unions comprising *all* workers in specific industry.

Do you agree with my points? Do you think you have captured them more accurately or less so?

The above is an example of note-taking – although my notes would in reality have been less literate and grammatical – but another good exercise is to try writing a continuous prose summary or précis of the same passage. Try doing this now. Your object will be to compress the argument into about 150 words, capturing all its most important points.

STOP   **20 minutes**

Discussion   How did you get on? My précis was as follows:

Britain's first permanent national trade unions developed in the period after 1850 from local organisations in tandem with the growth of national transport systems and national markets. They were conservative bodies embracing only highly skilled workers and were characterised by attempts to control apprenticeship, establish closed shops, unilaterally determine terms and conditions of employment and pay high friendly benefits. Changing economic and technological conditions meant that from the 1880s general workers previously regarded as 'unorganisable' joined unions in ever greater numbers. In distinction to the craft unions the general unions strove to organise all employees across industry, influenced by the fact that it was easier for employers to find substitutes for unskilled workers, and the socialist ideas of their leaders. A parallel development was the creation of semi-industrial unions in steel, coal-mining and rail transport, trying to recruit all those working in the particular industry.

Maybe – though this is unusual – you found the continuous prose summary easier than recording the points in note form – in which case you might adopt your study techniques accordingly. Let's try a similar exercise.

Read the following passage. Pick out the key ideas in each paragraph, perhaps by underlining the KEY WORDS. Reduce these the main points to one or two sentences. Then try to link them up in a concise version.

66   'The lecturers' sense of injustice was further exacerbated by the fact that despite attempts by the DES and the minister to fiddle the figures by switching baselines, the AUT has convincingly argued that university salaries have fallen 22 per cent in real terms since Mrs. Thatcher's policies began to bite. Anger was

further fanned when vice-chancellors blandly informed Sir Keith that for their part they accepted that nothing further than 4 per cent for 1985 could be done in the present wage round, even as university technicians were being offered more than 5 per cent; and as polytechnic teachers agreed an increase of 5 per cent from April 1985, with an additional 2 per cent from last December.

This last settlement would have ensured that if the 4 per cent on offer to lecturers *were* accepted, every point on the university lecturer scale – with the exception of the top point – would be below the equivalent on the polytechnic lecturer scale.

It was problems with wage scales which prompted the second element in the AUT's 1985 claim. Until the late '70's more than three-quarters of university of academics were promoted to senior lecturer during their careers, often before they reached the top of the ordinary lecturer's scale. Today, largely because of a limitation set by the University Grants Committee (UGC) – the body that acts as a buffer between academics and government and channels funds to the universities – not more than 40 per cent of staff in any particular institution can be in promoted posts. More than 40 per cent of university teachers are at the top of the ordinary lecturers' scale compared with 20 per cent a decade ago. Many will remain there for the forseeable future despite having senior lecturer qualifications.

To solve this promotion blockage the AUT proposed a single combined scale with relatively automatic progression. The authorities refused to establish a working party to look at it. Instead, the vice-chancellors produced their own proposals to replace the present two grades with four, thus creating the possibility of three blockages instead of one. Their counter proposals, described by UGC Chairman Sir Peter Swinnerton-Dyer as heralding the end of common pay scales and the beginning of market-related salaries, also included a five-year probation period instead of the present three years; and plans for closer assessment of lecturers, resonant of the controversial report from Sir Alex Jarratt, chairman of Reed International, urging tighter measurement of performance.

As the autumn term began and the universities – to protect themselves from higher national insurance contributions but with an air of finality – put the 4 per cent into pay packets, the AUT, looking particularly at the school teachers, decided that there was only one shot left in the locker. An emergency council meeting on 8th November authorised balloting on a series of one day strikes.

But the wages position in itself is far from the whole story, nor would it have been sufficient to have brought most university teachers out on the picket lines.

What *did* was concern for the future viability of Britain's university system. Funding has been cut by more than 10 per cent in real terms since 1980–81, involving the loss of £460 million and one in seven academic jobs. Staff-student ratios have declined by 6 per cent in the arts and humanities and by more than 11 per cent in the government's cherished science subjects. Universities are postponing essential building work, cutting back on essentials such as libraries and eating into reserves.

Despite the Prime Minister's assurance during the 1983 election of a period of level funding, last May's Green Paper merely promised further cut-backs, a shift of resources into science and technology and the possible closure of departments and entire universities. In its wake, the UGC asked universities to plan for a recurrent cut of up to 3½ per cent each year until the end of the decade, this to be implemented from an already shrunken base.

Extract from 'Lecturers in Arms' by John McIlroy, *The New Statesman*, Vol. III, 24 January 1986, pp. 11–12. **"**

STOP   30 minutes

Discussion   You should have ended up with something like this, though your summary might well have worked out longer:

Their union claims that university lecturers' salaries are down 22% on 1979 levels. Unrest is intensified by higher offers to other groups which affect parity and by a promotion blockage. Other immediate factors which have prompted the one-day strike are plans for longer probationary periods for university teachers and tighter measurement of their work. But the background – harsh government cuts in the resources going to universities – is an essential explanatory factor.

You will have noticed by now that the technique of compression is concertina-like: we can reduce this much or this much or this much, according to what we need from the speech or article, what we consider important and what we have the skill to capture. For example, you might have given details of other groups gaining superior wage increases, details of the promotion blockage, and so on. You have to decide on what you need and what you can efficiently manage. As you become more proficient in both your subject and your note-taking you will be able to expand what you note down from main argument and central examples to include more discussion, more illustration and more of your own comment. The ability to précis is important but there are some other techniques which will help you to take better and fuller notes.

Listening   3

Listening is a vital if overlooked skill. It is related to observation. Gather yourself up to listen as soon as the lecture or class begins. If you find it uninteresting see this as a challenge. Think about what is being said. Why do you find it uninteresting? Is it just the lecturer, not the subject? If so, see this as a challenge to make the lecture interesting for yourself.

The beginning and the end of a lecture are particularly important for information so guard against your mind wandering, whilst you are 'cold' at the start and tired at the finish. The longer you listen attentively the easier it gets. You can develop your sensitivity to the lecturer's signals by *watching* as well as listening. We have stressed the verbal cues to look for in discovering the structure of the lecture . . . 'I will start by . . .', 'and this is the significant point . . .', 'The main distinctions are . . .', 'The best conclusion is. . . .' With most lecturers you will soon become familiar with their style and this will make note-making easier. But also look for other signals, from using the blackboard, to banging the table, to pointing a finger before emphasising a key point. Practise listening by tape-recording radio talks and making notes from your recording.

The mechanics of note-making   4

1 Identification
You will have taken notes for intensive future use. For easy identification ensure that each set of notes starts on a *new piece of paper* and that they are clearly headed with

● The title of the lecture, book or article.
● The lecturer, author or source.
● The date of the lecture, book or article.
● The name of the publisher of a book or journal.
● The chapter number or title of a book.
● The full title of a journal or magazine with volume and issue number.
● The library classification number of a book or journal.

This might seem obvious. But the occasions when students have been unable to remember the source of important notes that they wish to use for essays or exercises or have been unable to track down the source to read further are too numerous to recount. Always fill in your full identification before you start your note-making.

2 Storage and retrieval
Most people find that the best major means of organising their notes is to use an A4 loose-leaf ring binder for each main subject. This means
● You do not have to carry your files around with you, simply your A4 notepad, avoiding the risk of losing valuable documentation.
● You can slot in new notes at any time without changing page number, etc.
● You can easily discard inadequate or rewritten notes.
● You have all your notes on a particular subject together in one place.
● You can divide your notes further into sub-categories through the use of dividers.

But *don't forget other systems:* at a certain stage many students find note-making on file cards a useful means of breaking down data for easy retrieval and cross-reference. Particularly where you are dealing with a large number of small discrete items, then, as with the looseleaf system, your cards are easily amended and updated. This method will be essential if, for example, you are a law student (to file cases) or are writing a thesis. Always file your notes *as soon as possible after your study session*. Think of the time wasted trying to track down that elusive set of notes you never put in your binder.

Finally, if your course involves the accumulation not only of books and but a mass of diverse materials, such as articles, pamphlets, reports, press cuttings and diagrams, you may feel the need for a filing cabinet and the large size filing folders. This might appear somewhat ambitious when you are first starting out as a student. In fact it is simply a development of the ring folder idea. Once you have been studying for several years you will have many ring folders and other study materials. Even if you have passed a particular study stage it may be useful to store all this material. Studying is a dynamic and sometimes unpredictable business and you will discover that only the rash state with finality 'I've finished with that'. You never know when you may need particular notes, articles or essays and your filing cabinet in a sense, is simply a large ring folder.

3 Layout

Ensuring your notes are attractively laid out can help you in note-making and ensure that later on your notes are a more effective method of learning.

(a) Writing on *only one side of the paper* may be expensive but many students have found it worthwhile. They are then able to use the other side of the paper for detailed additions, comments, notes from related books or articles or cross-references to other lectures.

(b) The use of *headings* imparts structure to your notes. It directs you to the key areas, shows you how the overall picture is linked together and acts as a vital aid to memory. With good notes if you remember the main headings you have the key to the highway of the subject and this then ignites recall of subheadings and details. **Number your headings**. Use **capitals** or **underlining** to make them stand out and catch the eye.

(c) Sometimes the lecture, book or article will have its own apparent structure. Sometimes it will not and you have to impose your own. So think in terms of *numbering*, (a), (b), (c); 1, 2, 3. Use different listing systems 1, 2, 3 for main points, (i), (ii), (iii) for sub-points or 1.1, 1.2, 1.3. Your numbering should be linked obviously to your headings.

(d) The use of *colours* and the development of a colour code are used by some students to make their notes more stimulating. If you include in your study kit different colour biros or felt-tip pens, you might use black to write your notes, blue to underline your headings and red for names, dates, key points. If you do this after you have made the notes it can aid your revision. It means that when you return to the code you will have a series of coded highlights which will make for greater interest and retention.

(e) The use of *indentation* and *spaces* can also help in creating effective notes. Always leave a large margin and space between each main section. Some students write on every other line. This not only gives visual force to your notes. It enables you to add details, comments and criticisms as you review them later.

(f) If you start main issues at the margin indent for sub-headings and indent again for further divisions. Again, this helps you locate specific points and makes the bone structure of the lecture or paper stand out for easy understanding and recall.

(g) *Visual aids* should not be overlooked. You may find that your own use of a short table, graph or diagram may be more effective for you than ten minutes of the lecturer's talk. Some students use asterisks * to highlight main points, arrows → to show interconnections or progress from one point to another, boxes □ or circles ○ to emphasise central points or even references or quotations. You can use these devices in your own way. Your code is your own, although remember to stick to it! Once again, the use of the symbols can help to show structure and flow of argument and make your work more interesting.

4 Language

When taking notes from speech you are under constant pressure. You are trying to do several things at once – listen, translate, question and write. Just as we have said that it is wrong to try to take down everything verbatim so for most of us it is inefficient to try to take everything down in continuous prose. Most of us use some personalised form of bastardised shorthand. Whilst you will want to develop your own dialect here are some abbreviations which are commonly used by students.

Using initials   HW instead of Harold Wilson, MCP instead of male chauvinist pig or simply S for Shakespeare, H for Hitler, H8 for Henry VIII.

Using symbols   > more than; < smaller than; – instead of but or rather; √ right, × wrong.

First part of word   The reaction was a pos(itive) one; Dept for Department; Min for Minister. *Eliminate unnecessary words.* Reaction pos. Leave out a, an, the and other small connecting words.

Omit syllables   regmntl cnl for regimental colonel; Dept Hd for departmental head; amnt, amount; bch, branch.

Common abbreviations   e.g.; cf; nb;.:   (because); via; gv; i.e.; pp.

5 Review

All the above points are vital to implement when taking notes. You cannot rely on writing them up from memory later. But it is vital that at the end of the day ideally, but at least at the end of the week, you go through the notes that you have taken, checking them for understanding and for future understanding using the guidelines that we have suggested; linking notes to the rest of your course; deciding which areas you need to develop; estimating what needs clarification or further work. The time for deepening understanding is whilst your notes and the experience that they stemmed from is still fresh in your mind. It is generally wasteful of time and effort to write your notes out again completely in a neater or more legible way. However, you may wish to rewrite parts of your notes using different methods.

Linear–Logical and Concept-Tree systems   5

Below you will see two different methods of making notes. Both involve note-making from the concluding part of a lecture on the Spanish Civil War fought between supporters of the Spanish republic and the nationalist rebels led by General Franco. The conflict raged from 1936 to 1939. What do you think are the advantages and disadvantages of the two methods?

Note-taking: Example 1
The Linear–Logical method

Why Franco succeeded
1 *Leadership*
(a) Franco's qualities.
(b) Leadership problems of Republicans.
2 *Army* N. Africa, W. Spain, supported almost totally.
(a) Professional
(b) Fighting untrained volunteers.
(c) Technology vs commitment, unequal battle.
3 *Foreign aid*
(a) 70,000 Italian troops, 10,000 German.
(b) Italian Navy vital as Spanish Navy supported Republic.
(c) Luftwaffe vital – new Junkers early on.
(d) Republic – few tanks from Blum.
(e) Enthusiastic but untrained volunteers – International Brigades.
(f) Russian military advisers but obsolete tanks and planes.
4 *Political conditions*
(a) Despite divisions
     Falangists
     Monarchists
     Conservatives
     Rebels able to focus on destruction of Republic.
     Crucial: Army control, *military unit.*
(b) Republicans could not reconcile difference to same degree.
     – Communists
     – Anarchists
     – Socialists
     – Liberal

    – Regional separation
    Internal faction fighting
    Led to
    Military disunity

Note-taking: Example 2
The Concept Tree

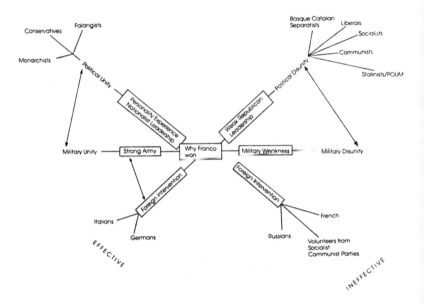

You obviously recognised easily the first method as it is the traditional and still most widely practised means of taking notes. Most of what we have said until now has indeed related to this technique. It is usually termed the *Linear Method* or the *Linear–Logical Method*. The notes are developed in a common sense structural *sequence*. The emphasis is completely *verbal* and the system is particularly appropriate for lectures and speeches, where at the start you do not know what the main point will be, how the points made will fit together and how relatively important they are. When you are getting only one chance to hear what the speaker says this is probably the safest method. Moreover, it has the advantage that notes made in this format can later be transformed into other modes not just for the fun of it but as a learning experience.

The system used in Example 2 is called the *Pattern* or *Concept-Tree System*. The emphasis here is *diagrammatic*. You turn your paper sideways and put the keyword, issue or concept smack in the middle of the page. You then add the main facts, arguments, explanations joining them to the central point by boxes or lines.

You can then add more and more lines, breaking down facts and arguments into finer detail, drawing interconnecting lines to show interaction and interrelationships. Many people find this system attractive as they discover that the visual impact of the pattern shape helps memory by simplifying, and stressing the relative importance of points and their interconnections. Many of us think better diagramatically than verbally. Other students feel safer with words and dislike the fact that the concept tree is restricted to one page and key words or phrases. Whilst additional information can be sketched in later there are limits, and I have heard some people say that they find it difficult later to recall examples and sub-arguments given by lecturers as distinct from the main thread that they have captured on their chart.

The Concept-Tree approach is just one form of diagrammatic note-taking. You can also develop flow diagrams, also very useful for showing interconnections between phenomena (see Example 3).

Example 3
Flow diagram illustrating stages in theory of economic growth

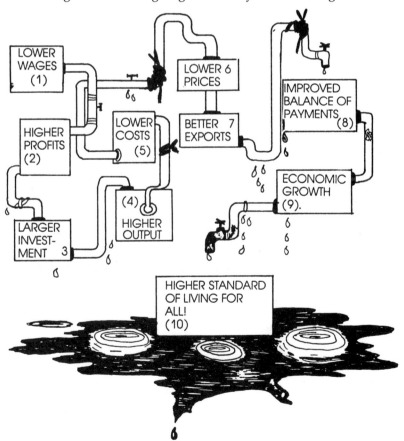

7 *Taking notes from lectures and from books*

Let's recap a little first. Before you attend a lecture you should be prepare for note-making. This involves:

Reviewing the previous lecture.

Attending any interim class.

Knowing what *this* lecture will deal with.

Doing some preparatory reading. This will psych you up in every way to get the best out of this lecture which will for you never be repeated

Not forgetting about handouts; documentation given to accompany the lecture. Relate your notes to any handouts. Wouldn't it be better if handouts were distributed the week *before* the lecture to aid preparation and ensure students start from a higher plateau? See if you can convince the lecturer to organise this system.

Once in the lecture be prepared to: CONCENTRATE, LISTEN AND THINK.

Sit at the front if you can't hear the tutor at the back.

Try to avoid distractions such as sitting near somebody who continuously comments in a humorous but irrelevant way, discusses what you should do afterwards or sits there doodling. Explain to friends that whatever happens afterwards you are going to use the hour of the lecture to best advantage and if required go off and sit by yourself.

Get the best out of your lecture by:

Using the techniques we have discussed to make good notes.

Jotting down your own thoughts and comments, cross-referencing to other parts of the subject.

Raising well thought out questions with the lecturer. If you don't understand a point or you want it developed then there is no time like the present.

Practice makes perfect. The more you get involved the better your experience will be.

We have been talking largely about making notes from the spoken word although we have used examples from books and articles to develop techniques. But as we said at the start you also need to take notes direct from the written word. Can you see any differences in making notes from lectures or from books? Are there any special considerations governing the latter task? Might one method of note-taking suit it better than another?

---

15 minutes   STOP

When you are taking notes from *printed materials* the task is less immediate. You have more time for thought, analysis and writing when taking notes from a book or article. Here:

Discussion

Make sure first of all that you have a good mental grasp of the material. If you understand it before you take notes the process will deepen your understanding. If you take detailed notes while you are reading you will miss some of the benefit.

If the material is new, then read it through thoroughly first. If the material is already known to you skim read it again to familiarise yourself with it. Don't start making notes until you understand each section or chapter and how they fit together.

Remember, as with lectures you are not simply making a précis but *translating* the material into your own language. This not only develops thinking and writing skills. When you do this successfully, you really *know* your material.

Once again the system you use is up to you. But one distinction between note-making from speech and writing is that, on the whole, the latter lends itself better to patterned diagrammatic note. However, as with lectures, many prefer to use the linear method and then later turn the notes into diagrammatic form to stimulate the memory and enable them to see the issue afresh.

Self-assessment exercises

Exercise 1
Without looking back over the chapter, can you list the main points we have covered in it?

Exercise 2
Below is an article from the *Guardian* (11 October 1985) which is an extract of a speech given by Sir Ian Gilmour, Conservative MP for Chesham and Amersham, to a Child Poverty Action Group meeting in Blackpool during the Tory Party Conference.

Using the Linear–Logical method, take notes on the article covering not more than one side of A4 paper. Then compare your notes with those offered in the guidance notes.

" Why poverty action is not an optional extra
Ian Gilmour MP
Socialists believe in equality, to be imposed by the dead hand of state power – equality of misery. Tories have traditionally believed in opportunity for all. So Labour would help the poor by making everyone else poor too – Tories want everyone to be able to acquire property.

This is an ennobling vision, because it promises an ultimate solution to poverty – a chance for the poor to have their full share of human dignity. But for it to operate, there must be hope. There must be a ladder of opportunity stretching all the way down. Everybody who is willing and able to work should share in this opportunity state.

But there will always be losers as well as winners, and they cannot be neglected. Genuine concern and action for the poor are the first casualties of doctrinaire politics. The rising socialist obsession with egalitarianism has provoked a polar opposite obsession with the so-called 'enterprise' culture amongst some Conservatives. Now I am all in favour of enterprise and entrepreneurs, but life can never be, or should never be, so one-dimensional that only those who maximise profit should get a place in the sun.

Creating and generating wealth are clearly vital steps in the jigsaw of the economy and in the maintenance of welfare services. You cannot provide for the increasing numbers of retired people and a more sophisticated modern health service and dealing with the problems of broken families in our inner cities without economic growth. Without the practical means, all the grandest of social objectives are still-born. Yet the production of wealth, goods and services is not an end in itself – rather it is a means towards the ultimate goal of all political endeavour, namely trying to create a better life for everyone.

Improving the condition of the people may sound a quaintly old-fashioned phrase in today's jargon-clad and dogma-dominated politics. But it is actually the inspiration, or should be, for most public service. Above all; it should be the guiding-light for Conservatives, because it is the key to the other great object of the party that Disraeli laid down: to maintain the institutions of the country.

Put at its most down-to-earth, those who wish to 'conserve' the fabric of society and avoid the shocks of revolutionary change must look to the contentment of all our fellow countrymen. The key to the survival of any social order is its ability to satisfy the aspirations of people in all walks or layers of life. The upwardly mobile artisans, professional and business classes are naturally enough an important, expanding army. They have skills, output, wealth and – of course – votes to contribute. I value their contribution as highly as any conservative politician.

Yet most thoughtful members of these prosperous sections in our society would be the first to acknowledge that their own futures depend upon a far wider cross-section of humanity; and that if their prosperity excludes a thickening wedge of less able or less fortunate people, then it is a partly sham prosperity, resting upon the very shaky foundations of social disaffection and discontent. If free enterprise does not offer hope to all of society, it will not be seen as a way of emancipation but will be regarded as the selfishness of the better off.

I have stressed the practical and self-interested case for the Conservative Party to give priority to the alleviation of poverty, since I hope that I hardly need to articulate the moral case. I think I can state that case in a few sentences. The acceptance of substantial poverty in a rich modern society with many resources and with first class communications is the anti-thesis of Conservatism and civilised behaviour.

Since Conservatives have no all embracing ideology like 'the revolution' or egalitarianism, they will, if they abandon their long standing commitment to gradual social reform, soon find themselves in a vacuum peering fixedly and myopically out at the Public Sector Borrowing Requirement, Sterling M3, and other unreliable indicators – which deserve a glance or two but not an obsessive stare and which are hopelessly inadequate guides to action or inaction.

Reverting to the practical case, I don't regard the relief of poverty and the maintenance of the Welfare State as optional extras or as luxuries to be indulged only when times are good. The Welfare State when properly divised and administered is not a handicap, a dead-weight on the economy. It should be the opposite. It should be an aid to the economy. By providing a measure of security, it helps society to adapt to change and it therefore promotes economic efficiency.

The best way of promoting economic efficiency, shoring up the Welfare State and reducing poverty is to reduce unemployment. That would greatly further all three of those objectives.

I could continue to think that modifications of policy are needed if we are to win the general election. The public has come to see unemployment as the crucial issue. Until it falls substantially they will not be impressed by talk of economic recovery. The election will turn on that as much as anything else. I hope that unemployment will fall during the next few months. We are after all having a good year. But the prospects for next year are less encouraging.

There are strategists who think it will be enough to win if unemployment is falling by next polling day. If we ignore all the heavy social and other costs of unemployment, maybe they are right. But that would be a high risk strategy. It would mean allowing unemployment to continue near its present level for quite a long time. And that in turn would entail allowing the popular conviction to grow that the Government was not sufficiently concerned about unemployment.

The conclusion must surely be that unemployment should be reduced, substantially, soon. Seasonally adjusted, it has risen by nearly a quarter of a million since the last election. So we have to reduce it by that amount before we are back where we started. We should start now.

Reform of the welfare state will have almost as much influence as unemployment on the result of the general election. It will greatly affect the way our party is seen by the public. One of the most disturbing findings of a recent public opinion survey was that more people now think our Party more extreme than the Labour Party. That, as we know, is quite wrong, but that is what they thought. A similar danger is the erroneous impression that we are the party of the rich.

Proper actions on poverty and unemployment will dispel all these myths and legends about the Party. They will be convincing proof that the future of the country and the interests of all its inhabitants are best safeguarded by Conservative government. And they will ensure that we win the election. Let us have them soon. **"**

Exercise 3
Produce a flow diagram of all the various stages in a process well known to you, for instance, servicing a car, decorating a room, raising a baby.

Exercise 4
Here is another kind of word-power exercise – this time to do with *synonyms*. A synonym is a different way of saying something: for example, a synonym of 'envy' is 'jealousy'. Naturally, each word has its own nuances and subtle shade of meaning, but a synonym must be a fairly close equivalent. Try to find synonyms for the words listed below. I would suggest that you attempt the exercise first of all without the aid of a dictionary, but then check your results against one later. In any case we offer our own checklist in the Guidance notes. And one further tip: make sure that the word(s) you offer are the same part of speech as the original. 'Envy' is a noun: it would be no use offering 'jealous', which is an adjective.

1 Argument
2 Behaviour
3 Certain
4 Delete

5 Enthusiasm
6 Fixed
7 Genuine
8 Harmful

Exercise 5
Take notes from a chapter of a textbook (approximately 12 to 20 pages), using whatever method you wish.

8 *Generating ideas*

Creative minds always have been known to survive any kind of
bad training   *Anna Freud*

Contents

Introduction

I want to start this chapter straight away with a simple exercise. If
you can easily ask someone to come and help, or ring someone up
who is long-suffering enough to listen for a few minutes, then
stand by to do so. If no one is available take out a piece of paper
and sit with your pen poised to write. Now, either talk to your
friend or write for four minutes on the subject which you will find
written upside down at the bottom of this page.

STOP   **4 minutes**

How did it go? Quite possibly you succeeded admirably and
produced a fascinating spoken or written account. Alternatively,
you might have started with a flourish but then found difficulty in
keeping going. Or you might have had the experience of many
adult students when this exercise is sprung on them: you might
have 'dried up', run out of ideas and sat feeling frustrated and
angry with yourself. Part of the explanation for this last
mentioned experience is being put on the spot in this way with no
warning; but part of it is often also the genuine non availability of
ideas. This almost certainly does not mean, however, that the
ideas and information were not there: merely that they were not
available when you wanted them. There is a simple device,
whereby you can summon these ideas to the forefront of your
mind. We call this 'brainstorming', a fairly common but perhaps
over-dramatic word for a very simple procedure.

Whales

Brainstorming   1

This is how you do it. Write the subject on which you need to generate ideas in the middle of a piece of paper. Let your mind relax and roam free around it. As words come into your thoughts write them down as quickly as you can. It can be helpful to generate a sense of urgency, to encourage the ideas to come as fast as they can – but you may find it easier just to relax and let the ideas find you rather than the other way round. Let your mind freely associate other ideas with the word last written down; don't worry if a few of the resultant words appear to be irrelevant but if you feel you have gone completely off the track then let your eyes return briefly to the idea written at the centre of the page.

Do this either on your own, or better still encourage someone to 'brainstorm' with you and shout out their ideas as they occur. You'll find that two, three or four people spark different ideas off each other. Even without this help you should find that the page fills up pretty quickly with a mass of ideas. Try it. Try brainstorming for three minutes on the subject of 'hats'.

---

3 minutes   **STOP**

Did it work? I hope it did. Try another subject: 'Aeroplanes'.

---

3 minutes   **STOP**

How did that go? Assuming it went all right *now* try talking to a friend or writing continous prose on either topic for four minutes (using your brainstorming notes as a resource if you wish).

---

4 minutes   **STOP**

If the device has worked, and it rarely doesn't, you should have managed this task with ideas to spare. Now let's try brainstorming another slightly more complex subject: 'City Traffic'.

---

5 minutes   **STOP**

Discussion   Have a look at what you have written and try to discern any patterns which might emerge. Maybe you cannot, and if so, don't worry in the slightest. But maybe you found that you tended to work through particular approaches or categories of things, perhaps without realising it. For example, you might have thought about a 'bus' and then gone on to 'car', 'lorry', 'bicycle', and 'taxi': in other words methods of transport. Your mind alighted on one and then 'associated' with others related to it. Alternatively, you might have written 'pedestrian' and gone on to think of 'crossing', 'subway', 'pavement', 'precinct', and 'escalator'. The mind tends to work in this way when brainstorming: you happen upon a topic and exhaust its associations before moving on to another.

Another tendency is to move from individual facts and ideas to wider questions connected with the topic. You might have written down the word 'congestion', for example, and gone on to write 'time-wasting', 'pollution', 'traffic management', 'need for improvements'. The mind tends to move here from the particular to the general: this is good because it helps broaden your approach, gives you more interesting things to talk or write about and maybe helps suggest a general structure which your talk or piece of writing might assume – more of this in a moment.

What I would like to ask you now is what other uses do you think this technique might have? Give it some thought for three to four minutes – you can even use the brainstorming technique to answer the question if you wish.

STOP   **3–4 minutes**

Discussion   I can think of three specific uses for this technique.
  (a) When generating ideas for a short talk or piece of writing – as we have seen.
  (b) When trying to think of ideas for the content of an essay.
  (c) When wishing to generate ideas on a particularly difficult topic, perhaps one on which you are stuck, say, midway through an essay.

In fact you can brainstorm when you need to generate ideas on anything at all: Christmas presents for relations, names for a new baby, new products for a company. The particular advantage of brainstorming is that it helps you reach the parts of your brain which other ways of thinking don't! If successful it casts a very wide net. It is also a kind of memory recall aid. In Chapter 4 you learnt that you remember best when you are able to establish associations between things. Brainstorming encourages you to make associations through enabling your mind to roam freely, picking up ideas from your conscious memory, but also moving into more dormant areas of your mind as well.

Remember, too, that a small group is generally more effective than an individual and it's a good idea to set yourself a time limit to help generate a little tension and excitement. The brain has to be alive and 'crackling' to be stormed effectively.

Organising your ideas 2

Assuming that your brain is now crackling nicely, let's move on to consider how you might use brainstorming in practice to help plan essays. Let me say at once that you don't necessarily need this technique: it is just something which helps if you find that the ideas are not flowing easily. Suppose you were asked to write a short essay on the subject of 'buying a new car'. Try brainstorming this topic for 4–5 minutes.

---

5 minutes STOP

Done that? Now I want you to move on to an important new stage: organising your ideas. Producing an essay plan from a jumble of ideas, facts and possible irrelevancies is not easy. Brainstorming has maybe solved an important problem by providing you with the raw material for your essay, but essays are much more complicated than short talks or written pieces. You cannot, for example, jump around from topic to topic as you might in a talk. We will be looking at essay plans in greater detail in future chapters (see volume II) but it should be obvious to you that a good essay proceeds in a logical, well-ordered way. They are usually divided into sections which deal with all the matters relevant to that section. To provide the basic elements of an essay plan from your brainstorming exercise, you need to organise your ideas into some kind of order. The way to do this is to look for *categories* into which you can sensibly divide your ideas. So here is your next exercise: try to find four or five categories which can accommodate all the *relevant* ideas produced by your brainstorming on 'buying a new car'. Before you start here are a few helpful hints.

(a) You need to look for the *connecting elements* between your items – what do they have in common? Can you discern any patterns?

(b) Try to identify some of those categories which, as we noted earlier, your mind may have worked through unconsciously. It could be that these categories, once identified, might help you with your essay, perhaps provide you with a section of it. Remember that you are looking for blocks of ideas and facts which can be built up to form the essay's basic structure.

(c) Look upon the exercise as trying to find a number of suitable boxes into which you can distribute the items you have written down. You may find that the first set of boxes you choose are not suitable and have to be rejected in the search for something more appropriate. It is like an intellectual puzzle: you have to work on it, wrestle with it maybe if it's a difficult topic, but it's very satisfying when it comes out right.

(d) As you transfer your ideas from your brainstorming page don't forget to add extra ideas if they occur to you, as they usually do, on the way.

Give yourself ten minutes or so on this topic. be prepared to scrap your efforts and start again if it is not going well. Don't worry if you have to make two or three attempts before you are satisfied.

STOP **10 minutes**

Discussion

My brainstorming on this subject is shown below. See how it matches and differs from your own.

cost of petrol   brakes   light   colour   VW
Ford   price   tyres   ashtrays   speaking dashboard
comfort   spare wheel   size of boot   wheel balance   bank balance
insurance   security   warranty
speed   number of gears
BUYING A NEW CAR acceleration   seat covers
performance   size   design   garage   dealer
British or foreign   kids   engine size
fuel consumption   overdraft
servicing   estate or saloon   hatchback   garage   radio   Fiat
bank manager   credit   three-wheeler   rust
comfort   sex appeal   depreciation   BL
second-hand value   sports-car

My subsequent organisation of ideas is shown below. See if you chose categories similar to mine: finance, design, performance, make.

1 *Finance* – cost, bank balance, overdraft/credit facilities, depreciation, second hand value, discount, insurance, warranty.
2 *Design* – type (hatchback, sports, saloon), comfort (seats, noise), shape (sex appeal?), internal details (dashboard, seat belts, radio), length (for garage), colour, security factors.
3 *Performance* – speed, acceleration, petrol and oil consumption, reliability, tendency to rust, gear change, brakes.
4 *Make* – British or foreign, cost of service and spares, previous knowledge of make, reliability of dealer.

Do you think my effort provides a suitable basic structure for an essay? The categories provide a structure and the constituent items the substance of each section. You may have cast your net wider and produced a more comprehensive coverage of the topic which touches on aspects which I have not mentioned – in which case, so much the better. However, I think my formulation is better than say the following set of categories:

1 Engine capacity
2 Economical motoring
3 Insurance
4 Cost
5 Make
6 Styling
7 Suitability of dealer

Do you agree? What is wrong with the above categories?

---

5 minutes   STOP

(a) The categories are not wide enough to cover all the points raised.

Discussion

(b) There are arguably too many categories to make up the sections of a short essay.
(c) Some of the categories could easily be joined together, e.g., 'insurance' and 'cost' are clearly related through the financial connection; 'engine capacity' and 'economical motoring' are also closely related and could be dealt with in the same section.

Let's try a slightly more contentious and therefore more complex question. Suppose you were asked to 'write an essay upon whether housework should be shared?' Try brainstorming this topic and then organising your ideas into categories which could form the basis of an essay plan.

---

30 minutes   STOP

Discussion   (a)   Have a look at my effort below at brainstorming this topic:

heavy work   light work   boring   'male' and 'female' roles
repetitive   houseproud
centralised housework?   tidiness
daily help   children
'earn'   fairness   travel   money   nanny
playgroups   labour-saving devices
(washing machines)   nursery schools
different culture – Asia, Africa, USA, Europe   washing up
Write an essay upon whether housework should be shared
dusting   sweeping   rotas   kids   time
different class attitudes (middle, working, upper)
changing values   work patterns
more women at work   servants
'women's work is never done'   paternity leave
big houses   flats   pets   cooking   pocket money

(b)   Now look at the categories I thought would be appropriate to help organise all these ideas.

1 Types of housework (washing up, use of modern machinery).
2 Traditional roles of women and men.
3 Attitudes differ according to culture and class.
4 Pressures for change (employment patterns, women's movement).
5 Suggested schemes for sharing (paternity leave, children 'earning' pocket money).

I found it all too easy to produce ideas on this – to me – very familiar subject! In my brainstorming I found I followed the pattern of writing down simple items in categories (my first item was 'washing up') and then moving on to the more complex ideas and arguments. My categories took a bit of sorting out – they always do. Note how I arranged them in a logical structure: I start with things which are necessary to explain what housework is; that is, introductory material, and then move on to consider the pressures for change and suggested schemes for sharing. Remember an essay should develop as it progresses, so when organising your ideas you should bear this requirement in mind.

Are you beginning to get the idea? Don't worry if you are still struggling. It takes time and practice to do this – especially the organisation of your ideas. Incidentally, the organisation bit, unlike brainstorming, is best done on your own: It requires hard thinking.

To give more practice try an even more sophisticated essay topic to brainstorm and categorise: 'Explain the causes of the inner-city riots in the 1980s'.

---

30 minutes   **STOP**

Below I give my brainstorming exercise: See how yours   *Discussion*
compares.

National Front   Pakistanis   government schemes
unemployment   burning buses   media   police
Handsworth   powder keg
Police constable Blakelock   Tottenham
police harassment of youth   batons
Douglas Hurd attacked
blood   stones   Moss Side
rastafarians   community relations   rubber bullets   shields
Mrs Thatcher's tough line   Mrs Jarratt
political agitation?   Brixton
Explain the causes of the inner-city riots in the 1980s
tear gas   police   racialism   Toxteth
South Africa   miners' strike   murder
violence   copy-cat effect   poor living conditions
governments say it's 'criminality',
opposition say it's 'social deprivation'
drugs   trigger event   alcohol   anti-establishment values
more blacks unemployed
Indian/West Indian rivalry   Enoch Powell
Lord Scarman   government complacency
no black representation in Parliament

Categories
By now, you will have drawn up your own categories but I want
to vary the exercise a little. Below I give a list of *possible* categories:
try and choose no more than seven which you think are the most
appropriate as an organising framework for the ideas produced
by my brainstorming of the topic.

1 Lord Scarman's report
2 Unemployment
3 Poverty
4 Legal
5 Cultural
6 Racialism
7 Economic
8 Police
9 Criminality
10 Law and order
11 Political
12 Social
13 Government explanations
14 Government complacency

175

15 Media
16 Social security
17 Extent and nature of riots
18 Trigger effect

STOP   **5–10 minutes**

Discussion   My categories were as follows:
1 Extent and nature of riots
2 Government explantions: criminality
Other explanations:
3 Economic (poverty, unemployment, housing)
4 Cultural (discrmination, interracial tension, 'alternative' immi-grant cultures)
5 Political (poor representation, poor police work, National Front, extremist agitators)
6 Media (publicity, notoriety, copy-cat effect)
7 Trigger effect (Mrs Jarratt, arresting of youths)
Can you see the logic behind my choice? The categories chosen provide a wide coverage of the topic. The first one gives some introductory or background material; the second offers the 'official' explanation whilst the third, fourth and fifth cover some of the fundamental causes of disorder offered by various commentators and authorities. The final two categories on the 'media' and 'trigger effect' look at the more immediate causes of the riots in the places where they occurred. I hope you can see that if you were now to sit down and write an essay on this subject you would not be short of ideas and would have a reasonably clear and systematic structure to follow. Even if the essay was very short it would be clear that you had thought it through carefully and you would almost certainly receive a favourable judgement from your tutor or examiner upon it.

3 *The Concept-Tree approach*

This is an alternative approach to the generation of ideas which you may find works just as well, albeit via a different process. You will already have encountered the Concept Tree in the chapter on note writing. The technique is simple. You proceed as with brainstorming by writing the topic in the centre of the page but you *select your categories first* and only then write in the detailed items. In other words, this approach moves from the general to the particular: the opposite procedure to the one considered so far. The term 'Concept Tree' – as we saw in the note-writing Chapter – comes from the fact that the categories are written in as 'branches' of the 'tree trunk' which is the topic being considered; the detailed points become the twigs or the leaves. As an example the exercise on buying a new car is given below.

Performance — Finance

Buying a New Car

Make — Design

Advantages of the Concept-Tree approach

Why bother with this approach? What advantages does it offer over the brainstorming in categorising techniques? Well, think about it yourself and see if you can think of any.

---

5 minutes   STOP

There are a few advantages: *Discussion*
1 It may suit your way of thinking in that you may prefer to work logically from general principles to particular examples.
2 If you are familiar with the topic its main elements may suggest themselves to you straight away. For example, the topic on inner-city riots is the kind of problem which can usually be analysed under headings like 'social, political, cultural, economic'. The Concept-Tree approach enables you to think through these implications straight away.
3 This approach is much quicker. Provided you can identify the right categories you can complete your clarification of the topic quite speedily: this makes the approach useful for examinations.

But there are disadvantages attached to the Concept-Tree technique. Can you think of any?

---

5 minutes   STOP

The most important disadvantage is that it can be less compre-   *Discussion*
hensive than brainstorming. You may think through five or six 'branches' but
(a) You may have chosen inappropriately and end up with very few or insignificant 'twigs'.
(b) You may miss out some major elements altogether.
Brainstorming offers you the possibility of generating *new* ideas whereas the Concept-Tree approach tends to utilise and organise

ideas which are already there. However, you are not faced with an either/or choice. You can use both techniques and see which suit in particular circumstances. The most important thing is to end up with the right result: the brainstorming and Concept-Tree techniques can both be instrumental to this end.

Self-assessment exercises

Exercise 1
Can you describe what points we have covered in this chapter, without looking back over it?

Exercise 2
Undertake a brainstorming exercise on the following three topics:
(a) 'Grass'.
(b) 'My attitude towards sport'.
(c) 'Cars should be banned from city centres'.

Exercise 3
Now organise your ideas produced above into categories. Go on to devise introductory and concluding points and organise your categories into essay plans. (We offer one sample essay plan in the guidance notes.)

Exercise 4
Brainstorm, organise, plan, and write up an essay on either
(a) 'The sentence given to offenders by the courts should seek to rehabilitate rather than to punish'. Discuss.
(b) 'Men are just as much "natural" parents as women'. Do you agree?

Exercise 5
Can you offer synonyms for the following terms:

1	Indirect	5	Oily
2	Laziness	6	Pleasure
3	Meeting	7	Real
4	Normal	8	Shake

What makes a good essay? 9

Reading maketh a full man, conference a ready man, and writing
an exact man   *Francis Bacon*

Contents

What makes a good essay?   **1**

So far you have learnt some important study skills like reading,
note-taking and generating ideas, but the really difficult part is
organising and expressing them in writing: most typically, in
higher education, in essay form. Part of the problem is that most
students are at first unsure of what to aim at, of what constitutes a
good essay. This chapter is designed to shed some light upon this
apparent mystery by asking you, first of all, to read an essay and
criticise it – as comprehensively, and indeed scathingly, as you
can. For this purpose we have selected an essay written in response to this question: 'Do you agree that capitalism is to be
preferred to socialism?' The essay produced by an anonymous
adult student is given below. You do not need to know a great
deal about political theory to appreciate its qualities as an argument. Just read the essay, making a careful note of both the good
points and the bad points.

Is capitalism better than socialism?
One of my uncles told me when I was a little boy that socialism,
like measles, is best got over when you are young. For several
years after that I waited for socialism to strike, but whilst mumps,
chicken pox and even measles came and went, socialism reso-
lutely avoided me. I can remember wondering what the symptoms might be: did one suddenly sprout long white hair and
develop a compulsive desire to address unwary groups of people
in a ranting style of speech? I'll never know. When a school boy I
learnt from George Bernard Shaw that 'If you are a capitalist at
twenty you haven't a heart but if you are a socialist at forty you

haven't a head.' This worried me a great deal as I considered lack of either qualities to be pretty disastrous, but to reverse one's beliefs in the space of two decades always seemed to me to be a tall order. Great believer in consistency I was, and still am. So political ideas for me have always been closely connected with physical states of health; being a hypochondriac I have always concluded that political agnosticism is the best guarantee of longevity.

Not such a bad guideline by which to rule your life when you think about it. Consider how many of the evil things in history have been done in the name of some 'ism' or other. The real 'ism' I am opposed to is 'extremism', or any belief which arrogates to itself the right to decide whether people should live or die. In this way millions have died during the last forty years. In the USSR perhaps 10 million died in Stalin's purges of the thirties, whilst as many again failed to survive the prison or forced labour camps to which their less than slavish intellectual beliefs caused them to be sent. In Germany six million Jews died as a direct consequence of Nazism and almost as many Germans died in their vain attempt to impose it on the world. In that same war, twenty million Russians died, four million Poles not to mention the French, British and American troops who gave their lives in defence of their own right to decide upon their form of government.

In our own system of government we have been successful in avoiding such unseemly displays of political commitment. Our history, since 1649 when we inadvertently executed our king, has been characterised by peaceful evolution even through the traumas of industrial and agricultural revolutions. Very sensibly politics is a subject frowned upon in most educated households. Not for us the endless intellectualising in coffee shops which gave birth to revolutions on the Continent. Politics, along with that other dangerous subject, religion, is banned from the after-dinner conversation agenda. Britain's secret is exactly that quality which activists denigrate: our apathy. This apathy is not born of ignorance or indifference (although I admit they might play a part) but good old British common sense. An informed aloofness from the bickering of party politicians is ever to be preferred. Even a cursory investigation of the current protagonists of socialism and capitalism illustrates the good sense of this maxim. On the right we have Mrs Thatcher. As far as I'm concerned this is the only thing 'right' about her. She already looks like a waxwork in Madame Tussauds. She speaks like a modern-day equivalent ôf Dickens's Mr Gradgrind and seems to have the moral sense of a Dalek. On the left we have Mr Tony Benn. Those large glassy eyes remind me of a fish, swimming around in the strange aquarium of the Marxist left. He is so earnest, so sure he knows what is best for me despite any feelings I might have myself on the matter that I would no sooner listen to him than fall off a wall backwards. My idea of hell would be to be locked up for eternity with Mrs Thatcher and Mr Benn. Which do I prefer? I strongly prefer neither. **"**

NOW STOP READING and make up your list of both the good and bad points in this essay before reading the discussion below.

STOP

What did you think of it?

Discussion

In its defence
1 It was quite amusingly and fluently written
2 For the most part the style was grammatically accurate
3 It made perhaps one or two relevant points
4 It was well presented, here in type (but the original handwriting was pretty awful).

On the debit side
1 The question was not answered either directly or thoroughly. This is hardly surprising as the title was copied out wrongly and the attempt to relate it to the full version in the last sentence was too little too late. The essay – if such a short and unsatisfactory piece of writing can be so described – dealt more with the evils of extremism then the relative merits of capitalism and socialism.
2 The essay had no coherent shape or structure – it rambled amiably from one anecdote to another and made no attempt to go through the subject-matter systematically.
3 The style, whilst lively, assured and readable, was prone to clichés, for instance, the 'measles' analogy, and whilst the chatty, personalised humour might appeal to some, it would certainly irritate those looking for a serious discussion of political ideas. In other words the style was not so much poor as inappropriate to the task in hand.
4 Sweeping generalisations were made with minimal real evidence cited in support. For instance, 'Politics . . . is banned from after-dinner conversation': what evidence is there that this dated assumption is still valid?
5 From what is written there is no evidence of serious reading or thought in the areas required. It would seem that the content has been drawn haphazardly from prejudices aired in the pub rather than gleaned painstakingly from books in a library.

Does your list of criticisms agree with the above? It probably does in major respects. It is much easier to see faults in other people's work than in your own, but if the foregoing essay's defects are so obvious to you, then you must also be aware of the elements which make a good essay. You have, in effect, already applied these standards of criteria in making your criticism – now you must try to articulate them.

STOP Make up a list of the qualities which constitute a good essay. *Do not read* the discussion before you have thought the problem through thoroughly.

2 *Elements of a good essay*

Discussion 1 **Appropriate style.** For an academic essay the third person rather than the first is preferred, though occasional use of 'I' is accepted by most tutors, especially when a personal view is specifically requested in the title. Remember such essays often seek a dispassionate appraisal of the evidence rather than your personal views, and the third person is usually, therefore, the more appropriate style. Beware also the use of humour – you come badly unstuck if a tired and cynical tutor or examiner decides he does not share your sense of it. But don't exclude it either: use it sparingly, and strategically, to give your essay life and buoyancy. Remember also that your essay should flow easily, drawing the reader's interest along naturally (even eagerly, if you can manage it!) with your arguments and ideas. Try to adopt the correct 'tone'. Don't talk down to your reader or seek to ingratiate yourself, but imagine you are addressing someone who is intelligent and reasonably, but not well, informed in the subject upon which you are writing. And remember that your style should be grammatically accurate: spelling mistakes, poor punctuation and sentence construction, mixed tenses and metaphors give a bad impression and dispose an examiner against your efforts from the outset. (see Volume II, Chapter 7, on written style.)

2 **Good presentation.** Make sure your essay is neatly written and presented. Researchers have shown that assessments given for the same work can vary by up to a whole grade (10%) depending upon the quality of the handwriting. If you are unlucky enough to have bad handwriting then either try to improve it (by no means impossible) or learn how to type (a useful skill for other purposes). Avoid submitting work which looks like a draft, with frequent crossings out, corrections and so forth. Remember tutors and examiners are only human and, quite understandably, will be disposed against your work if it is unsightly and hard to comprehend.

3 **Arguments or ideas well supported by evidence.** Essays should never be a series of unsupported assertions. Ask yourself always: 'Have I established this point sufficiently well?' If you have not or cannot then reconsider whether your approach is the correct one. If the evidence only enables a tentative conclusion to be drawn then say so – after all, most intellectual debate does not comprise clear contrast between black and white but, rather, infinite shades of grey. When you cite evidence, be sure that it is accurate – check your sources – and attribute accurately (usually via footnotes). Whatever you do, **do not plagiarise** – that is, incorporate other people's written words into your essay, trying to pass them off as your own. This is very tempting on occasions, especially when you feel you cannot improve upon an author's particular choice of words, but if you wish to use them, do so only between quotation marks and attribute the source – either in the text or footnotes. Plagiarism is after all, a form of cheating and is much frowned upon in education, not to mention all other branches of writing.

4 **Evidence of wide reading and understanding of the subject.** Essays are often set to encourage and direct your reading in the area studied – the literature of a subject, after all, **is** the subject in one sense of the word. If you show you have read widely and understood thoroughly you are demonstrating competence in the subject. Don't think you can base your essay upon just one book – this gives an impression of laziness and your essay in any case is less likely to be good if your range of sources is so narrow. On the other hand, do not get lost in too many books as this will take too much time, will confuse you and produce a poor end result. How many sources you can comfortably handle depends upon your own capacity, but a good rule of thumb guide for most essays in the social sciences and humanities is four or five major references. And here is another useful tip: put a list of books consulted at the end of your work, but don't try to compensate for inadequate reading with a long 'false' bibliography of books you have not really used: this is an old trick and is easily spotted by experienced tutors.

5 **Clarity of thought.** The hallmark of a mind which is working efficiently is clarity of thought; the ability, for example, to identify different types of issue and to argue them through logically; to organise material into a coherent essay structure; to make important distinctions and insights. If you are blessed with an excellent brain this will come relatively naturally but with effort and dedication we ordinary mortals can train our minds in specific areas to learn new ways of thinking and apply them rigorously.

6 **Originality of thought.** An essay which competently reviews

all the well-known arguments in a specific subject area and reaches a balanced conclusion may well be rewarded with a good mark but often the really high marks are given – deservedly – to the essay which displays that something extra: original ideas or an unusual, imaginative approach. Such essays seem fresh and exciting and tutors, fed up with the same old regurgitated content, are delighted to read something new. A word of warning is, however, appropriate here. Don't try to be different for the sake of it: you run the risk of appearing pretentious or, at worst, ridiculous. Being original is a risky business; it may not come off and you are well advised to play safe, as a general rule.

7 **Clear structure.** As we have seen in the section on essay plans, planning an essay is like building a house. It must have a solid foundation with a number of clearly defined rooms. Writing the essay is like leading a guest around your house, showing off its features. Nothing is more obvious to an experienced tutor than an essay with either no plan at all or a plan which is inadequate or poorly thought through. And yet *so many* students pick up their pens and start writing before they have thought how they are going to organise their ideas and arguments.

8 **Answer the question.** This requirement is virtually all the foregoing gathered together. If you have researched and planned the essay throughly, and written it up well, the chances are it will answer the essay question set pretty well. But it doesn't necessarily follow. Many students fail to understand the question (see Volume II, Chapter 1) and consequently answer it inadequately or write a great deal of irrelevant material. *You must be absolutely clear what the question means and ensure that your essay answers it directly and fully.* Ask yourself after each sentence, 'Does it contribute directly towards the answering of the question I have been set?' If it does not, then you may be advised to scrap it and think again.

The above eight elements or qualities are all important and to do well your essay would have to score well on several if not all of them. It is obvious, however, that some qualities are more important than others.

(a) Try to arrange the above eight elements in order of importance.

(b) Having done this, allocate to them the percentage you think they each deserve in the overall assessment of an essay, e.g. 10% presentation, 15% structure . . .

STOP   **15 minutes**

(a) The order I think appropriate is as follows:
   1 Answer the question
   2 Clear structure
   3 Style
   4 Evidence of wide reading
   5 Clarity of thought
   6 Well-supported arguments
   7 Presentation
   8 Originality
But . . . see comments below.

(b) This is more difficult as each tutor will have his or her own judgement, but we think most would agree that 'answering the question' is the prime requirement in any essay: we give it 20%. Structure is also vital: we give it 20%. So nearly half your marks are taken up by just these two! However, if you score well on these two the chances are you will have done reasonably well on the other criteria because – as you will have no doubt realised by now – they are all interrelated (except, probably, 'presentation'). We give in any case style, clarity of thought, well-supported arguments, presentation and originality 10% each. But this is an unreal exercise in many ways. Tutors and examiners are themselves less rational than my analysis suggests. In practice someone marking a truly original approach or analysis *which succeeds well* might give it a 'first' despite its structural and other weakness. Similarly a badly presented essay could easily be marked *down* by much more than 10%.

Discussion

Sample essays   **3**

Now read a second essay which also addresses the same question we have just considered and mark it according to the scale given above.

" Do you agree that capitalism is to be preferred to socialism?
The debate between advocates of these two rival ideologies has superseded the disputes over religious issues which, in earlier centuries, used to engage our ancestors. These two modern doctrines are secular, but they have semi-religious overtones which make definite judgements upon their respective merits, elusive or even illusory. Both are concerned with the organisation of the economy and both are products of the revolution in production techniques which took place in the eighteenth and nineteenth centuries.

Capitalism is based upon individuals or organisations trying to meet demand for certain goods or services in society, by establishing enterprises which sell them at a price which is competitive and makes a profit. If the enterprise is well run and efficient, its products will be bought by the public, its owners will prosper and its workers will receive good wages and secure employment. Socialism developed as a reaction to the capitalism which flourished in the nineteenth century. Its principal tenet is that workers should own and control the means of production and that the whole community should benefit from the fruits of their labours. Karl Marx believed that this was only possible after the working class had engineered a revolution which swept away the institutions and ideas of capitalism, but other socialists believed they could achieve their objectives through gradual, incremental reform of the capitalist system. These two schools of socialist thought have been called respectively, 'communism' and 'social democracy'. It is socialism which will be examined first.

Socialists argue that the economic system should serve the interests of all rather than those of the small group of entrepreneurs who own and control capitalist enterprises. They hope that such an economic system will succeed in changing social attitudes to make people more concerned about other people's welfare and less obsessed with the narrow selfish considerations of life in capitalist society. In other words they believe that capitalism distorts and perverts the innate tendencies in human beings to be compassionate and loving towards their fellows. Socialism aims to minimise and eliminate differences of income, status and power so that all will be more equal in rank, prosperity, and opportunity to perform different roles in society. Economic planning will ensure steady growth and abolish the absurdities of a market economy which, in the thirties, led farmers to burn food crops whilst people starved. No longer the slaves of some capitalist employer, workers in a socialist society can enjoy the dignity of sharing in and helping to shape collective enterprises.

The problem about socialism is that it has nowhere achieved these rather lofty objectives. In the Soviet Union and other communist countries the state has taken over the economy but the freedom and individual development which Marx foresaw have never arrived. On the contrary, political freedoms have been severely repressed and a grey uniformity of thought imposed throughout. Furthermore, industrial production, whilst increasing at a steady and constant rate, has not leapt ahead at the rate of capitalist countries like the USA and Japan. Social democracy, on the other hand, has been successful economically in Germany, Austria and the Nordic countries, but critics often claim that these

186

countries are only thinly disguised capitalisms. In the UK, so the critics say, the Labour Party's brand of social democracy has presided over a fall in Britain's position as tenth richest nation in 1960 to twentieth richest in 1980. The result has been that British workers now earn only half of their equivalents in capitalist America, France or Japan.

Critics of socialism also focus on the highly developed welfare systems which social democratic governments have developed. They claim that the provision of universal services encourages complacency; why should people help themselves when the state will do it for them? The individual's sense of initiative, it is argued, is sapped and his sense of responsibility for his actions eroded by a philosophy which assures him that 'society' rather than himself is to blame for his problems. The agencies established to implement this debilitating doctrine, develop into huge bureaucracies which are expensive, unproductive, ineffective and, ironically, heartless. Instead of being given the opportunity to earn their own living, the argument runs, citizens have to queue, cap in hand, for their welfare benefits, explaining and justifying themselves to doubting officials. Compared with more overtly capitalist countries, Britain has a disproportionately large bureaucracy for the collection of taxes and provision of services and by far the largest increases have occurred during the postwar labour governments. Additional bureaucracies were established to control industrial activity, thereby applying a straightjacket to economic growth and distorting the forces of the market.

People, like Milton Friedman, who championed the capitalist system, believe that market forces are natural and self-regulating: if left, unfettered by bureaucratic controls, to work their magic, they will transform ailing economies into vibrant expanding ones. Friedman argues that if able and energetic people perceive a demand, risk their own money, are allowed to establish a successful business and make a handsome profit, then economic activity will grow apace. Skill, energy and initiative will be rewarded by a rich financial return, 'And what,' Friedman would ask, 'is wrong with that?' The need to be competitive keeps prices down for the consumer whilst encouraging production techniques to be even more efficient and products even more advanced. Those who fail to compete go out of business but these are the rules of a game in which the consumer always wins. The self-interest of the entrepreneur therefore produces benefits for all. Friedman compares the material prosperity of his own country and Japan with the slow growth record of the communist bloc countries and others, like UK and India which have a history of government intervention in the economy. He concludes that capitalist free enterprise is always to be preferred.

Friedman, however, makes a tacit assumption that happiness is directly proportionate to the achievement of riches. Critics of capitalism reject this assumption, arguing that there should be more to life than the acquisition of goods and chattels, the development of competitive instincts and ruthless selfishness and the creation of false demands through insidious advertising. Under capitalism large groups of poor people suffer the indignity of selling their labour to a small group of the very rich. It reinforces inequality by giving disproportionate rewards to traditional professions like the law and the highly skilled technocratic jobs in industry; the rest have to accept low-paid, low status, uninteresting occupations. Through their influential jobs and social contacts the rich can protect their key roles in the economic and political systems and ensure that their children inherit the same privileged education. During recessions, the rich survive with scant discomfort whilst the poor suffer falling living standards and unemployment. By encouraging wholesale consumption, capitalism ravages the earth's resources at a suicidal rate and pollutes its beauty. By developing their activities abroad, big enterprises – often multinationals controlled by western countries – take over poorer economically vulnerable countries and initiate even more unpleasant forms of capitalism; for example, tobacco companies who face growing advertising restrictions in western countries, have been very successful in recouping their losses by converting Third World countries to the smoking habit.

Capitalism then, is the best guarantor of material plenty but it takes from the have-nots to give to the haves and ensures that they keep it. Socialism offers a shining mirror image to capitalism's defects but its bureaucratic machinery stultifies economic growth and its pursuit of equality frequently threatens freedom. Which then do I prefer?

Both have severe limitations but socialism's hopeful naiveté about human nature seems a preferable fault to capitalism's heartless exploitation of man's aggression and selfishness. But whilst capitalism is certainly not to be preferred to socialism, I would stop short of embracing the illiberal centralised control of communist countries. The social democracy of Sweden and Austria seem to draw upon the productive efficiency of private enterprise whilst distributing its benefits and safeguarding against its disadvantages along socialist lines. If such a system could be developed in Britain, then I would welcome it. **99**

15 minutes   When you have finished a careful reading of this   **STOP**
essay, write up your comments before going on to the discussion.

What did you think of it? What mark did you give it? Quite clearly   *Discussion*
this is a much better essay, but how good is it? We asked a lecturer
in politics at Manchester University to look at it and give his
reaction, assuming that it had been submitted to him as an
undergraduate piece of work. These are his comments:

> This is a high quality piece of work. It answers the question in an admirably
> balanced fashion and is clearly the product of considerable reading and
> thinking. The structure is straightforward and consistent throughout with a
> good introduction, a 'for and against' treatment of both ideas and a short
> conclusion which delivers the personal opinion which the essay title
> requested. The style is calm, measured, highly literate and grammatically
> accurate but, for my taste, is perhaps a little dense and solemn – it requires a bit
> more life. A bibliography would also have an advantage and for me the essay
> could have been a little longer for a subject of this scope. Presentation, of
> course, is excellent. I wish all my students' essays were typed. What mark
> would I give? A good upper second at least (65+%) – perhaps more, depend-
> ing on the course concerned.

Self-assessment exercises

Exercise 1
Without looking back over the chapter, can you list the eight most
important elements in what makes a good essay – and put them
in the order of importance we suggested?

Exercise 2
Here is another exercise in which we ask you to think clearly
about the meaning of a word. Which of the following definitions
of the word 'language' comes closest to what you understand to
be its meaning? Make notes on your choice, and explain why the
others seem to you less acceptable.

1 A form of expression.
2 A method of communication used by humans.
3 A series of interrelated symbols or messages which communicate a meaning.
4 The form of communication used by a particular human group.

Exercise 3
What follow are three sample essays on which you can check
your understanding of this chapter. Essay 1 is on 'The case for

and against private education in Great Britain' and has been written to illustrate some of the traps you can easily fall into when writing essays. Essay 2 is a vastly more competent treatment of the same subject – though it is not necessarily perfect. Essay 3 is an answer to the question 'Should there be censorship of sex and violence in the media?'

Use the checklist of points we offer in Section 2, 'Elements of a good essay', and make detailed critiques of these 3 essays, noting their strengths and weaknesses.

Essay 1
66 **The case for and against private education in Great Britain**
I think it is monstrous that private schools like Manchester Grammar School should be under attack when they have done such good work for so long. I have known a number of boys who went to such schools and they did wonders for them. Not just rich boys either, as is often claimed by those who are against private schools. Many families made enormous sacrifices to send their sons there and surely parents should be encouraged to do the best for their children, not discouraged by abolishing such schools.

Of course the truth of the matter is that these people who want to see private schools done away with are just jealous. They haven't the brains to go themselves and so they don't want anybody else to go. Either that or they were so busy spending their money on beer or bingo that there was none left over for important things like education. It is the same with taxation. Those who haven't done well (probably because they haven't tried) are jealous of those who have done well. So they want to take our money away with higher and higher taxes.

But the country needs people who will work hard and get ahead and private schools are just the places to get them from. If you look at the men who have got to the top, you will find that very frequently they have come from one of the famous private schools. This shows that the private schools are more successful at producing the best men.

What is more, it is not just the very clever child who benefits from the present private schools. A lot of parents who have children of average or below average ability are turning to private schools. This is because the state schools are so unsatisfactory. The discipline in them is hopeless, there is violence, bad language and no respect for authority. What is more the exam results are shocking.

What are parents to do who want their children to grow up decent and get a reasonable education? Of course they work for an alternative end and it would be dreadful if they were forbidden by law to spend their money to educate their own children. If somebody wants to buy a better house than their neighbours the law doesn't come along and say no you can't do that because everybody can't have a better house – so why should it over schools?

When you look at the politicians who say they disapprove of private schools you frequently find they have sent their own children to one. Either that or they have no children to send. It is like men and old women voting against abortion. Well they might since they are never going to be pregnant!

The people who do have children either do send their children to private schools or (if they are honest with themselves) would like to. When politicans get up in public and say they are going to abolish private schools they are simply vote catching.

I think any fair-minded person who has thought about the issues will agree with me that the private schools are doing a good job. That we should let them get on with it and encourage the state schools to emulate their success rather than looking for a solution in destroying them.

Of course some people say that it means that some children get an unfair start in life if they are able to go to a private school. But we all of us have to put up with some things which are unfair. I can remember when I was young there were lads who wanted to be taller. But they didn't grow so they couldn't join the police force because in those days you had to be a minimum height.

Life is unfair in many ways it just has to be accepted. Anyway, as I said before, if parents really wanted their children to go to private schools they could do without some of the luxuries and save up for them. **"**

Essay 2
" **The case for and against private education in Great Britain**
For the purposes of this essay, I intend to regard 'education' as 'education in schools'. I recognise, of course, that some parents prefer to educate their children privately at home totally outside any school system, state or private. But these situations raise different issues outside the scope of this essay and I shall confine myself, as stated, to private education in schools. I shall also assumed that the present system of registering schools, thus

ensuring minimum standards of safety and academic accepta-
bility, is going to continue.

The case for private education normally centres around two main
areas of discussion, firstly the question of the individual's
liberties and secondly the proven usefulness of private schools
themselves. I propose to enlarge upon these, dealing with
objections on the way, before moving on to the case against
private education.

Advocates of private schooling maintain that every individual
should have the right to spend his (or her), lawfully earned,
money as he wishes. Hence, if he decides to buy 'better' or simply
'different' schooling for his child that is his natural right. They
further argue that parents in particular have not only a right but a
positive duty to 'do the best' for their children. Any attempt,
therefore, to restrict or abolish private schools, undermines, not
only individual rights, but also the desirable relationship
between parents and children.

In response to those who point out that not every parent has
sufficient money to send their child to a private school and that an
unfair advantage is secured for some children, supporters of such
institutions counter with two arguments. Firstly, they advance
schemes like that of the 'assisted places', whereby the state provides scholarships at private schools for academically gifted
children, or those schemes whereby local councils pay for children with unsatisfactory homes to attend private boarding
schools. Secondly, they concede that such schemes, although
widening the opportunities, would not remove all differences of
opportunity for children, but claim that such differences must
inevitably exist in any foreseeably acceptable society.

The second main plank in the platform of those in favour of
private schools, is the long record of usefulness and, indeed,
excellence enjoyed by those schools. Their supporters point to
institutions like Manchester Grammar School and Westminster
reminding us that their world-wide reputations for academic
excellence have been acquired over hundreds of years. It is
argued that they provide the intellectually gifted individual with
an ideal environment in which to develop and the nation with a
constant supply of just the sort of innovators and leaders it needs.
At the other end of the scale, perhaps, the private school enthusi-
asts draw our attention to the provision made in such schools for
those children with physical, learning or personality difficulties.
It is claimed that the private sector provides a smaller, more
supportive framework for such children far better suited to their
needs than the large, state school which must, of necessity, cater

for the average.

The proponents of private education deny the claims that the existence of the private sector drains off the brightest pupils and the best staff from the state system. They point out in the first instance that only a very small proportion of children are educated privately and, as already stated, by no means all of these are academic 'high-fliers'. Secondly they maintain that the existence of, an admittedly small private sector, acts as an independent criterion, helping to keep standards higher in state schools and ensuring a stability in education impossible apparently in the politically influenced state sector.

Having outlined the case in favour of private education, I shall now discuss briefly the opposing viewpoint. This has two broad prongs of attack: firstly the socially divisive nature of private schools and secondly the fact that their existence serves to demoralize and debilitate the state system of education.

In the first place, the opponents of private education draw our attention to what they regard as the quite disproportionate influence exercized by a relatively small number of private schools. As evidence, they point out that in the traditionally powerful institutions of the country – parliament, the law, the civil service, the financial world and the board room – the vast majority of top positions are held by men coming from a couple of dozen private schools. Moreover, it is held, that although the majority of pupils at private schools do not, it is true, go on to become cabinet ministers or judges, they do tend to take up positions of influence in industry and the professions far out of proportion to the statistical probability for their age and intelligence quotient.

Bearing in mind that the private schools recruit largely from relatively rich, professional middle and upper-class homes, from the above-mentioned facts those opposed to private schools draw two conclusions.

Firstly, that the country is being run by men drawn from a very narrow, quite unrepresentative segment of society. Moreover, that the privileged aspect of their origins is being re-inforced by a highly protected schooling. This results, it is maintained, in a gap of understanding and sympathy, between those taking decisions and those having to follow them, which is unbridgeable and responsible, for example, to a large extent for the bad industrial relations in this country. Secondly, that in many cases men are being appointed from this privileged background, not on merit but as a result of influence. This in its turn breeds a suspicion of the disaffection towards the establishment on the part of the average citizen which is to the detriment of the whole nation.

Far from supplying the country with the gifted leaders it needs, the opposers of such schools say that they are, in fact, supplying us with leaders who are not always especially gifted academically and are rarely, if ever, able to understand the problems of the people they are supposed to be leading.

Moreover, whilst admitting that the private schools might provide a superior education for a privileged few, their opponents point out that they do so to the detriment of and at the expense of the vast majority of children who are, and always would be, unable to benefit from them. This, it is argued, is because of the previously discussed unfair advantage in the world of work a private school education gives a child. It is also the case because the so-called 'private' schools enjoy millions of pounds worth of support from the state both direct and indirect. Direct support is enjoyed in the form of the tax concessions which such schools receive through their charitable status. Indirect support is received in their draining off the best teachers who have been expensively trained at the state's expense.

In addition to this, the private school, by its very existence, provides an unfair standard of comparison with the state school; unfair because of its vastly greater resources and more specialised intake. Nevertheless, it is argued, the public make this unfair comparison and finds the state school wanting. This pressure serves, to distort the curriculum of the state school, which is involved in a hopeless attempt to imitate its rival; and to demoralize both staff and pupils in state schools because it is a contest they can never win.

Hence the anti-private school lobby says the private school undermines, both financially and morally, the state system which will never be able to function satisfactorily alongside it. These facts, it is argued, are sufficient to over-ride the rights of individual parents to spend their money on their child's education, in just the same way that we deny many other individual rights in favour of the good of the majority. It may be true, they admit, that a perfectly equitable society cannot be produced, but that is no reason why we should not move nearer towards such an idea.

In seeking to adjudicate between the competing claims on the issue it becomes clear that both sides agree on certain points. Firstly they both agree that some, at least, of the existing private schools do provide a very high quality of education for a small number of children. They also both agree that this number must always remain a minority and that they will have received an advantage in this respect over their peers. Beyond this common ground, the two sides differ radically in their opinions as to the effect that this priviledged minority has on the country and as to the relative value to be given to individual as opposed to communal rights.

It appears that the decision as to which set of arguments are found most persuasive will depend on the role one primarily accords schools: academic specialists or social integrators.

This, in its turn, may well hinge on whether one thinks society progresses by its front-runners dragging the rest behind, or whether one believes society moves forward only in so far as it provides opportunities for the vast majority. If the former, then one probably views schools primarily as academic specialists and would support the continuance of the private sector on the basis that they have centres of academic excellence which cannot be replaced. If the latter, then one would be inclined to place more emphasis on the school's role as social integrator and vote for the disbanding of the socially divisive private sector. The deeper reasons which lie behind a choice in one direction rather than another, would have to be the subject of another and much longer essay! **99**

Essay 3

66 Sex and violence in the media
First of all it will be assumed that by 'censorship' we mean the limitation of expression, distribution, and/or consumption by individuals or groups whose decisions are often arbitrary, irrevocable, and not subject to democratic control. Secondly, although 'media' includes newspapers, books, T.V. radio magazines, theatre, film etc I shall confine my observations and remarks to the telly and our wonderful daily newspapers.

First the case against censorship. This can be made on a number of different grounds: aesthetic, political, practical, moral, unnatural, etc. It's often been said that artists work better when under restraint or control: after all, Michaelangelo produced many of his sculptural masterpieces when working directly under the patronage of the Pope. Nevertheless, censorship always inhibits artistic talent and history has a number of embarrassing egs to offer. When James Joyces' *Ulysses* was first published (in Paris) it was banned in England on grounds of obscenity: now it is regarded as modern literary Classic. Similarly D. H. Lawrence's *Lady Chatterley's Lover* was prosecuted for obscenity in the English courts as recently as 1962: the case was lost, the novel is regularly taught in universities, and no appreciable decline in public morals standard has been recorded.

As I have just argued above, aesthetic values may be adversely affected by censorship – but the next point to be considered is: who will do the censorship? Who's values will be used as the basis for the moral code against which the works of art, newspapers or television programmes to be considered will be judged? Do we want the Mrs. Whitehouses of this world telling us what we can see? Do we hell! She can keep her opinions to herself I always think. It's true that we don't want to be bombarded by horrible visual images on our T.V. screens all the time, especially early in the evening when many young impressionable children might have been watching. Sociologists have shown us that young children are very susceptible to being corrupted and it is the responsibility of families and teachers and people who run T.V. stations to present decent moral standards.

Moral philosophy has argued since the 17th Century that the individual should have the right to make up their own minds regarding what is right and wrong. And in the mid twentieth century, with universal secondary education in Britain, it is surely possible to give each individual the chance to develop that sense of discrimination and that ability to make value-judgements which is all that is necessary to offset the possible corrupting effects of sex and violence in the media.

And why link together sex and violence? If by "sex" is meant normal healthy sexual behaviour between a man and a woman – this is altogether the opposite of 'violence' which involves one person hurting another. Moreover, the present system is not unbiased. Cries of protest are made if we even see a bit of 'bums and tits' on the screen, yet people are being killed at a fantastic rate in cops and robbers programmes and American westerns.

Two more intricate arguments against censorship. One, that scenes of sexual activity or violence act as a catharsis upon viewers and may even be salutary in the release from libido-inhibiting motor-armouring. Two, that the same images may serve as a healthy deterrent. Unfortunately its very difficult to find well researched substantiation for these arguments and therefore both of them have only the force of personal conviction or belief behind them. It might also be noted as a caution that the two arguments are in general contradictory ('catharsis' cannot simultaneously be a deterrent) and that applied to both sex *and* violence they might produce undesired results (would we wish to deter people from having satisfactory sexual relationships? Would Mrs. Whitehouse wish people to enjoy sexual catharsis?)

But surely *some* form of censorship is necessary and desirable. Most of us act as censors all the time – over our own behaviour, speech, manners.

I think any normal person would be disgusted if there were no restraints on civilized behaviour. We don't want to go back to the day's of Queen Victoria and 'We are not amused' etc. but some standards must be upheld.

Next, sex is only a necessary function, so why should we draw any more attention to it or make any more fuss about it than we would over going to the lavatory? People in the past didn't see it on T.V. or read about it, and they were a lot healthier and better off than now in our sick and neurotic society.

Many people want themselves and their children to be protected from the encroachment of excessive attention to sex and violence into the privacy of their lives. They can choose what to read individually, but on publically owned television stations their wishes ought to be respected by a policy of moderation which avoids catering for extremists. After all, anybody with minority or extreme views ought to be prepared to put himself to some trouble without complaint: a public service cannot cater quantiatively for everyone.

Perhaps the most telling argument in favour of censorship comes from the U.S.A. where on East coast T.V. Channels a murder is committed on screen every thirty-five seconds. This breeds an acceptance of violence as a 'normal' component of modern society which in that country results in one of the highest murder rates in the world.

Moreover in many of the American programmes broadcast in England violent murder is 'glamourised': it is commited by people the programme wishes us to admire ('Starsky and Hutch', 'Bonnie and Clyde'); it is artificially made 'necessary' or given a spurious justification ('Kojak') by not examining its root causes; or it is given a spectacular aesthetic gloss ('Straw Dogs', 'Apocalypse Now') which distracts attention from its moral implications.

The limitations of our own freedom of choice in the name of protecting others (or even ourselves!) is a perennial conundrum but as far as this particular question is concerned there may be two or three provisional conclusions. First, that sex and violence should be neither equated or confused. Next, that there may need to be different forms of censorship considered for each separate medium. That the interests of minorities (and the majority) should be considered in making judgements. That arbitrary censorship might be avoided by democratic safeguards and control. That 'public opinion' is not static. That many modern societies are multi-racial, multi-cultural, and have considerable sub-sections whose moral values are not those of the majority. For all these reasons (and many more besides) the question of censorship needs to be more carefully considered than the over-general terms of the question imply. **"**

Course review exercise

What follows is a list of questions relating to all of the chapters in this volume – which takes us up to half-way through the study programme. As usual, we would like you to be honest and rigorous: don't be tempted to look at the answers until you have come to the end of the exercise. And in common with the other exercises you have been doing so far – *write down* your answers.

This should be a useful guide to self-assessment. We don't expect you to come up with the correct answer to every single question, but the percentage of right answers will give you some guide to how well you have absorbed the lessons of the chapters in this volume.

Don't imagine that we are out to trick you or pose especially difficult questions. Everything will be based on what you have read in these pages. All we want to do is give *you* the chance to check that you have grasped some of the most important lessons in each chapter. And don't worry if you sometimes use slightly different terms to those we have used: just be honest with yourself when assessing your answers.

If there turn out to be some sections that you have understood less well than others, do not hesitate to go back over them. Re-read whichever chapters are concerned, and do the exercises again until you are sure of the points being made.

Questions
1 Can you list four of the most common problems facing the adult student?
2 List three of the advantages of being an adult student.
3 In what three general ways can studying be combined with everyday life?
4 List three of the study habits required for being an active student.
5 List three of the study habits which should help your powers of concentration
6 What 5 step process does the acronym SATRA stand for?
7 We gave seven advantages of studying in groups. Can you list four of them?
8 We listed fifteen guidelines for successful group discussions. Can you give six?

9 What are the two key elements required for developing the ability to speak in public?
10 Can you list five good points or features which might be used by a successful public speaker?
11 What are the three most important pieces of information we need about a book?
12 What does the expression SQ3R stand for?
13 We listed seven different kinds of reading. Can you name four of them?
14 Name the two most common note-taking systems.
15 List four ways of improving the layout of your notes.
16 What are the two most important stages of generating ideas?
17 List five of the eight features necessary in a successful essay.
18 What are the two most important requirements for an essay to be successful?

Answers to course review exercise

1 Any four from:

1 Lack of confidence	6 Negative family attitudes
2 lack of time	7 Lack of perseverence
3 Poor concentration	8 Doubts regarding future
4 Time lapse since last study	study
5 weak self-discipline	9 Lack of finance

2 Any three from:

1 Strong motivation	4 Effective management
2 Maturity	of time
3 Organising skills	5 Communication skills
	6 Perseverance

3 (a) Create more free time
  (b) Make more efficient use of existing time
  (c) Combine study with other activities

4. Any three from:
   1 Make notes on what you read
   2 Be prepared to summarise arguments as you go along
   3 Look up the meaning of words you don't understand
   4 If you do not agree with a point, make a note of your counter-argument
   5 Make a checklist of important names, dates, and events
   6 Try to relate what you are studying to other work you have done on the subject

5 Any three from:
   1 Good conditions for study
   2 No distractions

    3 Study routine
    4 Self-knowledge
    5 Confidence: a positive attitude
    6 Good planning and anticipation
    7 Discussion with your tutor and other students

6 SURVEY – AIM – TASK – REVIEW – ANALYSE

7 Any four from:
    1 Opportunity to interact with other students
    2 Group members can help each other
    3 A chance to try out ideas on others
    4 Benefit from the wide range of others' experience
    5 Can simplify complex tasks
    6 Practice in developing communication skills
    7 Opportunity for team approach and co-operation

8 Any six from:

1 Seating arrangements	9 Create a good atmosphere
2 Prepare	10 Be polite
3 Clarify your aims	11 Keep an open mind
4 Don't dominate	12 Appoint a chairperson
5 Don't be too negative	13 Be aware of roles
6 Listen carefully	14 Analyse performance
7 Encourage quieter members	15 Review what you have
8 Don't deviate	learnt

9 Confidence and practice

10 Any five from:
    1 Direct visual contact with audience
    2 Variety of tone and pitch in voice
    3 Range of features and expressions
    4 Use of visual aids
    5 Interest and enthusiasm in subject
    6 Clear speaking at reasonable pace
    7 Clear structure in lecture
    8 Occasional lightening of atmosphere
    9 Relate topic to audience
    10 Keep audience attention

11 AUTHOR – TITLE – DATE OF PUBLICATION

12 SURVEY – QUESTION – READ – RECALL – REVIEW

13 Any four from:

1 Surveying rapidly	5 Skimming
2 Sampling, or exploratory	6 Scanning or
3 Reading for entertainment	search-reading
4 Selective reading	7 Close and detailed reading

14 Linear–Logical and Concept-Tree

15 Any four from
   1 Use one side of paper only
   2 Use headings – and sub-headings
   3 Number your items
   4 Use colour-coding
   5 Use indentation
   6 Use plenty of spacing
   7 Use visual aids

16 Brainstorming and creating categories

17 Any five from
   1 Answer the question
   2 Clear structure
   3 Good written style
   4 Evidence of wide reading
   5 Clarity of thought
   6 Well-presented arguments
   7 Good presentation
   8 Original ideas

18 Answer the question, and provide a clear, sound structure

Results

I don't think it is necessary to be mathematical or too finely detailed about the results here. Assuming that you have been reasonably strict with yourself (after all, there is no point in cheating if you want to know how well you have performed) – then I would suggest that you could grade yourself as follows:

Number of correct answers
(51 possible maximum)

45 and over	Clearly this represents a highly successful study experience. You should have little problem with further study and should pass straight on to Volume II, *Thinking and writing*.
38–45	A good result. You can say that you have completed this part of the study programme.
30–38	Fair to good. You need to keep on working. Refer back to earlier chapters and brush up any areas of weakness.
20–30	Not a very reassuring result. Perhaps you should work through the chapters again more slowly.
Less	Don't despair. Either work back through the chapters again more carefully, or maybe try another type of course with more classroom contact and personal supervision from a tutor.

Guidance notes on self-assessment exercises

These are likely to be particularly useful to independent learners

Chapter 1

Exercise 1

This chapter covered:

1 *Our educational system:* its lack of support for adult students; the facilities and provision needed for adult students; the political reasons for the weakness of adult education.
2 *Problems of adult study:* lack of confidence, lack of time, poor concentration, time-lapse since last experience of study, poor self-discipline, negative family attitudes, lack of perseverance, lack of finance, confusion over direction of future study.
3 *The advantages of being an adult student:* strong motivation, maturity, organisation, effective use of time, communication skills, perseverance, the role of 'guilt'.
4 *Getting to know your own strengths and weaknesses:* social background and attitudes towards education; your own personal study strengths and weaknesses.

Exercise 2

These are some of the elements you may have included. Don't worry if some of them may appear in a negative manner: if you had enjoyed nothing but positive influences in your background, you probably wouldn't be engaged on this course.

1 *Parental influences:* the jobs, hobbies, cultural attitudes, and aspirations of your parents.
2 *Home environment:* possible stimulation of cultural atmosphere, books, learning, varied activities.
3 *Peer-group influence:* stimulation from brother(s), sister(s), friends.
4 *Primary school.*
5 *The 11-plus:* possible springboard or barrier to development.
6 *Secondary school:* secondary modern, comprehensive, grammar.
7 *Work and employment:* possible good or bad choice of career.
8 *Marriage and family:* possible stimulant or retardation of progress.
9 *Job change:* possible need for more qualifications.

10 *Personal growth or development:* desire for change, growing
interest in a subject.

Exercise 3
These are some of the skills you may have listed. Don't worry if
you have noted some which we do not mention. This list only
covers the most important, and this course will include mention
of others.
 1 Effective reading.
 2 Note-taking.
 3 Concentration.
 4 Clear thinking.
 5 Organisation of time.
 6 Generating ideas.
 7 Organisation of ideas.
 8 Working alone.
 9 Working in groups.
10 Planning a piece of work.
11 Clear writing.
12 Oral expression.
13 Confidence and perseverance.
14 Grammar and punctuation.
15 Examination skills.

Exercise 4
Here is a well-written and witty response to this exercise produced by an adult student, Ian Churton.

66 **A moment to remember**
I bought the ice creams at the interval. That was my big move. It
had taken most of my spending money as well. We were sat in the
middle upstairs, not in the 'one-and-nines'. They were the
double seats used by courting couples, at the end of each row
next to the wall. This way we were all together.

Baz was doing most of the talking, as usual. He was more confident, in fact you would think he had two girl friends and I was
his assistant. Every time I thought of something to say there was
an immense time lag before my mouth moved, and by then the
conversation had changed. I was confused.

This whole thing had begun last Wednesday, after school, when
we were all standing about the traffic lights, someone had said
there was a really good film on at the 'Elysian'. My mate Baz was
fixed up with Carol and so was Tich with some other girl. Baz said
'Who's going with Ian?' Jennifer Warren had said she would and I
had nodded and smiled. All fixed for Saturday night then.

I didn't have many clothes, so I went in my school trousers. My new red sweater was hiding an old school shirt with a good collar. I was carrying my mac. The 'old lady' said I had to take it.

We had met outside. Baz was wearing a swish jumper and his famous cavalry-twill trousers. I felt uncomfortable. When Jennifer walked up, I couldn't believe my eyes. She looked great. She had on a really nice suede jacket with very smart blouse and skirt, and it all matched. I felt second-hand.

The interval was over and the main film was starting. I wanted to put my arm round Jennifer, the way Baz had his round Carol. I had hardly said much and couldn't consider to have chatted her up. Maybe it was too soon. 'Go on do it you coward' a voice said inside. My arm froze. 'I'll do it in a minute' the other voice said. My arm relaxed a bit. 'You'll never get to kiss her' said the first voice. The internal dialogue went on. The film went on.

Next thing, there we were outside the cinema. It was foggy, 'I'll walk you home,' I told Jennifer. She said 'Ok.' Baz went off arm in arm with Carol. I walked along with Jennifer and we talked as we went.

I was relieved to be out of the cinema, and also glad that Baz had gone, so I might get a word in. I was feeling a bit more relaxed when that voice in my head said 'Why aren't you holding her hand?' 'I can't,' said the other 'easy just get hold of it. She'll think you daft if you don't.' 'I can't get hold of her hand if I didn't chat much or put my arm round her in the cinema.' 'Go on do it.'

We walked, we talked a bit and the internal dialogue went on. My hand remained frozen. She offered me a cough sweet. I accepted, too nervous to say no. I didn't really want one. We passed the traffic lights and Jennifer said she was Ok to walk the rest of the way alone. I insisted that I accompany her home. The conversation was almost non existent by now. We just walked on in the fog silently and separately.

Three hundred yards from her house, she announced, with relief in her voice, that she would be safe now and I'd better turn off down Highfield Road as I was miles out of my way. In seconds she was gone. I stood for a few seconds then set off down Highfield, for home.

The nervousness had gone, I now felt angry with myself. What a wally. My first girl friend hadn't lasted long. How was I going to find another one? What would I do if I did? Who cares? I lit up a comforting 'Woodbine' (my last one) and sauntered home in the mist hoping no one would remember what had just happened. **"**

Chapter 2

Exercise 1

1 *Creating more free time*
  (a) Re arranging daily activities.
  (b) Redistributing household tasks.
  (c) Less television, housework, pottering, socialising.

2 *Making more efficient use of existing time*
  (a) Plan what you do.
  (b) Create the right conditions for study.
  (c) Pace yourself.
  (d) Be an 'active' student.

3 *Combining study with other activities*
  (a) Listen to radio/tapes whilst doing housework.
  (b) Read or listen whilst travelling.
  (c) Review notes whilst relaxing.

Exercise 2

1 *Breakfast*
  (a) The three teenage sons could be taught how to get their own breakfast.
  (b) One hour, between 6.30 a.m. and 7.30 a.m. is then available to Mrs Griffiths for her own use.

2 *Morning*
  (a) Mrs G Spends one hour reading the newspaper, then as much again watching the television news. One of these could go, leaving her *another* hour free.
  (b) Shopping could be done less frequently – say every two or three days. More time saved.
  (c) Why not do the ironing in the evening, whilst watching television – two activities thereby combined in one?
  (d) If Mrs G follows suggestions (a), (b) and (c) she has the period between 10 a.m. and 1 p.m. free.
  (e) If the time taken over lunch is reduced to thirty minutes, she has another free hour.

3 *Afternoon*
  (a) Swimming may be healthy exercise, but maybe twice a week is enough.
  (b) The sons could take it in turn to exercise the dog.
  (c) The sons might also help with some of the household chores.

4 *Evening*
  (a) The household chores would surely be better done during the day.
  (b) Mrs G might then do some reading during the evening.

In general, Mrs G needs to rearrange her household tasks, avoid repetition, seek the co-operation of others – and then gather together the periods of time 'saved' into blocks for use as private study.

Exercise 3
   (a) Work may be onerous or unpleasant for some people, but there are also many who *enjoy* their work. Moreover, just because something is unpleasant (going to the dentist) or onerous (filling in a tax form) does not make it 'work'.
   (b) Most people work in order to earn money, but there are many people who work without getting paid at all (voluntary social workers, fundraisers for charity, the Women's Voluntary Service, St John's Ambulance Brigade).
   (c) Most work may be done as gainful employment completing specific tasks (baker, joiner, minder), but imagine having to dig over a garden fifty yards long: this too would be work, but unpaid. Alternatively, the *housework* done by a person living alone is not 'paid'.
   (d) This has the advantage of covering most possibilities – housework, the baker, the fundraiser, even going to the dentist. But it has the disadvantage of being rather vague and it doesn't take into account any notion of payment.

There is no right and wrong answer here. The exercise is simply devised to encourage you to think more clearly about the precise meaning of words which are used regularly in everyday parlance.

Exercise 4
You may find the response of a former student interesting.

❝ *The problems facing me as an adult student*
As a married woman with a young family, wondering whether or not to develop a second career, I am faced with several problems. The most important of these being the direction of my future studies.

Having already spent thirteen years in a very narrow field of study, and work, I now want to broaden my knowledge so that I can get a good idea of where my interests and abilities lie. I also want to give myself as much flexibility as possible in the job market. Having made some enquiries about various courses, I decided to enrol as an undergraduate with the Open University, but, I really have no idea whether this would be the most suitable course for me to take.

The second biggest problem facing me is lack of confidence, which mostly stems from ignorance. I have no idea at all of what is involved in taking a degree or other higher education courses, neither do I have any idea of my own strengths and weaknesses and, consequently, cannot judge how well or badly I might do.

The third problem is time. As much as I would love to devote myself to full-time study it is just not practicable. I have two young children aged two and four who need to be looked after. I have a husband who is working long hours, in an effort to produce the necessities and, hopefully, one or two luxuries in life, like study, but this leaves me with even less time for studying. There is the house to clean, meals to cook, clothes to wash, shopping, and visiting relatives etc. The only available time I have for study is in the evening and sometimes at the weekend, though I am not always at my best at these times.

Fourthly, there are financial problems, to an extent. Although my husband earns a good salary, the family budget does not allow for the provision of large course fees required for some of the H.E. courses.

Lastly, though I could not say that I would face any direct opposition, if I do go ahead with Open University course, I do not think I would get a great deal of positive support. My husband will happily go along with it, if it is what I really want to do, but I doubt that he would always make the necessary allowances or do more around the house. His relatives, whom I see regularly, whilst not condemning me outright, would consider that I was 'failing' in my role as wife and mother and being rather selfish. I suspect that my parents would be very patronising about it.

Really, the overall problem facing me is a universal one, what do I want out of life? What am I prepared to put in to it and how can I do it without upsetting anyone? **"**

Chapter 3

Exercise 1
This chapter has covered the following main elements:
1 Factors affecting concentration: three exercises
2 How to help your concentration
(a) Study habits
     Good conditions of study. No distractions. Good study routine. Self-knowledge. Confidence and positive attitude. Good planning and anticipation. Discussion with tutor and other students.
(b) Psychological aspects of concentration

Starting up. Varying your approach. Vocational interest
(c) Physical aspects of concentration
Sleep. Over-indulgence. Diet. Need for exercise
3 How to relax
Leisure pursuits. Breath control. Counting down to zero. Meditation. Muscle relaxation
4 How to build up your concentration
The Incremental Approach. Targets and rewards. Regular breaks. Avoiding last-minute rushes. SATRA (Survey, Aim, Task, Review, Analyse)
5 Memory
Information storage
Understanding the principles or basic ideas. Note-taking. Constant revision and review. Key words. Mnemonics. Association of ideas

Exercise 2
1 There is no evidence in the article that women are 'happy' to leave political activity to men – but plenty to suggest that the burdens of family care prevent them from being politically active themselves.
2 There is nothing necessarily 'natural' about women looking after children and old people: it is simply a convention that our society in general gives this role to them.
3 The article deals extensively with the problems women face in combining family care with work outside the home – but nowhere does it suggest that they have 'no problems' doing so.
4 There is no evidence in the article for any connection between work outside the home and political *awareness*. Indeed, one of the passages quoted points out that it is 'housewives without outside work commitments' who tend to predominate in the intermediate levels of political activity.
5 There is no evidence in the article to suggest that women are 'escaping' into full or part-time work. They *could* be (though it is more likely that the work is one extra burden), but the article does not say so.

Exercise 3
1 limit
2 inventory
3 dissipate
4 patent
5 saturnine
6 immunity

Chapter 4

Exercise 1
This chapter has taken you through:
1 The pros and cons of studying alone and in groups.
2 The role which group work should play in adult and higher education.
3 Good and bad group discussion in practice.
4 The roles which people play in groups.
5 Recommended guidelines for working in groups.
6 The desirability of active listening.

Exercise 2
No comment applicable. Consult your tutor if you have one.

Exercise 3
No comment applicable.

Exercise 4
1 gestation
2 oscillation
3 urban
4 cursory
5 allusion
6 belated

Chapter 5

Exercise 1
No comment applicable. Consult your tutor if you have one.

Exercise 2
No comment applicable. Consult your tutor.

Exercise 3
The letter which follows was written by former student Jean Brooks.

" The Headmistress
Cherry Tree School
Osborne Lane
Bilford

11 Staines Road
Bilford

Dear Mrs Ruddlestone

I am writing to tell you that I take exception to my daughter Anthea being sent home from school at lunchtime – apparently because she does not eat the meals that are provided. There are three reasons why I think this is quite unreasonable.

The first is that Anthea, like other members of our family, has chosen to be a vegetarian. I realise that the school meals service cannot cater for every single person's special taste, but I also think it is quite unjust for a child to be singled out and given what amounts to a punishment, simply because she will not eat meat.

The second is that both my husband and I have full time jobs, so there is nobody at home if Anthea is sent out of school. I think you will agree with me that it is courting an unnecessary danger to have an eight year old girl roaming the streets without any sort of protection.

And the third reason is that I am surprised that neither you nor any member of your staff got in touch with me before taking this action. Wouldn't a phone call or a note have been more appropriate?

Whenever possible in future I will give Anthea a packed lunch to bring to school, but in instances where that is not possible I hope we can come to some agreement over the best course of action for Anthea's sake. If you would like to telephone me at home any time after five o'clock I sincerely hope we can resolve this matter. **"**

Yours truly

Mrs J Brooks

Exercise 4
These are our own comments (all favourable), in no particular order.

1 The piece has both an arresting opening and a tidy conclusion, and the substance of what lies in between is organised in a clear, logical order. All these features create a strong sense of structure. The essay has obviously been carefully thought through and well organised.
2 The writing is clear and fluent, with plenty of variation in pace and sentence length. There is also good use made of the paragraph: each one contains a separate phase of the story.

3 There are some nice turns of phrase used to occasional effect: 'perpetually gloomy news', 'plethora of dead bodies'. This is the writing of someone who has a feeling for language.

4 There are some well-observed details ('the proprietor who always smoked cigars') which suggest that the writer is paying attention to the world and rendering it truthfully. The writing seems 'true to life' – as well as being entertaining and sometimes wryly amusing.

5 The subject-matter is an interesting mixture of sad and happy matters which are held in a delicate balance throughout. The lost brother somehow 'matches' the new-found husband-to-be, and the uncertainty of finding one is paralleled by the unexpected pleasure of the evening out – both underscored by the generally anxious atmosphere of wartime.

I hope this doesn't read like too dry and academic a comment on a piece of work we have included chiefly because we thought it so charming. Many of the features of good eassy writing will be dealt with later in Volume II.

Exercise 5
The main points covered in this chapter were:
1 Developing your confidence
  Practising short talks
2 How to prepare a short talk
3 How to deliver a short talk
  Good points and bad points in public speaking.
  Attention-winning devices. Relaxation
4 Different kinds of talks

Chapter 6

Exercise 1
1 27 in October 1974, and 19 in May 1979
2 None
3 30%
4 False. It is 'still only 80 per cent or so of men's pay'
5 'Some form of proportional representation'
6 The Single Transferable Vote system
7 8 out of 199
8 'As the importance of office increases the number of women declines'

Exercise 2
Compare your own draft letter with the one which follows:

66 Dear Mrs Sibley,

It is my unpleasant duty that I have to write this letter to you concerning your work as a cleaner. Recently I have noticed that your cleaning is not up to its usual high standard. On several occasions I have noticed chores which should have been done have been neglected. Every Friday it is your job to tidy the shoe cupboard under the stairs. Yesterday, I went in the cupboard and noticed that all the shoes were in disarray on the floor. Also Stanley has complained that his shirts have not been ironed correctly. On Sunday evening I was entertaining guests at an important dinner party, when Lady Pickton spotted dust on the window-ledge. This highly embarrassing incident was the final straw, and hence this letter to you. As I have very high standards at the Manor I cannot let this situation continue.

I hope you haven't got any problems which are worrying you and affecting your work. During the last three years I have found you a conscientious worker, who takes pride in all her work. However, I must make it perfectly plain that if your work doesn't improve I will be forced to dispense with your services at the Manor. Please have tea with me in the morning room at 11.00 a.m. on Friday, where we can discuss and rectify this situation. I will be most upset if I lose a friend as well as a cleaner.
Yours faithfully,
Lady Ascot 99

Exercise 3
1 prolix
2 dialogue
3 euphoria
4 flounce
5 genus
6 hedonistic
7 impede
8 ingenious

Exercise 4
Here is a sample preview:
Hicks and Hutchings *Literary Criticism: A Practical Guide for Students* (Edward Arnold, 1989)
This is a textbook and a working guide to literary criticism aimed principally at GCE A level students. Part One gives a quick summary of various theories of criticism; Part Two is a series of worked examples in which poems, passages of prose, and even playscripts and diary extracts are subjected to critical analysis; and Part Three offers answers to very common problems and

queries which arise in the 'A' level examination. The book *could* be used by the independant learner, because the origin of the examples studied in Part Two is concealed until the end of the book. There is also a useful glossary of technical terms. Cheap paperback edition.

Exercise 5
These were the main points you may have listed:
1 Types of books
2 Previewing the book
3 SQ3R – Survey – Question – Read – Recall – Review
4 Types of reading
5 Improving your reading speed
6 Using libraries
7 Kinds of library
8 Varieties of source materials
9 How libraries work
10 Catalogues
11 References

Chapter 7

Exercise 1
Here are the main points covered in this chapter:
1 Some of the reasons why it is essential for every student to think about and develop their own efficient means of making notes.
2 Some of the problems most students initially encounter in making notes from the spoken word in lectures and in classes.
3 Some of the basic skills of concentrating, listening, watching, compressing, that past groups of students have found very useful when taking notes from lectures.
4 Some of the basic techniques which will help you in your note-making exercise, such as the need to clearly identify your notes; employ an effective storage and retrieval system; develop a clear style of layout; create your own note-making language; and maintain a rigorous and regular review of the notes you have made.
5 Some of the different systems of note-making you may wish to employ in different situations, notably the Linear-Logical system and the Concept-Tree system.
6 The contrast between some of the rules for effective note-making from speech and some of the guidelines for effective note-making from written materials.

Exercise 2

Here is an example of notes on the article – roughly one for each of its paragraphs. (To aid understanding abbreviations have not been employed.)

1 Socialists level down – Tories give *all* chance to acquire wealth
2 But 'losers' in enterprise culture must be protected
3 Wealth must be generated to pay – but should be *means*, not end
4 Tories should improve conditions and maintain institutions (Disraeli)
5 Contributions of *all* should be valued
6 Prosperity of rich should not depend upon deprivation of others
7 Tories should not accept poverty and should support reform
8 State welfare should be an aid to economy by offering security during period of rapid changes
9 Unemployment should be reduced to promote economic efficiency
10 Tories should reduce unemployment to win the next election
11 Unemployment should be reduced *now* – otherwise public will think Tories do not care
12 Public perceives Tories as 'party of the rich'
13 Tory action on poverty and unemployment will dispel this idea

Exercise 3

Comment not applicable. Consult your tutor.

Exercise 4

1 Polemic, quarrel, altercation, hypothesis
2 Demeanour, deportment, conduct, manner
3 Definite, absolute, indisputable, inevitable
4 Erase, obliterate, expunge, excise
5 Vigour, zest, vivacity, ardour
6 Immovable, entrenched, rooted, embedded
7 Real, authentic, true, reliable
8 Damaging, corrupting, injurious, malignant

Exercise 5

Comment not applicable. Consult your tutor.

Chapter 8

Exercise 1
In this chapter we dealt with an introduction to the technique of brainstorming and have worked through some simple examples and then through some which were more complex. We then covered the problems of organising your ideas in a variety of ways, and finally considered the alternative Concept Tree approach to the generation of ideas.

Exercise 2
No comment applicable. Consult your tutor.

Exercise 3
Here is a sample essay plan for the essay 'Cars should be banned from city centres'.
1 Introduction – Popular idea, but may have unpopular consequences
2 Points 'for' –
(a) reduces pollution
(b) reduces congestion and possible accidents
(c) more pleasant environment
(d) use of buses environmentally better
3 Points 'against'
(a) large orbital roads required
(b) large city-edge car parks required
(c) deliveries to shops restricted
(d) possible loss of earnings to shops
4 Conclusion – could be pleasant, but extensive change in habits required. And has any city done it?

Exercise 4
No comment applicable. Consult your tutor.

Exercise 5
1 oblique, roundabout, vicarious, evasive
2 idleness, indolence, sloth, apathy
3 encounter, assembly, assignation, rally
4 orthodox, conventional, usual, established
5 fatty, greasy, unctuous, oleaginous
6 delight, enjoyment, gratification, rapture
7 actual, genuine, authentic, corporeal
8 quiver, tremble, vibrate, agitate

Chapter 9

Exercise 1
The most important elements of what makes a good essay are:
1 Answering the question
2 Clear structure
3 Appropriate style
4 Evidence of wide reading
5 Clarity of thought
6 Well-supported arguments
7 Good presentation
8 Originality

Exercise 2
1 It is true that 'language' is a form of expression – but then so are many other things. A shrug of the shoulders or a wink of the eye are expressions. So this definition is too broad: it is not specific enough.
2 The same is true of this definition. 'Language' is a form of communication – but then so are traffic lights, railway signals, and even 'body language'.
3 This is probably the best of the four, because it includes the important element of interrelatedness which characterises 'language' as a *system* for communicating meanings.
4 You can see that this definition recognises that there are many different languages – but in essence they all operate in the same way. And 'form of communication' is as unspecific as definitions 1 and 2: it is true, but doesn't say what it *is* exactly.

Exercise 3

Essay 1
You should have had no difficulty in spotting that this piece fails on a number of counts when measured against our checklist of 'What makes a good essay'. I will offer my own comments under each heading, against which you can compare your own.

1 Appropriate style
It is *not at all* appropriate – largely because of the excessive use of the first person pronoun ('I think . . . I have known . . .'). In addition it is also very opinionated and immodest: ('it is monstrous . . . parents should be encouraged'). There is also a hortatory or tub-thumping manner to the writing which is quite out of place in what is supposed to be a reasoned piece of argument.

2 Arguments or ideas well supported by evidence
It certainly fails on this count. There *are* some arguments (though

not all of them are to the point) but the 'evidence' to support them is either just personal opinion, subjective claim ('I have known a number of boys') or ill-informed prejudice ('exam results are shocking'). It *would* have been possible to produce *some* evidence to support these (rather bigoted) views – but the writer does not do so.

3 Evidence of wide reading and understanding the subject
There is no evidence of any reading at all – and although the writer obviously has strongly held views on the subject of private education, this is not the same thing as an *understanding* of it. There is no sign that the writer has ever considered any other views than the ones expressed, and no sign that any methodical study of the subject has been made.

4 Clarity of thought
There is very little of it. Almost all the arguments slither off the point they are trying to make, offer 'evidence' which does not prove the point at all, or are examples of what are called 'fallacious arguments'. To take one case – the comparison which is offered in the penultimate paragraph between a person's height and their educational opportunities. Both are offered as examples of life's possible unfairness which we ought to tolerate. But the argument is fallacious on two counts: a person's height is something we can do nothing about, whereas we can do something about educational opportunities; and not being able to join the police force because you are too small is only to be denied *one* career opportunity, whereas the quality of our education can affect many aspects of our lives and possible careers.

5 Originality of thought
Very little indeed. The 'essay' is a catalogue of bigotry and cliché (often the same thing). This sort of writing is too egocentric and ill-informed to be even competent, let alone original.

6 Clear structure
There is no introduction, no conclusion, and the separate paragraphs of argument have no particular logic to their progression. There is nothing linking them together, and they do not add up to a coherent point of view. There is no evidence that the piece of writing has been carefully planned in any way at all.

7 Answering the question
This is the most important shortcoming – because the case *against* private education is not considered at all. Only the last few paragraphs even mention that there could be a case 'against', but it is not presented or considered: the writer simply slurs the people who hold contrary views.

218

There are other flaws in the piece too, but I think the point has been made that it does not do well against our checklist. Are there any points in its favour?

Well, you could say that for the most part the writing is grammatically acceptable; the separate arguments are each put in a paragraph of their own; and somehow I suspect that with closer supervision the writer *could* have done better. Using our marking system, I would give this essay 35 out of a possible 100 – which is a 'close fail' (40 being the usual pass mark).

Essay 2
This is obviously a far superior piece of work on the same subject. I will give my own responses this time in the order which we suggested reflects the importance of each element. (The sequence does not really matter, so long as they are all given active consideration.)

1 Answering the questions
More or less full points for this element. The essay presents 'the case' – that is, the arguments both for and against private education. The arguments are well balanced, there is no wandering off the point, and there doesn't appear to be any bias or prejudice.

2 Clear structure
Full marks here too. There is a very clear introduction in which the limits of the essay are defined and the strategy of the argument is spelled out. Then the case 'for' is made, followed (at just slightly greater length) by the case 'against'. The essay is then rounded off with a very even-handed conclusion. This clarity and firmness of structure suggests that the arguments have been carefully thought through and arranged beforehand in a strong essay plan.

3 Style
There is an obvious attempt to be neutral and non-emotive here. The style is clear, dry, rather dispassionate and rigorous. This is perfectly acceptable, though personally I would have welcomed a little light relief or some small touches of decoration.

4 Evidence of wide reading
The person who wrote this essay is clearly well informed and is obviously used to handling intellectual concepts in a confident manner – but there *isn't* any direct evidence of wide reading, is there. One might have expected some statistics or the names of people who had written on the subject to be quoted.

5 Clarity of thought
I would score the piece very highly on this element. The control of the argument, the clear separation of ideas, and the fine discriminations being made all suggests it is being written by someone who thinks very clearly indeed. (It was in fact written by someone with an interest in philosophy.)

6 Well-supported arguments
If you look carefully you will see that each main point in the argument *is* supported with evidence in the form of further arguments or examples ('Their supporters point to institutions like . . . As evidence they point out that . . .') This 'support' does not *have* to be a statistical proof positive: it is just evidence that the claim *can* be illustrated and is more than the sort of rash generalisation we saw in Essay 1.

7 Presentation
Since the essay has been printed as part of this book we cannot expect you to comment here – but we can say that essays like this which show such clarity of thought are *almost always* well presented. And the converse is usually true: essays which are poorly and shoddily presented nearly always reflect scrappy thinking.

8 Originality
There isn't a lot of that here – but to be fair to the author the question is of a kind which asks you to 'Present the case for and against . . .'. This doesn't exactly encourage originality because it is asking you to rehearse arguments which have already been established through public debate.

Is there anything which could be said against the essay? Well – not very much. I personally find it a little stiff and formal ('It is argued . . . In seeking to adjudicate between the competing claims') but this is a matter of individual taste. I also think a few facts and figures could have added both interest and harder evidence, but this might depend upon the discipline being studied (sociology, philosophy, education).

As far as marks are concerned the piece obviously scores well on almost all elements. Being as severe as possible, I have come up with a total of 82 out of a possible 100, which puts it into the first-class category.

Essay 3

I hope you were able to see that this essay was something of a mixture – good points and obvious weaknesses jostling each other in close proximity.

1 *Answer the question*

Well – it *is* answered, but in rather a hit-and-miss fashion. You may have noticed that the title of the essay is not quite the same as the question set. This is nearly always a sign that the writer is not fully in control or is not paying full attention. Nevertheless, some of the pros and cons are debated, and there is a reasonable conclusion which focuses on the subject.

2 *Clear structure*

Some of the surface scrappiness may seem to conceal the fact, but underneath here there *is* a firm structure. It is as follows: introduction – arguments against – arguments for – conclusion. This sort of firm foundation can help support even the weakest set of arguments.

3 *Style*

The thing most obviously missing here is consistency of tone. A basically reasonable manner is flawed by all sorts of grammatical black spots: the use of abbreviations (e.g., etc.') colloquialisms ('telly', 'fantastic rate') inappropriate jargon ('libido-inhibiting') and sheer mistakes ('who will do the censorship?').

4 *Evidence of wide reading*

There is not much here in the way of statistics relating to the central issue, but there is a wide range of cultural references within the argument – to art, literature, cinema, sociology, and psychology. This might not be a high-level and tightly argued piece of work, but it reflects a fairly cultivated (if erratic) mind at work.

5 *Clarity of thought*

This is a little patchy. There are some perceptive ideas and observations, but they are not followed through very carefully. Having stated that the discussion would be limited to television and newspapers, the first argument is illustrated with an example dealing with sculpture. And the argument concerning catharsis and deterrence (which is quite interesting) is not spelled out as clearly as it might be. There are also one or two lapses into crude assertion – ('I always think . . . some standards must be upheld').

6 *Well-supported arguments*

The beginning and the end of the essay provide good examples of arguments backed up with examples from the worlds of literature and cinema – specific instances of the point being made. But the middle of the essay is a lot weaker in this sense. One notes that in this part a number of new questions are raised – instead of answering the one which has been set.

7 Originality
Once again, something of a mixture. One or two well-known points of argument are rehearsed, but there are also some interesting observations – for instance that 'sex' and 'violence' should be discussed separately, or that 'public opinion' is not a static phenomenon.

Allowing a moderate 6 out of 10 for presentation in my final tally under each heading, I come up with a total of 62 out of the possible 100 here. This may possibly seem rather high to you, but I would argue that although the flaws in this piece are very obvious, they are not seriously damaging.

Index